Mental
Health
in
Black
America

Mental
Health
in
Black
America

Edited by

Harold W. Neighbors
James S. Jackson

SAGE Publications
International Educational and Professional Publisher
Thousand Oaks London New Delhi

For information address:

 SAGE Publications, Inc.
2455 Teller Road
Thousand Oaks, California 91320
E-mail: order@sagepub.com

SAGE Publications Ltd.
6 Bonhill Street
London EC2A 4PU
United Kingdom

SAGE Publications India Pvt. Ltd.
M-32 Market
Greater Kailash I
New Delhi 110 048 India

Printed in the United States of America

Library of Congress Cataloging-in-Publication Data

Main entry under title:

Mental health in Black America / editors, Harold W. Neighbors, James
  S. Jackson.
    p.   cm.
  Includes bibliographical references and indexes.
  ISBN 0-8039-3539-0 (alk. paper).—ISBN 0-8039-3540-4 (pbk.: alk.
paper)
    1. Afro-Americans—Mental health. I. Neighbors, Harold W.
  II. Jackson, James S. (James Sidney), 1944-
  RC451.5.N4M45   1996
  616.89'0089'96073—dc20   95-50210

This book is printed on acid-free paper.

96 97 98 99 00 01 10 9 8 7 6 5 4 3 2 1

Sage Production Editor: Vicki Baker
Sage Typesetters: Yang-hee Syn Maresca & Andrea D. Swanson

Contents

Foreword

It is with great pleasure that I write the foreword to the third book in the Sage Empirical Series, *Mental Health in Black America*. As part of the research team that developed the idea for the National Survey of Black Americans (NSBA) and as coauthor, in the early years, of a number of the reports, papers, and subsequent proposals generated by this groundbreaking study, it has been impressive and a source of great pride to observe the explosion in research activity that Jackson, Neighbors, and their colleagues have generated over the last 20 years.

As the title suggests, this book focuses on the mental-health-relevant questions asked in the NSBA. Although much has already been written about this monumental undertaking (Jackson, 1991; Jackson, Chatters, & Taylor, 1993), a detailed description of the mental health implications of the NSBA has yet to be told. Although concerned with mental health, the NSBA did not attempt to assess the prevalence of discrete mental disorders. Rather, owing its intellectual legacy to earlier "omnibus" surveys conducted by the Institute for Social Research's Survey Research Center, including my own and colleagues' *Americans View Their Mental Health* (Gurin, Veroff, & Feld, 1960), the NSBA took a problem-focused approach to how African Americans coped with the stress in their lives. Specifically, this study examines two important aspects of black mental health: (a) the distribution of personal problems, psychological distress, and feelings of happiness and satisfaction, and (b) the manner in which African Americans cope with and adapt to the problematic situations they face. This includes exploring processes such as the effect of group identification on self-esteem, the effect of discrimination on self-efficacy, and the protective role of the family and community networks on psychological distress. Help seeking and the use of informal as well as professional (health, medical, and specialty mental health) services were also of central concern to those of us who planned and conducted the NSBA. The study focused on the assessment of mental health needs and with how those needs were being met.

The topic of help seeking provides an excellent segue for placing the NSBA within the larger psychiatric epidemiologic context. The study was conceptualized in the late 1970s, before the National Institute of Mental Health (NIMH) Epidemiologic Catchment Area Program, and it did not attempt psychiatric diagnostic classification using survey methods. Rather, it approached the assessment of mental health need, and the seeking of help to address this need, from the experience and perspective of the people being assessed. The NSBA is fundamentally a comprehensive description of mental health from the lay, black cultural perspective—what African Americans *themselves* think about issues of mental health.

To truly appreciate what a monumental and historic feat the NSBA was, one has to think back to the tenor of the 1970s. This was a time still heavily influenced by the radicalism of the 1960s. In 1977, when planning for the original NSBA began, we were not that far away from the urban civil disorders and the subsequent federally funded research attempts to understand and control these protests. Nor were we very far removed from the research backlash that resulted from the publication of the Moynihan Report. These and other social forces combined to create a pessimistic atmosphere for social science research on African Americans during the 1970s.

Nowhere was this negative perspective on minority social science research more evident than in the mental health arena (Kramer, Rosen, & Willis, 1973). Comer (1970) wrote that black communities were exploited to advance the careers of students and researchers, but little effort was made to use research findings to benefit black "laboratory communities." Comer also warned that if things did not change, "It is likely that needed future research and evaluation in black communities will not be possible" (Comer, 1970, p. 9). In this era, social scientists were seen as agents of the white power structure—outsiders who entered black communities only to advance personal goals. This viewpoint contributed to a growing hostility toward universities in black neighborhoods. This caused concern and alarm among those of us who saw the potential utility of social science research, particularly if it was conducted in a culturally meaningful manner.

In what can now be recognized as one of the earliest attempts at conducting culturally sensitive social research, a number of social scientists called for the

inclusion of more African American investigators in the planning and imple-
mentation of their own research studies, in order to address issues and
priorities that were of importance to African Americans themselves (Cannon
& Locke, 1977; Kramer et al., 1973). Within this context, the NSBA can truly
be appreciated for the revolutionary study that it is.

The NSBA provided monetary compensation for the time spent by each of
the 2,107 black respondents who so graciously responded to an interview that
averaged almost 2 hours in length. The NSBA interviewers were African
American—and in many cases, they were indigenous to the very communities
under study. The interviewers were instructed to go to great lengths to explain
the nature and purpose of the study. Most of the senior research staff and
research assistants were African American. This study provided hands-on
training opportunities for the new cadre of black social scientists who would
be called on to conduct the kind of research that many whites were concluding
they could not and should not do without the input and collaboration of black
scholars (Blauner & Wellman, 1973; Jackson, 1991).

Here, the NSBA and its subsequent offspring, the Program for Research on
Black Americans, really shine. The hands-on training provided by the original
NSBA spawned a three-generational study of black families, a national study of
black youth, four national black election studies, an epidemiologic survey of
prisoner mental health, and three follow-up data collections on the original 2,107
NSBA respondents. More important, however, is the fact that because of these
studies, the Program for Research on Black Americans has supported more than
22 doctoral dissertations and 60 postdoctoral fellows and has trained more than
70 graduate and undergraduate students, the bulk of whom are African American.

In short, this study and the research program it generated have played a major
role in our national movement, in less than a generation, from a period when the
predominance of white researchers in the studies of black life led some to argue
for the elimination of research on blacks to a period of black and white social
scientists working together on meaningful, useful, and culturally grounded social
research on African Americans. This historic role is equally as important as the
tremendous substantive contributions that the Program for Research on Black
Americans has made to our understanding of black American life.

If I may inject a personal note, although I derive great satisfaction from
whatever I may have contributed to the NSBA, I have to admit that I can claim
no credit for the vision that created the broader program of research and
training that gives this enterprise its historic significance. If anything, I tried
to limit it. When I first started working with them, James Jackson was an

assistant professor and Woody Neighbors was a graduate student on whose doctoral committee I served. I was concerned about their careers. I remember arguing with James Jackson against his plans to write the proposal for a summer training institute that would bring African American graduate students and young scholars to Michigan to analyze and publish data from the NSBA. I pointed out the overload on him and the lack of career rewards for training. He looked at me and said, "This is what it's all about." In an academic environment that is increasingly focused on "unique" individual contributions, my association with the people in this research program over the years has taught me the greater rewards of research that is communal in its process and values.

In closing, let me say that Neighbors and Jackson should be highly commended for putting together an excellent collection of thought-provoking chapters that address African American mental health issues from a wide variety of perspectives. I suspect that professors will find this to be an excellent teaching tool for their classes, and students will find the book will stimulate their thinking about how best to study and address the mental health needs of black Americans. I strongly recommend this book as required reading for anyone interested in stress, coping, and the mental health of African Americans.

Gerald Gurin
*Professor Emeritus of Higher
Education, Research Scientist
Emeritus, Institute for Social
Research, University of Michigan*

References

Blauner, R., & Wellman, D. (1973). Toward the decolonization of social research. In J. A. Ladner (Ed.), *The death of white sociology* (pp. 310-330). New York: Vintage.

Cannon, M., & Locke, B. (1977). Being black is detrimental to one's mental health: Myth or reality? *Phylon, 38*, 408-428.

Comer, J. (1970). Research and the black backlash. *American Journal of Orthopsychiatry, 40*, 8-11.

Gurin, G., Veroff, J., & Feld, S. (1960). *Americans view their mental health.* New York: Basic Books.

Jackson, J. S. (Ed.). (1991). *Life in black America.* Newbury Park, CA: Sage.

Jackson, J. S., Chatters, L. M., & Taylor, R. J. (Eds.). (1993). *Aging in black America.* Newbury Park, CA: Sage.

Kramer, M., Rosen, B., & Willis, E. (1973). Definitions and distributions of mental disorders in a racist society. In C. Willie, M. Kramer, & B. Brown (Eds.), *Racism and mental health.* Pittsburgh, PA: University of Pittsburgh Press.

Preface

Mental Health in Black America is the third in a series of empirical volumes based on the National Survey of Black Americans (NSBA) conducted in 1979-1980 by the University of Michigan's Institute for Social Research. This volume continues the series initiated in *Life in Black America* (Jackson, 1991), which provided a general overview of the life circumstances of African Americans at the beginning of the 1980s, and *Aging in Black America* (Jackson, Chatters, & Taylor, 1993), which applied a life span framework to the physical, social, and psychological aging of older African Americans.

The present volume extends this prior work to research on mental health, coping, and help-seeking behavior. Prior to the successful completion of the NSBA, the majority of psychiatric epidemiologic investigations focused on ethnicity and culture and did little more than compare blacks and whites. Although certainly an appropriate starting point for descriptive psychiatric epidemiology, the continued reliance on this race-comparative paradigm contributed to the mistaken impression that African Americans were a monolithic group and could be understood only in relation to how they differed from whites. The NSBA successfully challenged this as the only means of understanding or studying the mental health of black people. The NSBA has substantially increased our knowledge by providing a framework and opportunity to explore differences in the distribution of and approaches to coping with stressful personal problems *within* the African American population.

Mental Health in Black America focuses on important issues relevant to the social psychiatric epidemiology of African Americans before the Epidemiologic Catchment Area (ECA) study was conducted. As a result, rather than assessing the prevalence of discrete mental disorders, this volume focuses on the social and psychological correlates of coping with serious personal problems, the distribution of psychological distress, and help seeking, including the use of specialty mental health care, general medical care, and informal social support networks. In this respect, *Mental Health in Black America* owes its intellectual roots most directly to the classic Joint Commission on Mental Illness and Health study, *Americans View Their Mental Health* (Gurin, Veroff, & Feld, 1960). The central questions here are very similar to those addressed by *Americans View Their Mental Health:* Are there group and individual differences in how stress and problems are conceptualized, and if so, how do these differences influence help-seeking behavior?

Each chapter of *Mental Health in Black America* provides a selected but comprehensive overview of an important mental health issue facing African Americans. Topics such as gender differences, family support, marriage, alcohol abuse, hypertension, and stress denial, to name a few, are covered. Each chapter also includes a multivariate analysis of the topic using data from the NSBA. The final chapter provides a summary of selected topics addressed in the individual chapters. This chapter also updates these issues through the analysis of follow-up panel data collected on the original NSBA respondents over a 13-year period.

The work reported in this volume has been supported by research grants from the National Institute of Mental Health, the National Institute on Aging, the Ford and Rockefeller Foundations, and the Carnegie Corporation. Institutional and individual postdoctoral grants were also instrumental in this work and were provided by the National Institute of Mental Health, the National Institute on Aging, and the Rockefeller Foundation. Financial and moral support was provided by Steven Withey, then Director of Survey Research Center; Robert Zajonc, then director of the Research Center for Group Dynamics; and Thomas Juster, then Director of the Institute for Social Research. We would also like to acknowledge the special role played by Patricia and Gerald Gurin in helping to establish the Program for Research on Black Americans.

Finally, we would like to acknowledge the contributions of Sally Oswald, who had major responsibility for coordinating the production of this manuscript, as well as the previous volumes in the series. We would also like to acknowledge the tremendous contribution made by Myriam Torres, who had primary responsibility for directing and supervising all data management and data analysis activities. We would like to thank Phyllis Stillman for her proofreading and editing skills and Ain Pili Boone for her extensive contributions in the areas of data analysis and graphic presentation. We are also deeply indebted to Elizabeth Chase, Dale Jerome, Estina Thompson, and Monica Wolford for contributing valuable time and energy to the completion of this book.

Harold W. Neighbors
James S. Jackson
University of Michigan

References

Gurin, G., Veroff, J., & Feld, S. (1960). *Americans view their mental health.* New York: Basic Books.

Jackson, J. S. (Ed.). (1991). *Life in black America.* Newbury Park, CA: Sage.

Jackson, J. S., Chatters, L. M., & Taylor, R. J. (Eds.). (1993). *Aging in black America.* Newbury Park, CA: Sage.

1

Mental Health in Black America
Psychosocial Problems
and Help-Seeking Behavior

Harold W. Neighbors
James S. Jackson

Mental Health in Black America is an edited volume of empirical research studies on the emotional and psychological well-being of adult African Americans. A unique feature of this book is that all of the chapters are based on statistical analyses of a nationally representative data set, the National Survey of Black Americans (NSBA) (Jackson, 1991; Jackson, Chatters, & Taylor, 1993). Specifically, this is a book that details the self-reported stress of being black in America while at the same time documenting the cultural resources African Americans draw on to overcome adversity and maintain a positive, healthy perspective on life. Each chapter presented in this volume stands alone as a complete work and, as a result, each author makes a unique contribution to our understanding of African American mental health. Thus, these chapters need not be read in any particular order but can be sampled according to the interests of the reader. If, on the other hand, these chapters are read in sequence, one will discover a discernible thread that weaves these writings together into a coherent fabric describing the varied coping strategies and survival mechanisms intrinsic to African American life.

This book differs from other edited volumes on African American mental health in that all of the chapters focus on one research study. Many of the previous books on black mental health are compilations of nonquantitative, conceptual overviews of important mental health topics (e.g., Gary, 1978a; Wilkinson, 1986) or contain sources of data that vary widely in scope (e.g., Friedman, 1994; Ruiz, 1990). Although NSBA is used throughout the entire book, a variety of mental health outcomes are explored, including psychological distress (i.e., symptomatology), life happiness, life satisfaction, hypertension, and problem drinking. One of the more frequent ways that blacks choose to cope with stress—seeking help from family, friends, and professionals—is also the subject of in-depth exploration. Emphasis is given to the special problems of certain demographic target groups known to be at increased mental health risk (e.g., women, the unemployed, and the elderly).

The NSBA cross-sectional study attempted to address some of the major limitations in the existing literature (Jackson, Tucker, & Bowman, 1982). The NSBA was initiated in 1977 (Jackson, Tucker, & Gurin, 1987). Funding for the study was provided by the Center for the Study of Minority Group Mental Health, National Institute of Mental Health, and the Ford Foundation. The NSBA is a national probability household survey based on the distribution of the African American, noninstitutionalized population in the continental United States. The final sample consisted of 2,107 self-identified black Americans 18 years of age or older. The survey was conducted over a 7-month period in 1979 and 1980 (Jackson, 1991). The size and representativeness of the sample permit systematic investigation of the heterogeneity of the adult black population.

Substantively, this omnibus survey was concerned with major social, economic, and psychological aspects of black American life. The questionnaire included items on family and friend relationships, community life, religion, racial identity, political attitudes and participation, mental health, informal and formal help resources, and job and employment history. The 2,107 face-to-face household interviews were conducted by an all-black male and female professional interviewing staff that was trained and supervised by the Survey Research Center at the Institute for Social Research (Jackson, 1991; Jackson & Hatchett, 1986; Jackson et al., 1982, 1987).

In summary, *Mental Health in Black America* is composed of three distinct but related substantive areas. The book begins with a positive focus—exploring happiness and life satisfaction. Then it segues into an exploration of how these quality of life indicators are related to health problems and diseases (e.g., excessive drinking and hypertension) afflicting African Americans. Once the dynamic tension between life quality and stress is established, an extended, in-depth perusal of the various coping mechanisms (anger expression, denial, prayer, social support, and problem solving) used by blacks to deal with adversity follows. Chapters 2 and 3 focus on the broad psychological and sociological factors that are related to overall quality of life. The second section of the book (Chapters 4 through 7) focuses on the manner in which many of these psychosocial factors contribute to the disproportionate number of health problems that burden the black community.

The third and final section of the book (Chapters 8 through 12) examines how African Americans attempt to solve problems they face in life. Specifically, Chapter 8 examines coping strategies such as prayer, avoidance, and active problem solving, whereas the last four chapters investigate the decision to turn to others for help. For Chapters 9 through 12, the authors each provide a slightly different perspective on describing the help-seeking behavior of African Americans, detailing how blacks use informal support networks (both family and nonfamily) and documenting contact with professional services such as community mental health, psychotherapists, and the police. In short, after completing this book, readers will come away with a deep sense of respect for the resilience of African Americans and a clearer understanding of how blacks have been able to accomplish so much in the face of pervasive prejudice and discrimination.

Public Mental Health and African Americans

The major impetus behind the idea of a groundbreaking study like the NSBA was the overreliance on race-comparative studies as the main basis of social scientific knowledge about African American behavior (Jackson, 1989, 1991; Jackson et al., 1982). This created problems for researchers interested in a more detailed inspection of the special mental health needs of blacks (Graham, 1992; Jackson, 1993; Wilkinson & King, 1989; Yee, Fairchild, Weizmann, & Wyatt, 1993). Although race-comparative studies provide many useful leads about where future research is needed, they are limited in many respects. Because of the small numbers of African Americans sampled in most population surveys, comparative studies often are unable to describe the heterogeneity of mental health problems and help-seeking behavior within the black population (Veroff, Douvan, & Kulka, 1981).[1] As a result, they present a circumscribed view of African Americans that provides unintentional support for all too familiar stereotypes.

Concerned health researchers have argued for quite some time that African Americans should be sampled in much larger numbers to arrive at more reliable estimates of mental health problems (Hahn, 1992; Jackson et al., 1982). It is especially important to study representative samples of African Americans when previous investigations have documented substantial ethnic differences in mental health status. The obvious solution is more comprehensive research on the epidemiology of African American mental health problems and how blacks cope with those problems. This book responds directly to these shortcomings. It represents the first community survey of mental health and help-seeking information ever conducted on a nationally representative sample of adult African Americans.

The study of African American mental health has been an important and controversial issue since the early 1600s (Fischer, 1969). Historically, the question of African American mental health has been used politically as a justification for slavery, as a "scientific" rationale for segregation, and to reinforce the concept of black racial inferiority (Williams, 1986). With the Community Mental Health Movement's emphasis on the elimination of inequities in access to treatment, African Americans have been a priority for the delivery of mental health services for the past 35 years (Neighbors, 1987; Wagenfeld, Lemkau, & Justice, 1982). Before those services can be effectively targeted, however, more information on how mental health problems are distributed within the black population and how blacks use professional health services is needed (Jackson, Neighbors, & Gurin, 1986; Neighbors, 1984b; Snowden, 1982; Snowden & Cheung, 1990; Snowden & Holschuh, 1992).

Mental health researchers, planners, and service providers generally agree that African Americans are at high risk for the development of mental health problems. This assumption is based on at least three bodies of empirical research. The first is the set of social indicators that show that blacks are economically disadvantaged relative to whites (Braithwaite & Taylor, 1992; U.S. Department of Health and Human Services [DHHS], 1985; Williams & Collins, 1995). The second is the body of literature connecting changes in macroeconomic variables to the precipitation of stressful economic life events and eventual negative changes in mental health status (Brown & Gary, 1988; Catalano & Dooley, 1983; Dressler, 1986; McLoyd, 1990). Third, findings from epidemiologic community surveys comparing blacks and whites reveal that African Americans score higher on measures of psychological distress (Jackson & Neighbors, 1989). There is, however, some ambiguity as to whether the higher rate of distress among African Americans is due to the stress of racism or the fact that blacks disproportionately reside in the lower socioeconomic strata (Kessler & Neighbors, 1986; Neff, 1985; Warheit, Holzer, & Arey, 1975; Warheit, Holzer, & Schwab, 1973). The idea that the effects of ethnicity on mental health might be explained by the fact that so many blacks are poor only heightens the need for and practical importance of an in-depth investigation of African American mental health.

An important feature of this book is the underlying theoretical orientation that guides the analyses and serves as a unifying theme for this diverse collection of chapters. These chapters all employ a stress and adaptation approach to understanding the problems confronting African Americans (Myers, Bastien, & Miles, 1992). The concepts of stress and adaptation are viewed as characterizing a discrepancy between the demands impinging on a person and the capacity to effectively cope with those demands (Myers, 1982). Such discrepancies are commonly associated with the onset of psychological distress. This orientation places an equal amount of emphasis on environmental and situational factors as possible causes for psychological distress as it places on personal explanations (Neighbors, Jackson, Broman, & Thompson, 1996). The stress model also focuses attention on one of the more positive aspects of African American mental health—successful problem solving (Neighbors, Jackson, Bowman, & Gurin, 1983).

Historically, studies of race and mental health have failed to consider the role of black coping capacity (Franklin & Jackson, 1990). For example, despite the fact that African Americans are disproportionately exposed to social conditions considered to be antecedents of psychological disorder, data from epidemiologic community surveys do not always show that blacks exhibit higher rates of psychological distress than whites (Neighbors, 1984a; Williams, 1995). These findings might be explained by cultural differences in the ways in which blacks and whites cope with stress (Dressler, 1985a; Kessler, 1979b; Ulbrich, Warheit, & Zimmerman, 1989). Thus, there is a need for research that examines African American mental health in a more comprehensive manner than previous efforts. This research must take into consideration the prevalence of emotional distress, the stressors that blacks face, and the coping strategies used to adapt to those stressors. The approach to mental health taken in the NSBA does precisely that, and the findings presented in this book will answer many important questions about African American mental health and coping.

Although it is clear that the mental health status of African Americans is an important issue, there is less agreement about how to improve the emotional well-being of the largest minority group in the United States. Traditionally, mental health practitioners have waited to intervene until people were already psychologically troubled. The fact that assistance is not always provided for all who need it has led some to argue that increased access to mental health services is needed for those in psychic pain (Neighbors et al., 1992; Takeuchi, Bui, & Kim, 1993; Wu & Windle, 1980). It is important to note, however, that many mental health scholars also see social stress as the primary cause of mental health problems among African Americans (Hilliard, 1981). Thus, epidemiologic research should also be directed toward diminishing stress through the creation of healthier psychological and physical environments (Cannon & Locke, 1977; Williams, Lavizzo-Mourey, & Warren, 1994).

Philosophically, the research reported in this book is influenced by both viewpoints. First, this book agrees with the assumption that much promise resides in a public health approach to preventing large numbers of African Americans from succumbing to the stresses of racism, oppression, and poor economic conditions. This is the basis for the strong social epidemiologic focus taken in most of the chapters in the book. On the other hand, there will undoubtedly be a continuing need for tertiary treatment interventions for blacks with serious personal problems. Thus, a number of chapters explore the help-seeking behavior of African Americans, and one in particular focuses on the clinical implications of psychotherapy. Equal emphasis is placed on understanding the importance of clinical and social factors affecting who seeks professional help as well as those more likely to use informal social contacts.

This central interest in a public health approach to dealing with African American mental health results from the recognition that, although many constructive steps have been taken to increase the access blacks have to mental health services, the U.S. mental health care system continues to struggle to meet the emotional needs of African Americans (Griffith & Baker, 1993). It is apparent that continued reliance on a treatment mode of mental health intervention alone will not be enough to meet the needs of hard-to-reach ethnic minorities. As a result, there is a need to move toward a model of intervention that has as its primary goal the prevention of serious emotional difficulties (Bell, 1987; Neighbors, 1990). To develop and implement a public health model of mental health prevention with blacks, however, the epidemiologic knowledge upon which to base those prevention efforts must be obtained. At present, that knowledge base remains inadequate (Adebimpe, 1994; Brown, Eaton, & Sussman, 1990; Williams, 1995).[2]

Overview of the Chapters

Chapters 2 and 3 highlight various factors that affect quality of life and psychological well-being. Chapter 2, written by Carolyn B. Murray and M. Jean Peacock, is titled "A Model-Free Approach to the Study of Subjective Well-Being." As Murray and Peacock eloquently point out, the large amount of information gathered in the NSBA allows for a more in-depth exploration usually not possible with typically small data sets on blacks. Although they admit that "ransacking" large data sets is cumbersome, time-consuming, and costly, Murray and Peacock present an efficient data analysis procedure using a sophisticated statistical technique, the Automatic Interaction Detector, as a way of empirically searching data to identify an initial set of predictors to explain subjective well-being among African Americans. They show that stress is important in explaining subjective well-being and that African Americans 55 years old and older are more satisfied with their lives than African Americans under age 55. Family closeness and the number of helpers living in one's neighborhood are also found to be important predictors of subjective well-being.

In Chapter 3, "Stress and Residential Well-Being," Gayle Y. Phillips examines the role that stress and housing quality play in explaining neighborhood satisfaction among African Americans. Her chapter answers the question of whether objective, physical residential characteristics, perceptions of neighborhood services, and the location of one's residence explain housing quality and neighborhood satisfaction. Phillips finds that the important correlates of neighborhood satisfaction differ for men and women. Women are more concerned than men about safety and crime as major neighborhood problems. Overall, neighborhood satisfaction increases because of the maintenance and improvement of residential conditions, which can be facilitated by participating in neighborhood groups.

Chapter 4 also focuses on quality of life and provides a transition from the positive side of African American mental health to the more negative—how problem drinking exacerbates a host of physical and mental health problems. In the chapter, "Problem Drinking, Chronic Disease, and Recent Life Events," Isidore Silas Obot makes an important contribution to the implications of alcohol abuse among African Americans by presenting epidemiologic data on the breadth of health and social problems that negatively affect the life of the drinker, the immediate family, and society at large. Obot's penetrating analysis provides a comprehensive description of those African Americans who drink too much and, more important, the medical and social consequences of problem drinking.

Chapters 5 and 6 describe some of the more problematic aspects of black life by detailing the impact that serious personal problems can have on mental health. In Chapter 5, "An Analysis of Stress Denial," Rhoda E. Barge Johnson and Joan E. Crowley argue that their reading of the racism and stress research leads to the conclusion that it is virtually impossible for any African American to reach adulthood without having experienced at least one significant stressful life problem. To their surprise, however, these authors discover that a sizable percentage of the NSBA sample reported never having been seriously upset by a personal problem. Thus, Chapter 5 provides an important exploration of those African Americans who claim to have no problems at all. Johnson and Crowley ask the provocative question, "Are these people incredibly lucky, highly efficacious in their coping capacity—or are they living in a perpetual state of denial?"

Diane R. Brown has written extensively on the epidemiology of depression and anxiety among African Americans. In Chapter 6, "Marital Status and Mental Health," Brown focuses on whether married black men and women cope with stress differently than blacks whose marriages have fallen apart. Brown does not stop there, however. She also answers the question of whether getting married in the first place has any advantage at all over never marrying—a lifestyle choice that is more and more a viable alternative for African American women. The major objective of Brown's analysis is to explore the relationship between marital status and psychiatric symptoms among adult African American males and females. The results of the analyses in Chapter 6 show that, although marriage may be better for one's mental health than being separated or divorced, marriage is not any better than having never married. Apparently, the lives of many African American adults are psychologically healthier in terms of minimizing the impact of stressful problems if they marry and stay married or if they never marry at all.

The overt and covert racist insults that all African Americans at one time or another are subjected to cause tremendous internal anger and turmoil, especially when it is not always possible to act on that anger. It is also well-known that hypertension is the great "silent killer" of both male and female African Americans. In "The Association Between Anger-Hostility and Hypertension" (Chapter 7), Ernest H. Johnson and Larry M. Gant examine the relationship between hypertension and the expression of black anger toward those responsible for igniting those feelings. Johnson and Gant predict that hypertension is highest among those African Americans (male and female) who hold their feelings of rage inside rather than let it out. Johnson and Gant's chapter finds support for a relationship between hypertension and anger. They also reveal some rather surprising results with respect to gender and urbanicity that they speculate may be due to the actual method of measurement (self-report) used in the NSBA.

Although African Americans are extensively exposed to stressful life circumstances, they typically show levels of psychiatric symptoms that are no higher than those of whites. This paradox has attracted much attention in the psychiatric epidemiologic literature (Kessler, 1979b; Williams, 1995). In Chapter 8, "Coping With Personal Problems," Clifford L. Broman argues that black coping capacity is the understudied factor that ameliorates the impact of stress on African American mental health. Broman points out that, despite this very promising line of reasoning, there are surprisingly few empirical investigations focused explicitly on how African Americans cope with blocked opportunities and disappointments. Broman examines the different coping strategies African Americans use to deal with personal problems. His results show that blacks use a variety of coping strategies but that such strategies vary tremendously depending on the type of personal problem confronting the individual and personal characteristics such as gender and social status. Chapter 8 provides a strong argument for additional studies of how blacks cope with stress. It also represents a forceful testimony to the unique contribution of African American culture to the dynamics of survival.

Previous analyses of the NSBA have shown the importance of informal social networks for African Americans (Chatters, Taylor, & Neighbors, 1989). In fact, Chatters et al.'s research has clearly documented the significance of kin and nonkin sources of assistance in coping with personal problems. Their studies describe the complex system of exchange provided by the black extended family and close friends. In Chapter 9, "Kin and Nonkin as Sources of Informal Assistance," Robert Joseph Taylor, Cheryl Burns Hardison, and Linda M. Chatters expand on their previous gerontological research on family support by focusing on the informal networks of younger and middle-aged blacks as well. Chapter 9 also explores the use of informal help in a comprehensive fashion by actually differentiating the importance of family as opposed to friends and neighbors as sources of help in response to a serious personal problem. The findings reported by these authors reinforce the importance of the black family in providing the first line of assistance, especially for health problems. Taylor et al. caution, however, about the possible overreliance on family helpers for health problems and provide evidence that people are more likely to use nonkin helpers for interpersonal problems.

Chapter 10 also addresses help-seeking behavior, but this investigation focuses exclusively on black women and explores the combined use of informal and professional help. Cleopatra Howard Caldwell argues that because it is impossible for professional helpers to service all blacks in need of assistance, it is necessary to distinguish among those African Americans who truly require professional help and those who will be fine with a little help from family, friends, and neighbors (Neighbors & Jackson, 1984). Caldwell's analysis, "Predisposing, Enabling, and Need Factors Related to Patterns of Help-Seeking Among African American Women," will aid efforts designed to augment mental health services by identifying additional community supports. This chapter also highlights the personal characteristics of those black women who will benefit most by using informal help alone compared to those who need a combination of informal and professional help.

In Chapter 11, Vickie M. Mays, Cleopatra Howard Caldwell, and James S. Jackson offer a unique and insightful clinical perspective on how and why black women utilize mental health services for help with problems. "Mental Health Symptoms and Service Utilization Patterns of Help-Seeking Among African American Women" explores black women's use of community mental health centers and private psychotherapists while focusing more specifically on the importance of ethnic group consciousness, religiosity, and cultural resources in the use of mental health services. This chapter provides an in-depth analysis of help seeking by exploring more than the demographic correlates of the decision to seek help. Rather, it examines the implications of treatment once black women make contact with the professional therapist (e.g., exploring black women's preference for African American therapists). This chapter clearly shows the need to know much more about African American women's use of mental health resources in order to design clinical services that are gender sensitive and culturally specific.

The relationship between African Americans and law enforcement has been the center of much attention and debate. The message seems to be clear—blacks and the police do not get along. In Chapter 12, "The Police: A Reluctant Social Service Agency in the African American Community," Patricia A.

Washington provides a refreshing look at this important topic. Washington demonstrates that despite much media attention, the role that police officers play in responding to the problems of African Americans has not received the amount of rigorous empirical investigation it deserves. Chapter 12 combines quantitative and qualitative approaches to investigate the use of police assistance as a help resource during stressful situations. The chapter operates under the premise that some African Americans in distress do indeed request assistance from the police—but only after exhausting other available help resources. It is also significant that many of the requests for police assistance do not directly involve matters of law enforcement. Washington's insights into how and why some African Americans are inclined (sometimes compelled) to turn to the police with personal problems will challenge many of the attitudes and beliefs we hold regarding the role of law enforcement in the lives of African Americans.

In Chapter 13, we turn to a more dynamic view of the changes in some key indicators of African American mental health over the volatile period of the 1980s. Analyses in this chapter are based on the NSBA that followed the original 1980 NSBA respondents and interviewed a substantial number of them on three additional occasions—1987-1988, 1988-1989, and finally in 1992. Our purpose in this last chapter is to continue the exploration of the important themes focused on in the main sections of the book. Thus, we examine the individual changes over the 13-year period from 1979 to 1992 in sources of positive life well-being, the distribution and nature of physical and mental health difficulties and life dissatisfactions, and the nature of the coping resources and ways of coping employed by African Americans in maintaining healthy psychological lives. An overriding concern in this last chapter is the manner in which African Americans' emotional and psychological life may have shifted in response to the press and stressors engendered through a period of adverse economic, political, and social circumstances (Adams, 1996; Jackson & Adams, 1992).

Conclusions

More than two decades ago, the National Institute of Mental Health concluded that it was impossible to provide precise descriptions of the frequency of mental health problems among African Americans due to a number of methodological difficulties in the measurement and compilation of mental health statistics (Kramer, Rosen, & Willis, 1973). Mental health data had not been routinely collected in a systematic way by race. Data that were available by race were most often dichotomized as white-nonwhite. The majority of studies used measures developed and validated on white populations to provide estimates of incidence and prevalence (Adebimpe, 1981, 1994; Dressler, Viteri, Chavez, Grell, & Dos Santos, 1991; Flaherty et al., 1988; Malgady, Rogler, & Tryon, 1992). Furthermore, researchers could not be certain that the meanings of diagnostic categories were equivalent across racial groups (Bell & Mehta, 1980, 1981; Neighbors, Jackson, Campbell, & Williams, 1989). Thus, mental health planners had no way of knowing what needs African Americans had for mental health services and how adequately those needs were being met.

It is true that we now have much more data on the distribution of discrete mental disorders among African Americans than we did 25 years ago. This is primarily due to the publication and distribution of the Epidemiologic Catchment Area Program's regional results (Freedman, 1984; Robins & Regier, 1991) and analyses of those data focused specifically on African Americans (Brown, Milburn, Ahmed, Gary, & Booth, 1990; Sussman, Robins, & Earls, 1987; Williams, Takeuchi, & Adair, 1992a, 1992b).[3]

In conclusion, when all of the chapters in *Mental Health in Black America* are viewed together, the result is a portrait of African American mental health unlike any picture painted to date. There have been a number of important texts focusing specifically on minority mental health that have, over the years, made important contributions to the field of minority mental health (e.g., Dressler, 1991; Friedman, 1994; Gary, 1978a; Ruiz, 1990; Snowden, 1982; Thomas & Sillen, 1972; Willie, Kramer, & Brown 1973). It is fair to say, however, that never before has there been such a comprehensive collection of nationally based empirical investigations that have addressed the concept of African American mental health from so many perspectives, nor has there been a book whose results are relevant to so many different segments of the African American community.

Mental Health in Black America contains findings that confirm what many blacks intuitively feel they already know. The book also contains some surprises. Many of the conclusions contained herein will challenge some of our conceptions of black life. Actually, the fact that a book about black mental health contains counterintuitive findings should not be very surprising. The truth of the matter is that if there is any one topic that blacks, like many other Americans, avoid discussing, it is mental health. Unfortunately, there remains considerable stigma and embarrassment surrounding terms such as *crazy* and *nervous breakdown.* Fortunately, many of the people interviewed for this book were able to overcome such obstacles and talk freely about the serious personal difficulties they have had to confront as African Americans. Thus, this book addresses the topic of mental health directly from the responses of a nationally representative sample of African Americans telling their own stories of how they cope with the inevitable stresses and strains of being black in America. It was the role of the authors to take these stories and provide a coherent and comprehensible presentation. We think you will agree that they have succeeded admirably.

Notes

1. To quote Veroff and his colleagues (1981) discussing the methodological difficulties in specifying the relationship of race to mental health in a multivariate context:

> With a larger sample of blacks in each year, we could detect changes that have occurred. However, the confounding of education level or occupation or income with race in our small sample severely handicaps our analysis. Education and income are powerfully related to well-being. When we filter out these effects and look at race effects net of such status factors, we are straining our analytic technique, given the small size of the black sample. It takes a very large year difference to achieve significance when group size is small. When we control income and/or education, we simply do not have enough left to reach significance. (p. 432)

2. For example, one early problem with the epidemiologic literature on race and mental health was that too many studies relied on admission to treatment as the operational definition of mental disorder. Treatment rate studies have been harshly criticized as being inadequate for estimating the distribution of psychological problems because of variability in black help-seeking behavior (Adebimpe, 1994; Cannon & Locke, 1977; Fischer, 1969, among others). Personal feelings of distress are not always defined as a mental health problem. Even when distress is so defined, it does not always lead to the use of professional help, much less contact with a mental health resource (Neighbors, Caldwell, Thompson, & Jackson, 1994). In short, treatment rate studies raise more questions about the help-seeking process than they answer about the distribution of psychological problems in the African American population.

3. We still lack comprehensive national epidemiologic information about rates of psychiatric disorders by race in the United States, although that situation too is about to change once the results of the National Co-Morbidity Survey (NCS) become more widely distributed (Kessler et al., 1994). Interestingly, Kessler et al. found that blacks had lower rates of mood and substance use disorders. In fact, there were no disorders that were consistently higher for blacks than for whites (p. 13).

2

A Model-Free Approach to the Study of Subjective Well-Being

Carolyn B. Murray
M. Jean Peacock

Mental health is most frequently assessed through objective evaluations that consider individual adjustment and coping capabilities. Important, too, are subjective evaluations that provide researchers and mental health workers with information pertaining to how the individual feels "inside" about life situations. Self-assessments can be categorized under the rubrics "subjective well-being" or "psychological well-being." Positive self-evaluations are related to mental health or mental well-being, whereas negative self-evaluations may indicate distress or mental disorder (Franklin & Jackson, 1990).

Until recently, research on African Americans' perceived life quality was limited to small and nonrepresentative samples. In addition, most of the available research examining the quality of life construct compared African Americans to Euro-Americans without considering the appropriateness of methods and procedures across different populations (Jackson, Chatters, & Taylor, 1993; Jackson, Tucker, & Bowman, 1982). Furthermore, larger studies were based on comparisons between representative samples of Euro-Americans and nonrepresentative samples of African Americans.

The National Survey of Black Americans (NSBA) (Jackson, 1991) allows for the exploration of subjective well-being within a large representative sample of African Americans. The NSBA's research design addresses many of the problems that have plagued the "quality of life" research such as the lack of sample representativeness and reliance on small sample sizes. In addition, the NSBA employs theoretically sensitive models, instruments, and procedures appropriate for African Americans (Jackson et al., 1982).

The large amount of information gathered in a well-designed and well-executed survey, such as the NSBA, permits a level of exploration not possible with other more restricted data-gathering procedures. Advantages achieved through development of appropriate conceptual frameworks and new data collection procedures, as well as through redefining constructs, however, may be stifled by restrictive assumptions at the data analysis level. Although theoretical models or assumptions guide research analysis, restrictive assumptions may result in a loss in the richness of the data, a restriction of possible interaction effects, and an increase in predictive error. On the other hand, ransacking large data sets is cumbersome, time-consuming, and costly. A model-free data analysis approach, the automatic interaction detector (AID), is proposed in this chapter as a viable solution to both restrictive assumptions and time-consuming procedures (Sonquist, Baker, & Morgan, 1973). Prior to searching the data for the purpose of identifying an optimal model to explain subjective well-being, however, some theory must be initially applied to aid in the selection of predictors.

Indicators of Psychological Well-Being

Why some people are happy and others are not has been the subject of scientific inquiry for some time. Three decades ago, a comprehensive literature review conducted by Wilson (1967) cited numerous studies designed to measure and define the well-being construct often assumed to be a function of varying degrees of happiness. Even as early as 1930, Watson (cited in Wilson, 1967) reported that good health, high job morale, a happy home, and positive relationships with others were factors significant to happiness. Wilson's own conclusions supported such correlates, but his research also implied that happiness in life was available only to the privileged. According to Wilson, "the happy person emerges a young, healthy, well educated, well paid, extroverted, optimistic, worry free, religious married person with high self-esteem, high job morale, modest aspirations, of either sex and a wide range of intelligence" (p. 294).

In a similar vein, Bradburn and Caplovitz (1965) and Bradburn (1969) defined well-being in terms of happiness but conceptualized happiness as a product of two affective components. Specifically, Bradburn concluded that psychological well-being may be viewed as a person's position on two independent dimensions—one of positive affect and the other of negative affect. Thus, it appears logical to conclude that the degree to which one is high on well-being is contingent on the extent to which that individual has experienced positive as opposed to negative affect.

Methodologically, the relative independence of positive and negative affect was challenged in the psychological literature but was eventually supported by Bryant and Veroff (1982) and by Diener, Larsen, Levine, and Emmons (cited in Diener, 1984). Diener suggested that measurement scales may be at fault in studies that failed to replicate Bradburn's (1969) findings. For one reason, results derived from frequency data showed that positive and negative affect were strongly inversely correlated. If scales assessed only emotional intensity, however, the results indicated that the two types of affect were strongly positively related. Finally, if the scales tapped both frequency and intensity, then mean levels of affect were being measured, suggesting near independence between positive and negative affect.

A third dimension of well-being, life satisfaction, has been defined by Neugarten, Havighurst, and Tobin (1961) and by Andrews and Withey (1976). In research with an aging population, Neugarten et al. outlined the domain (as reflected in the life satisfaction rating scale) as the extent to which an individual takes pleasure from whatever activities constitute everyday life, regards life as meaningful and accepts resolutely that which life has been, feels he or she has succeeded in achieving his or her major goals, holds a positive self-image, and is relatively happy and optimistic.

In summary, a social psychological perspective provides both theoretical and empirical support for the following dimensions of psychological well-being: (a) happiness, defined as high intensity and duration of positive affect; (b) unhappiness or distress, which can be defined as high intensity and duration of negative affect; and (c) life satisfaction—cognitive judgments about one's life using one's own standards as the baseline for comparison.

Correlates of Psychological Well-Being

Age. One of the most pervasive stereotypes in American culture is that, in contrast to young and middle-aged persons, elderly persons are less happy or satisfied with life. It was assumed that social, physical, and psychological losses that accompany the transition to old age would account for a subsequent dissatisfaction with life (see Rosow, 1967). Early research findings supported this notion (Gurin, Veroff, & Feld, 1960; Rosow, 1967), but more recent research has challenged this work with reports of virtually no age effects (Spreitzer & Snyder, 1974) or reports of positive correlations between age and satisfaction (Campbell, Converse, & Rodgers, 1976; Hertzog & Rodgers, 1981; Medley, 1980). Thus, examinations of the relationships between age and subjective well-being have focused primarily on the direction and magnitude of the relationship and the identification of the intervening variables that account for that relationship.

For older African Americans, the "double jeopardy hypothesis" suggests that minority group status adds another layer of problems that further tax well-being (Murray, Khatib, & Jackson, 1989). On the other hand, the main competing perspective, the "age-as-leveler hypothesis," suggests that majority-minority differences as determinants of well-being are reduced in later life (Janson & Mueller, 1983). Specifically, although young African Americans (ages 25-44) usually scored lower on dimensions of well-being than young Euro-Americans (Andrews & Withey, 1976), middle-aged and older African Americans reported no difference (Hertzog & Rodgers, 1981) or reported higher morale than their Euro-American counterparts (Messer, 1968). It is now generally agreed that, traditionally, African Americans accept age and look forward to the rewards of advanced years. In summary, the literature suggests that although age is positively associated with satisfaction for both African Americans and Euro-Americans, the relationship is more pronounced among African Americans (Jackson, Chatters, & Neighbors, 1986).

Stresses and Problems. Any change in life that requires a person to adapt to new circumstances can cause stress, including beneficial change. Especially troublesome are negative events such as health, money, and personal problems. For instance, people with a large number of events regarded as bad were more likely to report physical and emotional problems 6 months later (Dohrenwend, Krassnoff, Askenasy, & Dohrenwend, 1978; Sarason, Johnson, & Siegel, 1978). In addition, uncontrollable negative life events (death of a loved one, job loss, and sudden illness) were directly associated with depression (Dohrenwend & Dohrenwend, 1974b).

An inverse relationship between well-being or mental health and life events is well documented. The analysis provided by Williams, Ware, and Donald (1981) is noteworthy in that their data were longitudinal and were based on a representative sample of 2,234 respondents. Among other findings, the results supported the prediction that life events negatively affected mental health over time. Moreover, problematic interactions were found to be negatively related to life satisfaction (Brenner, Norvell, & Limacher, 1989).

An examination of the social well-being for African Americans demonstrated a very serious difference in living conditions and access to resources compared to Euro-Americans (Kiyak & Hooyman, 1994). African Americans tend to be more poverty stricken, less rewarded (and more discouraged) in seeking employment, less able to afford decent housing, and more debilitated in terms of health problems than their Euro-American counterparts (Murray et al., 1989). The inferior social, political, and economic conditions that African Americans encounter may result in differential processes underlying the development of subjective expressions of well-being (Jackson, Chatters, & Neighbors, 1986).

Not enough information is available that reports the impact of stressful life events on African Americans. Even fewer studies systematically address stressful life differences between African Americans and Euro-Americans (Dohrenwend & Dohrenwend, 1974b). Several competing theories address this issue. Michalos (1980) predicted that life satisfaction will decline as a function of the gap between an individual's aspirations and his or her assessment of actual accomplishments. It might be expected, then, that for African Americans, a group whose life accomplishments have been restricted by systemic forces, the effect of stressful life events would be clearly exhibited (Jackson, Chatters, & Neighbors, 1986; Krause, 1993; Neff, 1985).

An opposing theory suggests that adjustment factors may operate that abrogate any gap relationship to reported satisfaction. For instance, Campbell et al. (1976) wrote,

> Aspirations do in fact become adjusted to reality, as witnessed by the low aspiration levels of the poorly educated and the shrinkage of aspirations with aging. At the same time, however, we have shown that statements of satisfaction in all the domains investigated, as well as the more global reports of happiness and overall satisfaction with life, appear quite responsive in the expected ways to benign and adverse changes in life situation. (p. 208)

A third theory argues that perceptions of societal inequity may be a more salient process underlying satisfaction than gaps in aspirations, expectations, and attainments (Carp & Carp, 1982c)—that is, another consideration might be that cultural or ethnic differences or both exist in perceptions of what is stressful. For instance, an impending birth to an unwed teenage daughter might be perceived as more stressful by Euro-Americans than by African

Americans. On the other hand, being stopped by the police for a minor traffic violation might be perceived as more stressful by African Americans.

Finally, self-evaluations might have been mediated by social comparison differences. Specifically, when evaluating subjective well-being, do persons of different ethnic and social classes compare themselves with similar others, an ideal other, or neither? Given that few, if any, studies have considered these possibilities, the effects of stressful life events on the subjective well-being of African Americans are questionable at best.

Social Support. A third correlate of well-being is social support (Bell, Leroy, & Stephenson, 1982). Research has found that life satisfaction correlated positively with total sources of social support (Brenner et al., 1989). Moreover, greater levels of life satisfaction were reported by those with no consistent sources of negative interaction and by those with more total sources of social support. Numerous cross-sectional and longitudinal studies are in agreement, suggesting that the absence of social support negatively affects well-being. For instance, marriage is probably a resource fostering life satisfaction at all ages (Campbell et al., 1976), although its normative importance varies across the life course. Being unmarried is more acceptable during young adulthood before stable life patterns have been established and is least acceptable during the middle years (Levinson, 1978). Being married is also a resource during old age, but the lack of a marital partner is not likely to be stigmatizing because of high rates of widowhood (Lopata, 1973). Thus, being married is most likely related to subjective well-being for middle-aged persons, least strongly related for young adults, and moderately related for older adults (George, Okun, & Landerman, 1985).

George et al. (1985) proposed that social support is more important for young and old adults than for the middle aged. The basis for their assumption is that a greater proportion of the middle aged are married than are young and older adults, lessening the need for social support outside the marital dyad. In addition, they pointed out that middle-aged people tend to be more strongly attached to the social structure via formal social roles (e.g., occupational and community roles) than are younger and older adults.

Although both observations are also true for African Americans (Crohan, Antonucci, Adelmann, & Coleman, 1989), it is to a lesser degree because of the high number of single parent households, premature widowhood, and high unemployment and underemployment rates (Thompson & Peebles-Wilkins, 1992). For instance, Brown and Gary's (1985) investigation of 91 married and 183 nonmarried African American females found that family members and extended kin were the primary source of social support irrespective of marital status. This body of literature appears disjointed, however, as evidenced by both main and interaction effects of social support.

In summary, it seems to be important for one to feel part of a network that causes the individual to perceive that he or she is cared for and loved. This network operates to mediate or "buffer" life events, thereby decreasing vulnerability to such strains. For African Americans, however, the impact on life satisfaction of the various constellations of social support is not clearly explicated in the literature. Because of the restrictive nature of the data, small sample sizes, and inappropriate methods, the literature on subjective well-being among African Americans is questionable at best. With regard to the predictors of subjective well-being, the present focus is on age, stress, and social support. Although the empirical data examining the effects of these predictors of subjective well-being are flawed, the literature is consistent in its assertion that they do play an important role.

The analytic approach that follows results in the development of a model for explaining subjective well-being in a large representative sample of African Americans by determining how these predictive variables relate to this phenomenon, under what conditions, and through what intervening process.

A Model-Free Approach

The automatic interaction detector (AID) program (Sonquist et al., 1973) was employed to help explain which factors predicted subjective well-being. AID searches large data sets for complex and interacting relationships in prediction of an interval-scaled dependent variable. Unlike regression, AID does not impose assumptions of linearity and additivity (i.e., the absence of interaction) or symmetry. To use the AID program, one must specify a dependent variable, a set of predicting characteristics, and some strategy parameters. In place of restrictive assumptions, reliance is on a prearranged procedure that begins with the most stable and dependable finding (division of the data set on that predictor that reduces the variance of the dependent variable the most) and works down to less dependable and less powerful findings on smaller subgroups. The goal is not to exhaust all the information in the predictors but to discover how they work.

The program operates sequentially, imposes a minimum of assumptions on the data, and does a great deal of searching. (The program prespecifies a strategy of the search process so that it is reproducible.) Theory is involved in the selection of explanatory variables, their hierarchical ranking, and in the interpretation of the results. AID was specifically used to relate the dependent variable, subjective well-being, to a set of independent variables: age, whether one or more of nine problems had been experienced over the past month, and the various social support variables. The program scans all possible dichotomous splits on a given independent variable and retains the one that explains the greatest fraction of the variance of the dependent variable.

Dependent Variable. Subjective well-being was measured by the following questions: "Taking all things together, how would you say things are these days—would you say you're very happy, pretty happy, or not too happy these days?" and "In general, how satisfied are you with your life as a whole these days? Would you say that you are very satisfied, somewhat satisfied, somewhat dissatisfied or very dissatisfied?" The happiness and life satisfaction items were combined into a factor that represented the dependent variable.

Independent Variables. The independent variables were age, negative life events, and social support items. Age was partitioned into two levels: persons 18 to 54 years old and those who were 55 years of age or older. Regarding negative life events, the respondents were asked to answer "yes" or "no" to whether they had experienced each of nine day-to-day stresses or problems (e.g., health, money, family, marriage) within the past month. The independent variable for stressful life problems was based on whether the respondent reported experiencing zero to nine day-to-day stresses over the past month.

The social support independent variables were (a) degree of family closeness, (b) amount of family contact, (c) number of friends they could call on, (d) frequency of contact with friends, (e) number of neighbors they could visit or call on, and (f) how often they visit with neighbors.

Results

The variable that proved to be most important in explaining subjective well-being among African Americans was whether or not the respondent reported experiencing any problems over the past month, and the best division of the variable was between one or more problems and no problems. Respondents who reported experiencing no problems in the past month, as indicated in Figure 2.1, reported the highest levels of satisfaction with their lives (mean =

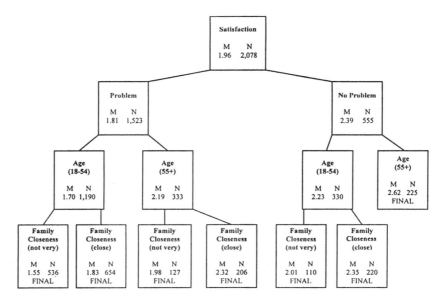

Figure 2.1. Means and Sample Sizes for Subjective Well-Being, by Negative Life Events, Age, and Family Closeness

2.39), which was in contrast to respondents who reported one or more of the nine problems over the past month (mean = 1.81).

The AID program then further divides the sample and assesses all of the predictors for importance in explaining who, among those reporting problems, are more likely to report higher subjective well-being. It repeats the process on the population that reported not having had any of the nine problems in the past month. Although persons reporting no problems over the past month have higher subjective well-being than persons who reported at least one problem, within the no-problem and the problem groups persons 55 years of age and over reported higher subjective well-being than did persons under the age of 55.

Age was important to both the problem and the no-problem subgroups and had similar effects within each group. This indicates that the effects of age on a respondent's reported subjective well-being do not depend on whether problems were experienced over the past month—that is, there appears to be no interaction between having experienced problems and age. Figure 2.1 shows that the main predictor of subjective well-being was whether the respondent experienced problems over the past month. Being over 54 years of age also contributed within each of the subgroups. More specifically, the older group (55+ years of age) was more likely to report positive subjective well-being.

After the four problem/age subgroups have been created, the program next assesses the six social support variables in separate analyses for explanatory power within each of these subgroups. New, smaller subgroups are created and searched. This process continues until splits either result in subgroups that are too small or the splits themselves do not explain some minimum amount of the total variance (usually 0.5%) of the dependent variable (Morgan, Dickinson, Dickinson, Benus, & Duncan, 1974).

The AID program generates a diagram showing a successively finer set of population subgroups, defined by the sequence of divisions that created them. If the effects of the independent variables are additive, then the same predictors should appear symmetrically in the branches of the diagram and with similar effects. If, however, different subgroups are divided on quite different predictors or their effects are different, this lack of symmetry implies interactive effects. If an AID program is run using age, negative life events, and family closeness and another is run using age, negative life events, and family contact as independent variables, a noninteractive model for life events and age would first split the sample by problem and no problem and then by the two age groups for each analysis prior to any other decomposition of the sample by family closeness or contact. This is, in fact, what happened for all six analyses.

The analyses revealed that some but not all of the social support variables were important predictors of well-being. Figure 2.1 indicates that family closeness is important for three of the four subgroups. The exception was the no-problem respondents who were 55 years of age or older. In all three subgroups, the sample was further divided into two groups—those close and those not very close to family. The closer the family members, the more likely the respondent reported higher subjective well-being.

Figure 2.2 shows the results for the number of neighbors respondents could visit or call on. Number of neighbors was an important predictor only for persons with problems who were 55 years of age or older. The higher the reported number of neighbors, the higher the respondent's reported subjective well-being for this problem and age group. Family contact, number of friends, frequency of contact with friends, and how often neighbors were visited did not appear as important predictors of subjective well-being in this population.

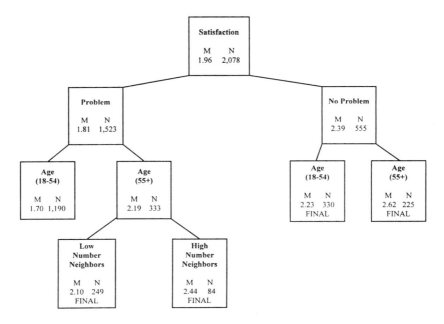

Figure 2.2. Means and Sample Sizes for Subjective Well-Being, by Negative Life Events, Age, and Number of Neighbors

For each of these factors, the AID program stopped after the four age group splits.[1]

Discussion and Conclusion

The variable that proved to be most important in explaining subjective well-being for African Americans was whether the respondent reported experiencing any problems over the past month, and the best division of the variable was between one or more problems and no problems. For both subgroups, persons 55 years of age or older are more likely to feel more satisfied with their lives in comparison to those who are under 55 years of age. Finally, different types of social support interact differently with the problem/age subgroups.

Family closeness and number of neighbors—but not family contact, number of friends, frequency of contact with friends, and how often visits with neighbors—explained subjective well-being. Specifically, family closeness explained subjective well-being for all the problem/age groups with the exception of persons 55 years of age or older who reported no problems. Individuals who reported that their families were "close" also reported higher subjective well-being. In line with the literature, it appears that the quality of interaction (i.e., family closeness) is more important than the frequency of interaction (i.e, family contact, number of friends, frequency of contact, and how often visits with neighbors) (Rao & Rao, 1983).

Interestingly, for persons 55 years old or older who report no problems, neither family closeness nor frequency of contact is an important predictor of subjective well-being. This finding is in contrast to the previously discussed assumption that social support is more important for young and old adults than for middle-aged adults (George et al., 1985). Explicating these results is the finding that for persons 55 years of age or older who report having problems, persons reporting higher subjective well-being also report having more neighbors. Thus, it appears that for older people with problems, both degree of closeness and number of neighbors are important, whereas neither is important for older adults without problems.

With regard to elderly persons without problems, one study found that persons who stay to themselves are usually homeowners and have what they consider adequate income (Stanford, 1978). Moreover, this behavior was especially true of those persons who were healthy and felt they could be independent. In summary, for older people without problems, social support does not appear to be an important contributor to subjective well-being. Further research on the mental health aspects of these findings is in order.

Another purpose of this chapter was to describe a model-free approach—the AID program—to identify and analyze relationships, specifically for surveys with a large number of cases. In particular, the AID approach was employed to investigate subjective self-evaluations of psychological well-being in African Americans. Traditional investigatory frameworks, procedures, and theoretical assumptions are of questionable legitimacy for use with African Americans (Jackson et al., 1982). This approach was efficacious in discovering indices or complex constructs that explain how age, stress, and social support are related to subjective well-being for African Americans without imposing restrictive assumptions on the data.

Once the importance of each predictor on each subgroup is discovered, the predictors can be introduced into a linear model that can be estimated and tested by the usual procedures. This testing, however, can be performed only on a fresh independent set of data and not with the data used to select the model (Morgan et al., 1974). The separation of the searching and testing is crucial and may be made possible by designating two random samples—one for the application of the AID program and the other for significance testing of the model generated.

The program should not be viewed as a panacea for all the problems that plague data analysis procedures, especially those that pertain to the study of African Americans. Sonquist et al. (1973), however, wrote,

> The general principle of the AID program is an application of a prestated, if complex, strategy simulating the procedure of a good researcher in searching for the predictors that increase his/her power to account for the variance of the dependent variable. (p. 1)

The AID program and other model-free approaches should go far in increasing our scientific knowledge and providing mental health workers with pertinent information to facilitate optimal African American mental health.

Note

1. Due to the similarity of the results, these diagrams are not shown.

3

Stress and Residential Well-Being

Gayle Y. Phillips

The quality of residential well-being among African Americans is an important emerging theme within the quality of life research literature (Deane, 1990). The housing and neighborhood quality of African Americans, for example, are not as good as those of whites (Struyk & Soldo, 1980), although the small number of African Americans included in these samples limits the generalizability of the findings. According to 1990 census data, blacks are more likely than whites to be renters (rather than homeowners) and many African Americans reside in declining residential areas. Stipak and Hensler (1983) discovered how residing in declining neighborhoods was a source of dissatisfaction whether black or white or low or high income. Blacks are also more likely to reside in poor-quality housing (U.S. Department of Housing and Urban Development, 1979).

Stressors emanating from the residential environment have been used to explain residential mobility, either directly or indirectly, through housing or neighborhood satisfaction (Brown & Moore, 1970; Brummell, 1981; Clark & Cadwallader, 1973; Kasl & Harburg, 1972; Marans, 1976; Speare, 1974; Varady, 1983; Wolpert, 1966). Blacks, however, frequently encounter institutional barriers and experience economic constraints limiting moves to improved residential environments (Fairchild & Tucker, 1982). Obstacles thrown in the path of aspirations for the upward social mobility represented by moving to a "better" neighborhood are stressful, and such stress emanates not only from the residential environment but also from discrete life events

(Baum, Singer, & Baum, 1981; Dohrenwend & Dohrenwend, 1974b; Evans, 1982; Fischer, 1984; Lazarus & Folkman, 1984; Levine & Scotch, 1970; Miller, 1989; Taylor, 1982). Stressful life events produce adverse effects on mental or residential well-being. Cox (1978) discussed the potential negative effects of stress on the quality of life and on psychological well-being. Cannon and Locke (1977) disclosed how racism, a chronic stressor, produced a negative effect on the mental health of blacks. Clopton (1978) and Gary (1978b) discussed the adverse relationship between stress and the quality of the residential environment of blacks. Dressler (1987) examined mental illness, preventive intervention, and delivery of interventions within the context of a southern black community.

Stress and neighborhood satisfaction are explored in this chapter by examining two questions: Do subjective social indicators, objective social indicators, personal attributes, and location of residence explain neighborhood satisfaction directly or indirectly through housing quality? Do subjective social indicators, objective social indicators, personal attributes, and location of residence explain neighborhood satisfaction directly or indirectly through stress? The conceptual model contains the hypothesized relationships of this study (Figure 3.1). The subjective social indicators, objective social indicators, personal attributes, and location of residence are hypothesized as having direct effects on neighborhood satisfaction and indirect effects through housing quality and through stress. Among African Americans, the subjective and objective social indicators that explain neighborhood satisfaction may be different for males and females or for residents of urban and rural areas. For example, women, in contrast to men, tend to view safety and crime as major neighborhood problems (Campbell et al., 1976; Carp & Carp, 1982a).

Subjective Social Indicators

Subjective social indicators are residents' perceptions and evaluations of their residential environment. These indicators were derived from the results of factor analysis (Phillips, 1991). Three factors emerged from the factor analysis of 11 subjective social indicators: neighborhood crime-police relations, neighborhood services, and neighborhood social relations. Indices based on the variables loading high on each factor were created for each one. A fourth concept, neighborhood groups, was also explored. Several questions

Exogenous Variables   **Intervening Variables**   **Endogenous Variables**

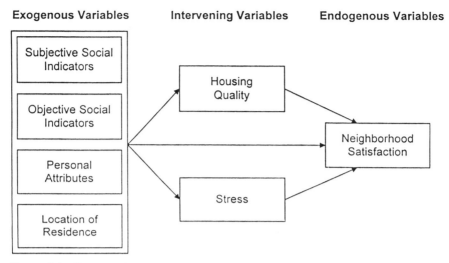

Figure 3.1. Conceptual Model of Neighborhood Satisfaction

from the National Survey of Black Americans (NSBA) (Jackson, 1991) were combined to create the variable neighborhood groups.

Neighborhood Crime-Police Relations

The index of neighborhood crime-police relations contains four subjective social indicators and has a Cronbach's alpha coefficient of .66. In general, respondents were somewhat satisfied (42%) rather than very satisfied (25%) with police protection (Table 3.1). About 28% of the respondents viewed crime problems as occurring fairly or very often, and 46% evaluated drug use and selling to be a fairly to very serious problem. A surprisingly high number (85%) of the respondents got along with the police. Previous research has shown that dissatisfaction with the police or problems with crime or drugs in the neighborhood decreases neighborhood satisfaction (Ahlbrandt & Cunningham, 1979; Campbell et al., 1976; Galster & Hesser, 1981; Lawton, 1978; Louis Harris and Associates, 1978; Marans, 1979). Police satisfaction, problems with crime and drugs in the neighborhood, and police-resident relations compose the index of neighborhood crime-police relations. The index of neighborhood crime-police relations is hypothesized to have a direct positive effect on neighborhood satisfaction.

Table 3.1 Neighborhood Crime-Police Relations

Crime-Police Relations	%	N
Police protection satisfaction		
Very satisfied	25.2	523
Somewhat satisfied	41.7	866
Somewhat dissatisfied	20.5	425
Somewhat dissatisfied	12.6	261
Total	100.0	2,075
Crime problems		
Never	12.2	251
Hardly ever	26.0	536
Not too often	33.6	693
Fairly often	15.0	309
Very often	13.2	273
Total	100.0	2,062
Drug problems		
Not serious at all	25.4	401
Not too serious	29.1	461
Fairly serious	19.4	307
Very serious	26.1	413
Total	100.0	1,582
Police-resident relations		
Very well	36.6	722
Fairly well	48.2	953
Not so well	9.7	192
Not well at all	5.5	109
Total	100.0	1,976

Neighborhood Services

Three subjective social indicators of public services comprise the index of neighborhood services. This index has an alpha coefficient of .44 and consists of satisfaction with garbage collection, schools, and public transportation (Table 3.2). Respondents were asked, "In general, how satisfied are you with [garbage collection, schools, and public transportation] around here?" The response categories ranged from very satisfied to very dissatisfied. Overall, respondents exhibited positive attitudes toward neighborhood services. A full 79% were either very or somewhat satisfied with garbage collection, whereas 76% were very or somewhat satisfied with schools. A slightly smaller per-

Table 3.2 Neighborhood Services

Services	%	N
Garbage collection satisfaction		
Very satisfied	48.6	986
Somewhat satisfied	30.6	621
Somewhat dissatisfied	11.3	229
Very dissatisfied	9.5	193
Total	100.0	2,029
School satisfaction		
Very satisfied	34.0	618
Somewhat satisfied	42.4	768
Somewhat dissatisfied	15.6	283
Very dissatisfied	8.0	146
Total	100.0	1,815
Public transportation satisfaction		
Very satisfied	32.0	600
Somewhat satisfied	35.2	660
Somewhat dissatisfied	14.1	264
Very dissatisfied	18.7	352
Total	100.0	1,876

centage (67%) were very or somewhat satisfied with public transportation services. High levels of satisfaction with neighborhood services are likely to result in high levels of neighborhood satisfaction. This is consistent with previous research (Ahlbrandt & Cunningham, 1979; Lawton, 1980b; Marans, 1979).

Neighborhood Social Relations

The index of neighborhood social relations includes three subjective social indicators: residency status, neighborhood friendliness, and number of neighbors visited. The alpha for this index was .41 (Table 3.3). Half (50%) of the respondents had lived in their neighborhoods for 10 years or more, whereas only 5% had lived there for less than 2 years. About 58% viewed neighbors as friendly or somewhat friendly. Half (50%) of the respondents said they had only a few neighbors they knew well enough to visit or call on; some respondents (12.5%) visited no neighbors. Neighborhood social relations are hypothesized as having a positive influence on neighborhood satisfaction, which is consistent with previous findings (Ahlbrandt, 1984; Campbell et al., 1976).

Table 3.3 Neighborhood Social Relations

Social Relations	%	N
Residency status: "Have most of the people in this neighborhood lived here more than 10 years, from 5 to 10 years, from 2 to 5 years or less than 2 years?"		
10 years or more	49.6	897
5-10 years	32.9	596
2-5 years	13.0	235
Less than 2 years	4.5	81
Total	100.0	1,809
Neighborhood friendliness		
Friendly neighbors	17.0	352
Somewhat friendly neighbors	41.3	855
Unfriendly neighbors	41.7	862
Total	100.0	2,069
Number of neighbors		
Many	20.0	421
Some	17.8	373
A few	49.7	1,044
None	12.5	263
Total	100.0	2,101
Neighborhood group participation		
Aware of groups and involved	14.8	312
Aware of groups and not involved	23.1	486
Not aware of groups so not involved	62.1	1,306
Total	100.0	2,104

Neighborhood Groups

Although it did not emerge during the factor analysis, the impact of neighborhood groups was explored. The neighborhood group participation variable was created by combining two questions asked of respondents: "Are there any groups in the neighborhood (block clubs, community associations, social clubs, helping groups, and so on)?" and "Are you involved with any of these groups?" (Table 3.3). The response categories created from these two questions are: neighborhood participation, neighborhood nonparticipation, and neighborhood group unawareness. Neighborhood participation means that respondents are aware of neighborhood groups and participate in them (14.8%). By contrast, neighborhood nonparticipation means that respondents are aware of neighborhood groups but opt not to participate (23%). Neighbor-

hood group unawareness means that respondents are unaware of neighborhood groups and thus are not participants (62%).

Problems evolving from or pertaining to the residential environment are
predictors of neighborhood participation. Thus it makes sense to explore
whether participation in neighborhood groups has any relationship with
neighborhood satisfaction. Cox and McCarthy (1980) found a significant
relationship between neighborhood problems and neighborhood activism.
Ahlbrandt (1984), however, discovered a nonsignificant association between
belonging to a neighborhood group and neighborhood satisfaction. Orbell and
Uno (1972) showed that blacks were more likely than whites of similar status,
in similar urban areas, to deal with residential problems by voicing their
concerns rather than by moving; this effect increased with length of residence
for blacks (see also Ahlbrandt & Cunningham, 1979; Miller, Tsemberis,
Malia, & Grega, 1980; Wolpert, 1984).

Objective Social Indicators

Objective social indicators used in this study are the interviewers' ratings
of the residential environment. Interviewers were instructed to note, to the
extent possible, the presence of specified residential attributes in the neighborhood and surrounding area. These residential attributes ranged from respondents' housing quality to the presence of commercial buildings.

Based on the interviewers' ratings, 65.6% of the respondents' houses
required major or minor repairs (Table 3.4). The vast majority of respondents
lived in low- and moderate-income neighborhoods and the yards in the
neighborhoods were maintained well—74% reported yards that were very or
fairly well maintained. Although few respondents resided in government
housing projects (5.9%), more single-family dwellings (80.5%) than multidwelling units (37.1%) existed in these neighborhoods. Another 15.2% of the
neighborhoods had vacant land, abandoned buildings (15.7%), parks (8.4%),
schools (11.9%), or government and commercial buildings (19.8%).

Not all objective social indicators are expected to directly or indirectly
explain neighborhood satisfaction. In previous research, however, many were
significant in explaining individual or collective residential satisfaction
(Campbell et al., 1976; Zehner, 1977). The objective social indicators have
somewhat limited objectivity because of their source of origin—the interviewers' ratings. They are, however, useful in understanding the dimensions

Table 3.4 Objective Social Indicators

Interviewer's Ratings	%	N
Housing quality: "Are the structures in need of repair?"		
No repairs needed	34.4	706
Minor repairs needed	42.9	880
Major repairs needed	22.7	466
Total	100.0	2,052
Estimated neighborhood income		
Low (under $10,000)	47.5	968
Medium ($10,000-$25,000)	44.9	914
High (over $25,000)	7.6	155
Total	100.0	2,037
Yard upkeep		
Very well	25.7	522
Fairly well	48.5	986
Poorly	12.9	261
Very poorly	5.3	112
No front yard[a]	7.4	150
Total	100.0	2,031
Government housing project		
Yes	5.9	120
No	94.1	1,909
Total	100.0	2,029
"Look at the structures in R's neighborhood and check as many as apply."[b]		
Multidwelling units (apartments, townhouses, etc.)	37.1	779
Single-family dwellings	80.5	1,688
Boarded-up or abandoned buildings	15.7	330
Vacant land only	15.2	319
Park	8.4	176
School or government buildings	11.9	249
Commercial buildings	19.8	416

a. Yard upkeep was recorded to exclude no front yard from the multiple regression analyses.
b. Only "yes" responses are reported. "No" responses are calculated by subtracting N (yes) from the total N.

underlying neighborhood satisfaction (Campbell et al., 1976; Morgan, 1978; Zehner, 1977).

In summary, there is a scarcity of research utilizing objective and subjective social indicators to analyze and monitor intragroup differences and the residential well-being of blacks. Findings from this study will contribute to the efforts of social scientists to collect objective social indicators that are independent from subjective assessments and to use equivalent measures of the objective and subjective environment to determine the level of congruence or incongruence in explaining and monitoring residential well-being over time (Andrews, 1981; Carp & Carp, 1982b; Lee & Marans, 1980).

Personal Attributes

In addition to residential social indicators, personal attributes have made independent contributions in explaining neighborhood satisfaction. This analysis explores five personal attributes that are hypothesized to have both direct and indirect effects on neighborhood satisfaction: age, marital status, tenure status, household income, and household size. Seventy-two percent of the respondents were under 55 years of age. Forty-two percent of the respondents were married. Nearly as many respondents were renters (47%) as were homeowners (49%). Others (4%) resided in alternative housing arrangements. In 1979 and 1980, 51% of the respondents had incomes under $10,000, 27% had incomes ranging from $10,000 to $19,999, and 22% had incomes of $20,000 or more.

The literature indicates that all of the personal attributes exert some effect on residential satisfaction. For example, the elderly tend to be more satisfied with their neighborhoods than the nonelderly (Campbell et al., 1976; Lawton, 1978). Homeowners are more satisfied with their neighborhoods than renters (Marans, 1979; Struyk & Soldo, 1980). Marital status, household size, and household income are also related to neighborhood satisfaction (Campbell et al., 1976; Galster & Hesser, 1981; Marans & Rodgers, 1975).

Location of Residence

According to census data of 1980 and 1990, more blacks reside in the South than in other regions (O'Hare, Pollard, Mann, & Kent, 1991). The housing quality of blacks in the South is not as good as that in other regions (Dillman & Hobbs, 1982; Lawton, 1980a; Mayer & Lee, 1980; Struyk & Soldo, 1980). Urban and rural residents have been found to experience similar stressful life events (Miller, Bentz, Aponte, & Brogan, 1974; Webb & Collette, 1979). One question this research focuses on is the extent to which location of residence explains neighborhood satisfaction directly or indirectly through housing quality or through stress.

Stressful Life Events

Stress is an intervening variable in the conceptual model of neighborhood satisfaction (Figure 3.1). The multivariate analyses will seek to answer whether subjective social indicators, objective social indicators, personal attributes, and location of residence explain neighborhood satisfaction indirectly through stress. In this chapter, stress was measured by counting the total number of problems respondents experienced in approximately the past month. Specifically, respondents were asked to indicate whether problems on a list had happened to them within that period of time. The list includes problems with health, money, job, family, marriage or relationships, children, or people outside the family; being a victim of a crime or the police; and being treated badly because of race. Overall, respondents reported few problem stressors. For example, 52.7% experienced no or 1 problem, 43.2% experienced 2 to 5 problems, and only 4.1% experienced 6 to 10 problems.

Neighborhood Satisfaction

Expressing high levels of satisfaction with the neighborhood while simultaneously evaluating some residential conditions as problems raises questions about what explains neighborhood satisfaction (Campbell et al., 1976; Marans, 1976; Marans & Rodgers, 1975). Thus, the dependent variable in the conceptual model is neighborhood satisfaction (Figure 3.1). Notwithstanding other conceptual and methodological issues, a general assumption is that feeling good about the neighborhood means being satisfied with the neighborhood. Neighborhood satisfaction was measured by asking, "In general, how do you feel about this neighborhood?" The response categories range from very good to very bad. Most respondents felt fairly good (56.5%) about their neighborhood, whereas 32.5% felt very good; only 11.0% felt fairly or very bad about their neighborhood.

Multivariate Analysis

Based on the descriptive data presented previously, the multivariate analysis seeks to show which indicators (subjective social indicators, objective social indicators, personal attributes, and location of residence) explain neighborhood satisfaction for this national sample of blacks. It will also clarify the

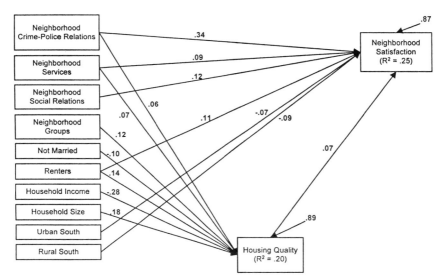

Figure 3.2. Subjective Social Indicators, Personal Attributes, and Location of Residence

roles that housing quality and stress play in neighborhood satisfaction. Path analysis was necessary to answer these questions. This is a statistical technique enabling the decomposition of direct, indirect, and total effects of hypothesized causal relationships (Alwin & Hauser, 1975; Asher, 1976; Blalock, 1971; Duncan, 1966; Finney, 1972). The results reveal similarities and differences in the exogenous variables used to explain neighborhood satisfaction for males, females, and total sample.[1]

Subjective, Personal, and Location Effects

The results indicate how the exogenous variables directly or indirectly relate to neighborhood satisfaction through housing quality (Figure 3.2). The exogenous variables are neighborhood crime-police relations, neighborhood services, neighborhood social relations, neighborhood groups, age 55 years or over, not married, renters, household income, household size, urban South, rural South, and rural non-South, with urban non-South as the excluded comparison group. All multiple regression equations and path coefficients are significant at the .05 level except for the path coefficient between housing quality and neighborhood satisfaction. The exogenous variables such as age and rural non-South are not in the path models.

The model shown in Figure 3.2 was also run separately for males and females. For males (figure not shown), neighborhood crime-police relations produce the strongest impact on neighborhood satisfaction (i.e., the absence of crime and satisfactory police relations). Positive perceptions of neighborhood social relations also directly increase neighborhood satisfaction. For males who do not rent, all significant personal attributes along with the location of the residence explain neighborhood satisfaction indirectly through housing quality. In contrast, males who rent express high levels of satisfaction with their neighborhoods independent of housing quality. The insignificant path coefficient between housing quality and neighborhood satisfaction minimizes indirect effects for males; the findings suggest, however, that low-quality housing lowers the level of neighborhood satisfaction for unmarried males and for males with low and moderate incomes. In the rural South, quality housing increases neighborhood satisfaction for males; this is not true for other locations of residence. Males with large households (four or more persons) who reside in high-quality housing are most likely to be satisfied with their neighborhoods.

A somewhat different pattern emerges for females (figure not shown). Neighborhood crime-police relations has the strongest association with neighborhood satisfaction, as it does for males. Neighborhood services and neighborhood social relations also have direct positive associations with neighborhood satisfaction. Renting has both a direct and an indirect association on neighborhood satisfaction for females, but the indirect association is reduced because of the size of the path coefficient between housing quality and neighborhood satisfaction. For females, neighborhood groups have a positive indirect association with neighborhood satisfaction; this is not true for males. It may be that participating in neighborhood groups for problem resolution facilitates the improvement or maintenance of housing and neighborhood quality or both. This hypothesis is supported by past research (Bachrach & Zautra, 1985). Females with low or moderate incomes respond similarly to males with respect to the quality of housing and its effect on the level of neighborhood satisfaction. Housing that needs repair negatively affects the level of neighborhood satisfaction for females in the urban South. Lower levels of neighborhood satisfaction prevail more among females in the rural South than among females residing in other areas. Age and marital status are not statistically significant explanatory variables for neighborhood satisfaction among females.

When looking at the total sample, the small size of the path coefficient between housing quality and neighborhood satisfaction minimizes indirect effects on neighborhood satisfaction. Neighborhood crime-police relations and neighborhood services both directly and indirectly explain neighborhood satisfaction. Respondents in the South, both urban and rural, are less satisfied with their neighborhoods than those in other areas. Neighborhood groups have a positive, indirect association with neighborhood satisfaction for unmarried respondents and for those with low and moderate incomes. Age is not statistically related to neighborhood satisfaction or housing quality either when looking at the total sample or when the sample is broken down by gender.

In summary, either directly or indirectly, some subjective social indicators and personal attributes significantly explain neighborhood satisfaction as does location of residence. The direct effects are stronger than the indirect effects. The size and, in some cases, the insignificance of the path coefficients between housing quality and neighborhood satisfaction reduce the strength of the indirect effects. Neighborhood crime-police relations, neighborhood social relations, and renting as opposed to owning a home directly explain neighborhood satisfaction. Renting has an indirect association through housing quality as do household income and household size.

Some gender differences, moreover, are noticeable. Neighborhood services have a direct association with neighborhood satisfaction for females but not for males. Neighborhood groups have an indirect association with neighborhood satisfaction for females but not for males. The location of residence has different direct and indirect effects for males and for females; across the total sample, however, low levels of neighborhood satisfaction exist among respondents in the urban and rural South. The pattern of direct and indirect effects shifts when examining the total sample. On the basis of R^2 values, other exogenous variables excluded from the multiple regression equations also help to explain neighborhood satisfaction and housing quality. The R^2 values, however, are within the range of findings from previous studies.

Objective Attributes

The results of the direct and indirect effects of objective social indicators on neighborhood satisfaction are shown in Figure 3.3 (only the significant

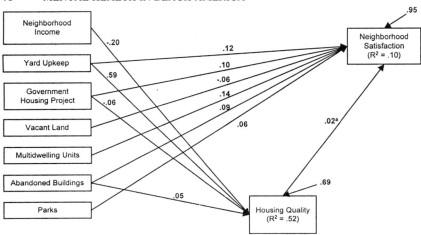

Figure 3.3. Effects of Objective Social Indicators for Males
a. This is the only path coefficient that is insignificant; .05 level of significance for all others.

exogenous variables are shown). All multiple regression equations and path coefficients are significant at the .05 level of significance except for the path coefficients leading from housing quality to neighborhood satisfaction. Multidwelling units exert the strongest direct effect on neighborhood satisfaction. When the same model was run separately by gender, the presence of multidwelling units in the neighborhoods, in essence, does not decrease neighborhood satisfaction. Yard upkeep, followed by neighborhood income, have the strongest indirect effects. Government housing projects and abandoned buildings also have indirect associations with neighborhood satisfaction. The direct and indirect effects are somewhat different in some cases for males, females, and the total sample. For males, the indirect effects suggest different meanings because of the negative path coefficient between housing quality and neighborhood satisfaction. Overall, the path coefficients between housing quality and neighborhood satisfaction produce suggestive rather than statistically significant effects.

For females and the sample as a whole, the findings are almost identical; the only difference is the size of some path coefficients. Having well-maintained yards, for example, positively explains neighborhood satisfaction both directly and indirectly. Living in government housing projects has a direct positive effect and an indirect negative effect. The presence of abandoned buildings does not decrease the levels of neighborhood satisfaction either

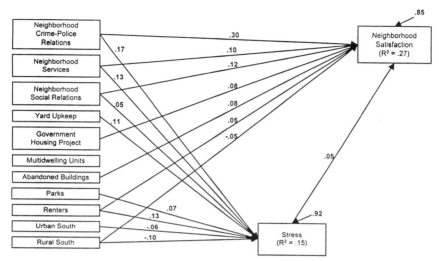

Figure 3.4. Effects of Stress, Residential Social Indicators, Personal Attributes, and Location of Residence for Males and Females

directly or indirectly. The presence of parks exerts a positive direct effect, whereas the presence of vacant land has a negative direct effect.

In summary, some objective social indicators are useful in uncovering some direct and indirect dimensions underlying neighborhood satisfaction. Unlike previous findings, the presence or maintenance of some residential attributes does not decrease neighborhood satisfaction. Caution, however, should prevail in generalizing beyond these findings because of the small R^2 values for neighborhood satisfaction, because of the insignificant path coefficients between housing quality and neighborhood satisfaction, and because of the source of origin of the objective social indicators.

Stress

Stress, measured by the number of problems (0-10) experienced by respondents in approximately the past month, plays an important role in explaining neighborhood satisfaction (Figure 3.4). Collectively analyzing most of the significant exogenous variables that directly contribute to neighborhood satisfaction uncovers the role of stress as an intervening variable. Except for the path coefficient between stress and neighborhood satisfaction for females, all others are significant at the .05 level. All multiple regression equations are significant at the .05 level of significance. This model was also run separately for males and females.

The exogenous variables explored in the model for males are neighborhood crime-police relations, neighborhood social relations, multidwelling units, abandoned buildings, housing quality, and renters. Multidwelling units and housing quality are not significant contributors. Neighborhood crime-police relations exerts the strongest effect both directly and indirectly. Renting also has both direct and indirect positive effects. Experiencing none or few stressful life events has a positive relationship with levels of neighborhood satisfaction for males.

The exogenous variables included in the path model for females are neighborhood crime-police relations, neighborhood services, neighborhood social relations, yard upkeep, government housing projects, multidwelling units, abandoned buildings, housing quality, renters, and the three locations of residence. Neighborhood crime-police relations, neighborhood services, neighborhood social relations, yard upkeep, and government housing projects have both direct and indirect effects. Neighborhood crime-police relations has the strongest direct and indirect effect. Substantively and indirectly, experiencing few or no stressful life events has a positive effect on the relationship between the significant residential social indicators, as do renting and neighborhood satisfaction; they produce a negative effect, however, for females in government housing projects and in the rural South.

When looking at the total sample, all exogenous variables used in the path model for females are included along with vacant land and parks. Neighborhood crime-police relations exerts the strongest direct and indirect effect. Among females, neighborhood services and neighborhood social relations explain neighborhood satisfaction both directly and indirectly. Among males, renting has both direct and indirect effects. When looking at the entire sample, unlike breakdowns for males or females, rural South has both direct and indirect negative effects; urban South has an indirect negative effect. On the basis of the findings, experiencing more than a few stressful life events decreases the levels of neighborhood satisfaction for respondents in the urban and rural South.

In summary, stress is an important intervening variable in explaining neighborhood satisfaction. The extent of the direct and indirect effects of stress, however, vary by gender and across the total sample. The small R^2 values, however, suggest that other phenomena strongly explain the relationship between stress, residential social indicators, personal attributes, location of residence, and neighborhood satisfaction.

Conclusions

This chapter has focused on the overall residential well-being of African Americans revolving around the direct and indirect dimensions underlying neighborhood satisfaction. By gender and across the total sample, the results of the path analyses reveal how subjective social indicators, objective social indicators, personal attributes, and location of residence explain neighborhood satisfaction, directly or indirectly, through housing quality and stress. The direct effects exert the strongest effect; some R^2 values are small but significant and compare with previous findings. The cross-sectional data used in the path models should be considered before generalizing. No multicollinearity of any considerable effect exists among the exogenous and endogenous variables.

The findings have implications for policy interventions and for future research. Overall, residential well-being increases through maintenance and improvement of residential conditions, which can be facilitated by neighborhood residents and through policy interventions. For instance, participating in neighborhood groups has a positive association with neighborhood satisfaction through housing quality when looking at females and the sample as a whole. This finding suggests that respondents participating in neighborhood groups have better quality housing than respondents who do not participate. About 5% of the population actively engages in forms of citizen participation (Checkoway & Van Til, 1978). Previous research identifies the conditions under which blacks, in contrast to nonblacks, engage in forms of citizen participation such as working with existing neighborhood groups (Ahlbrandt, 1984; Louis Harris and Associates, 1978; Verba & Nie, 1972; Warren, 1975). Promoting neighborhood participation is perhaps one way to maintain and improve residential well-being.

Formulating policy interventions for housing and neighborhood development may be another way to increase overall residential well-being. Some of these policies may exist but may need to be reassessed to focus on groups identified as having lower levels of residential well-being, such as low- and moderate-income neighborhoods and respondents who reside in government housing projects. On the basis of the present findings, respondents in the urban and rural South would also fit these criteria because they are less satisfied with their neighborhoods than other groups and are experiencing more than a few stressful life events. Miller et al. (1974) and Webb and Collette (1979) disclosed how urban and rural residents experienced similar stressful life events. Large sections of the South are rural, and more blacks reside in the South than in other regions according to census data (O'Hare et al., 1991). Other research has suggested the need to study various models and indicators of residential life quality in rural areas (Dillman & Hobbs, 1982; Lawton, 1980a; Scheidt & Windley, 1983).

African Americans express positive feelings about their neighborhoods, but stress appears to play a role in contributing to their overall residential well-being. Future research should investigate the dimensions underlying residential well-being, including housing quality, stress, and other phenomena that were not part of this research, by location of residence and by gender. Such research should also include nonblacks for comparison, bearing in mind the need for representative samples for the results to be generalizable to the population as a whole. Incorporating equivalent measures of residential social indicators in such research will likely contribute to an understanding of the dimensions underlying residential well-being among African Americans and other groups. The findings presented in the chapter reveal that we have only scratched the surface in understanding neighborhood satisfaction and its impact on black communities.

Note

1. All previously described nominally scaled variables were entered into the regression analyses as dummy variables. All ordinally scaled variables were entered as coded except in cases in which the response categories had to be reversed. The same was true for all interval variables (e.g., household size). Except for housing quality, neighborhood income, yard upkeep, and neighborhood satisfaction, the scoring for all of the other objective indicator variables was 1 if present and 0 if not.

4

Problem Drinking, Chronic Disease, and Recent Life Events

Isidore Silas Obot

The abuse of chemical substances, especially alcohol, is an old problem (el-Guebely & el-Guebely, 1981; Seller, 1985). In recent years, the problem has increased in scope and has resulted in expressions of international concern (Naranjo & Bremer, 1993). In 1981, the alcoholic beverage industry was worth $170 billion and had a global advertising expenditure of $2 billion (Cavanagh & Clairmonte, 1985). The tremendous growth of the industry in recent years has been accompanied by diversification and expansion into new markets. Beer, spirits, and wine manufacturers are selling food and tobacco products both in their traditional markets of Europe and North America and in the developing countries of Asia, South America, and Africa (Cavanagh & Clairmonte, 1985).

Increased production and marketing of alcoholic beverages have been associated with increased per capita consumption in many countries. Also, a declaration by an international group of researchers that "changes in the overall consumption of alcoholic beverages have a bearing on the health of the people in any society" (Bruun et al., 1975) has been borne out. Available evidence shows that the prevalence of alcohol-related pathologies has increased in many regions of the world, including Africa and Asia (Obot, 1991), within certain groups in North America (Bettes, Dusenbury, Kerner, James-Ortiz, & Botvin, 1990; Harford, 1992), and in the United Kingdom (McKeigue & Karmi, 1993). The problems have not only increased within the stereotypi-

45

cal at-risk economic groups but have become normalized. Skid row inebriates and declared alcoholics have now been joined by an expanding group of "middle class cirrhotics and drunken drivers" (Makela, Room, Single, Sulkunen, & Walsh, 1981).

The effects of alcohol abuse are alarming. Measurable economic cost of the problem in the United States is estimated to be more than $70 billion per year (Rice, Kelman, Miller, & Dunmeyer, 1990). Much of this is attributed to time lost from work and reduced productivity due to sickness, medical expenses, and premature death. Alcohol accounts for up to 125,000 deaths each year in the United States. There are many other consequences of excessive alcohol consumption, and some of them are not easily measured. These include family and community disruptions, grief from the death of spouses and loved ones, homicides, accidents, legal problems, and strained interpersonal relations.

Availability, international trade practices, and aggressive marketing techniques are not sufficient explanations for increased alcohol consumption and alcohol-related problems in developing countries or among African Americans in the United States. In many developing countries, growth of disposable income, rural-urban migration, urbanization, and the increased consumption of industrial liquor in place of traditional beverages have contributed to the observed malaise (Moser, 1980). Also, the dislocation in traditional social and religious structures that often accompany modernization may encourage the use of alcohol to reduce tensions, anxiety, hostilities, and general psychological distress (Bettes et al., 1990).

Many studies have attempted to address ethnic and racial differences in the use of alcohol, but these studies are hampered by methodological limitations that render their findings imprecise (Cheung, 1990-1991; Heath, 1990-1991). In a national probability sample of 2,058 adults, Midanik and Clark (1994) found that alcohol use was significantly lower among whites in 1990 than in 1984. No significant trends were found among Hispanics and blacks over the same period. Nonwhites, however, seem to be overrepresented among those who experience the complications of alcohol abuse and alcoholism—for example, alcohol-related automobile accidents (Popkin & Council, 1993) and withdrawal symptoms (Robyak, Byers, & Prange, 1989).

The purpose of this chapter is to contribute to the important discussion on alcohol abuse among African Americans by presenting data on alcohol-related problems from the National Survey of Black Americans (NSBA) (Jackson, 1991). In what follows, the term *problem drinking* will be used interchangeably with *alcohol abuse* to refer to a pattern of alcohol consumption that is likely to lead to or has already resulted in negative consequences for the drinker, the family, and society at large.

Prevalence of Alcohol Abuse and Related Disorders in the United States

Surveys of alcohol use show that 65% of adults and more than 80% of 12th graders report use of alcohol in the "past year" and 50% and 57%, respectively, in the "past month" (National Institute on Drug Abuse, 1991a, 1991b). Males report more drinking and heavier alcohol consumption than females. Apparent consumption is more than one ounce of absolute alcohol (two drinks) daily for people 14 years or older, but it is estimated that the 11% who constitute the heavy-drinking group consume more than one half of all alcoholic beverages sold (Malin, Coakley, Yaelber, Munch, & Holland, 1982).

Heavy drinkers are obviously at greater risk of health and social problems than light and moderate drinkers. Drinking-related health problems are, in fact, widespread. One estimate is that 16% of Americans have reported some problem associated with alcohol within the past 3 years. About 4% report more than trivial problems (American Psychiatric Association, 1987). If consequences other than health problems are taken into account, these rates would be much higher.

Both physical and mental health problems have been attributed to excessive alcohol consumption. The mental health problems include alcoholism, alcohol psychosis, and mood disorders. Physical problems are many and include malnutrition (a condition that arises because alcohol generates a large caloric yield but supplies no essential nutrients), liver cirrhosis, pancreatitis, gastrointestinal disorders, toxic alcohol heart, perinatal and pediatric problems (e.g., fetal alcohol syndrome), nervous system disorders, and malignancies of the mouth, pharynx, esophagus, and the large intestine (Seixas, 1980; U.S. Department of Health and Human Services, 1990).

The contribution of alcohol to some of these problems is, in some cases, quite extensive. Alcohol is the direct cause of death from alcoholism (100%), alcoholic psychosis (100%), and cirrhosis (90-95%). It contributes significantly to death from homicide (47-70%), suicide (25%), motor vehicle accidents (30-40%), and accidental falls (44%) (Malin et al., 1982; Murphy & Wetzel, 1990; Naranjo & Bremer, 1993).

These consequences are prevalent among all groups of abusers, but certain characteristics of the person or environment seem to determine the type and pattern of disorders (Herd, 1990). For example, differences in socioeconomic status and urban or rural residence seem to influence the nature of reported disorders (whether acute or chronic). Therefore, it is possible that variations in the prevalence of drinking problems between black and white men are associated with differences in the sociocultural context of drinking and relative socioeconomic status (Herd, 1994). What seems clear at the moment is that the research among African Americans indicates a higher prevalence of some alcohol-related problems than can be explained solely by rates of consumption of alcohol.

Problem Drinking Among African Americans

The following questions predominate the literature on problem drinking among African Americans: What are the differences between the rates of drinking and problems related to drinking between African Americans and whites? Why do African American men drink excessively more than African American women? What are the social consequences of drinking among African Americans?

There is some disagreement in the literature on the degree of alcohol consumption among African Americans compared to whites. Depending on time and the population surveyed, lower (Harper, 1976) and higher (Bailey, Haberman, & Alkane, 1965; Brunswick, 1977; Rachal, Hubbard, Williams, & Tuchfeld, 1976) rates have been reported for African Americans. What seems to be indisputable is that the proportion of abstainers is higher among African Americans than among whites, mainly because of the high proportion of abstainers among African American women. After controlling for socioeconomic status, Lillie-Blanton, Mackenzie, and Anthony (1991) found that white women with 12 years of education or more were heavier drinkers than black women with similar educational backgrounds.

Another consistent finding is that particular problems associated with problem drinking are disproportionately represented among African Americans. For example, Herd (1994) presented findings from a national probability survey of drinking that showed that alcohol-related problems were higher among black men even though they did not have significantly higher rates of heavy drinking or drunkenness than white men. In some urban areas, the rate of cirrhosis of the liver is higher for nonwhites than for whites. Malin et al. (1982), in a survey with samples from facilities in Washington, Baltimore, Philadelphia, New York, Detroit, Chicago, and Los Angeles, found that, for all ages, cirrhosis mortality rates among African Americans were nearly twice those for white Americans. Rates for those in the 25 to 34 years of age group were found to be as much as 10 times higher for African Americans than for whites.

In a review of the literature on African American alcoholism, King (1982) cited data that showed that the prevalence rates of death from cirrhosis in the African American population had increased from 5.8 per 100,000 in 1940 to 20.4 in 1974. Secondary diagnosis of alcoholism increased from 40% to 50% among hospital patients. In this review, which covered the period from 1977 to 1980, King stated that the problems and consequences of African American alcoholism had become worse over the years: "What we see is an increasing use of alcohol at an earlier age by youth and a growing intensity of use by women, with serious implications for fetal alcohol syndrome" (p. 403).

Data on other problems also indicated very high mortality and morbidity rates among African Americans. In 1980, the homicide rate for African American males was 66.6 per 100,000 compared to 10.9 per 100,000 for white males. In 1991, the rates were 72.0 and 9.3, respectively, and the total numbers of victims were 10,628 and 9,581, respectively (U.S. Bureau of the Census, 1994). If 50% of the homicides are attributable to alcohol, more than 5,000 African Americans lost their lives in 1991 because of alcohol abuse. Significant relationships between problem drinking and disrupted marriages and multiple hospitalizations for acute alcohol psychoses at ages below 45 years have also been reported (Rosenblatt, Gross, Malenowski, Broman, & Lewis, 1971). These and similar findings led Harper (1976) to declare, "Alcohol abuse is the number one health problem and the number one social problem in black America" (p. 1). The situation remains unchanged today.

In an analysis of the problem, Harper (1976) attributes African American drinking behavior and problems to the following factors:

1. African Americans have ambivalent reactions to alcohol that are manifested in the extreme behaviors of total abstinence and heavy drinking.
2. In African American communities, alcohol is widely available and easily accessible.

3. Because of economic frustrations from unemployment, drinking becomes a means of escape from an unstable economic condition.
4. African American men drink to escape a general feeling of distress associated with racial discrimination. Drinking becomes a social activity in the peer group.
5. African American women drink far less than men because of family responsibilities, parental and religious teachings, dislike of alcoholic beverages, and lack of exposure to drinking situations.

These reasons serve to explain the differences in alcohol-related problems between African Americans and whites. The focus is on the historical and social experiences of African Americans that are vastly different from those of whites. A more persistent issue than African American-white differences in rates of alcoholism and alcohol abuse, however, is the nature of health and social problems associated with drinking among African Americans and how this question has been addressed in research studies.

Concerns about the dearth of research on African Americans in the literature on alcoholism have been expressed from several quarters (Harper, 1976; King, 1982; National Institute of Alcohol and Alcohol Abuse, 1979). Criticisms of the available studies have also been expressed (Cheung, 1990-1991; Heath, 1990-1991). The criticisms address the following issues: (a) Most studies have been comparative in nature, using white norms as reference and treating African American alcoholics as deviants; (b) samples with limited numbers of African Americans are often used; (c) many studies deal with captive African American subjects in hospitals, clinics, and prisons; (d) important variables such as socioeconomic status, education, residence (rural-urban) have not been clearly used in analyses; and (e) African American values have been neglected.

Using the NSBA, it is possible to address some of these issues. It provides the data set for the analyses of the biopsychosocial impact of problem drinking among African Americans. One general and two specific questions were addressed in the study:

1. What is the nature of problem drinking among African Americans?
2. What are the demographic and personal variables associated with problem drinking?
3. What are the health and psychosocial consequences of drinking among African Americans?

Methods

Measures of African American Problem Drinking

The data set from the NSBA contains information on a wide range of issues related to the lives of African Americans. Information on substance abuse was gathered with questions related to specific substances from a cross-sectional sample of the adult African American population ($N = 2,107$).

The question regarding alcohol asked specifically about the health consequences of drinking. Each participant was asked, "Have you been told by a doctor that you have a problem with your health because of drinking?"[1] The proportion of respondents who answered yes to this question was 3.5% ($n = 73$). The extent of alcohol use and mortality due to specific diseases could not be determined from this study. The data set did, however, provide information on morbidity from many other self-reported health problems. It is fair to assume that the "true" prevalence of problem drinking and physical health problems was much higher than the rates of diagnosed problems in this sample.

Measures of Chronic Health Problems

There were two measures of health status—one dealing with general health satisfaction and the other with the presence or absence of specific disorders. Respondents were shown a list of health problems. After looking over the list, they were asked "whether a doctor has told you that you have that problem." Information on health satisfaction was gathered with the question, "In general, how satisfied are you with your health?" Responses to this question were very satisfied, somewhat satisfied, somewhat dissatisfied, and very dissatisfied.

Measures of Recent Life Events

Information on psychosocial problems was gathered in a similar manner. Respondents were asked, "Please tell me whether or not these things have happened to you in the past month or so?" The list included problems in the following areas: money, job, family or marriage, people outside family, children, victim of crime, police, and love life.

Demographic and Other Variables

The following information was available for each respondent: gender, age, place of residence (urban or rural), marital status, family income, education, employment status, region of residence, perception of the neighborhood, and participation in religious activities.

Data Analysis

To answer the questions posed, both bivariate and multivariate analyses were conducted. The association of diagnosed problem drinking and health-psychosocial problems was examined with chi-square analyses. Dichotomous regression with the logit model was used to assess the probability of being diagnosed a problem drinker given certain demographic and background variables. The dichotomous regression program provided a multivariate technique for holding all other independent variables constant while assessing the effect of one demographic variable on the probability of being designated a problem drinker.

Results

Demographic Variables and Problem Drinking

Chi-square analyses were conducted to examine the relationship of various demographic and background variables to problem drinking. The relationship of problem drinking to selected demographic variables is presented in Table 4.1. Gender, age, residence, education, and employment status were significantly related to problem drinking. Table 4.1 shows that male respondents were more likely than female respondents to be diagnosed as problem drinkers. This is consistent with the established finding that males use and abuse alcohol more than females (Malin et al., 1982). Age shows a curvilinear relationship to problem drinking, with the highest rate occurring among those 35 to 54 years of age. People with diagnosed alcohol problems also tended to be the least educated, live in urban areas, and be unemployed. Family income and marital status did not yield significant relationships.

Table 4.2 shows the relationships of various background variables to problem drinking. All four of the variables show strong significant relation-

Table 4.1 Demographic Variables and Problem Drinking

	Percentage of Problem Drinking	*N*	χ^2
Gender			
Male	5.9	792	22.80***
Female	2.0	1,306	
Age			
18-34	2.2	857	9.09*
35-54	5.1	648	
55+	3.6	590	
Residence			
Urban	4.0	1,658	7.42**
Rural	1.4	440	
Education			
0-11 years	4.8	913	12.79**
High school graduate	2.6	649	
Some college	1.2	334	
College graduate	2.2	182	
Marital status			
Married	3.8	875	0.88
Not married	2.9	752	
Never married	3.4	465	
Family income			
Under $5,000	3.7	458	2.02
$5,000-$10,000	4.3	468	
$10,000-$20,000	3.1	490	
$20,000+	2.7	412	
Employment status			
Working	2.3	1,194	12.20***
Not working	5.1	904	

*$p < .05$; **$p < .01$; ***$p < .001$.

ships to problem drinking. Specifically, problem drinking increased as respondents' perceptions of their neighborhoods changed from very good to very bad. People who went to church every day or weekly were least likely to have a drinking problem. Problem drinkers were also more likely to smoke and were less satisfied with their health.

A multivariate dichotomous regression analysis was conducted to examine the separate effects of each demographic variable on the dependent variable of problem drinking. The adjusted probabilities of being a problem drinker

Table 4.2 Background Variables and Problem Drinking

	Percentage of Problem Drinking	N	χ^2
Neighborhood perception			
Very good	2.6	680	16.41***
Fairly good	3.1	1,180	
Fairly bad	6.8	147	
Very bad	9.6	83	
Religiosity			
Every day	0.0	87	16.56***
Weekly	1.6	681	
Few times/month	4.3	585	
Few times/year	4.9	370	
Less than once a year	5.2	365	
Smoking problem			
Yes	13.2	129	38.40***
No	2.8	1,965	
Health satisfaction			
Very satisfied	2.4	1,083	34.70***
Somewhat satisfied	3.1	679	
Somewhat dissatisfied	5.9	254	
Very dissatisfied	14.1	78	

***$p < .001$.

are presented in Table 4.3. The findings indicate that gender, residence, education, perception of the neighborhood, smoking problems, and participation in religious activities were significantly related to problem drinking.

Table 4.3 indicates that, after controlling for all the other variables, male respondents had a higher probability of being problem drinkers than female respondents. The 95% confidence intervals for both males and females do not overlap, indicating that the two are significantly different. There is also no overlap for urban and rural respondents or for those with and without a smoking problem. The adjusted probabilities indicate that living in an urban as opposed to a rural environment and having a smoking problem are closely related to being a problem drinker. The overlap observed in the 95% confidence interval for other significantly related variables is slight and negligible.

In summary, the bivariate and multivariate analyses show that certain demographic variables are closely associated with the diagnosis of problem drinking. Specifically, being male, living in an urban area, having less than

Table 4.3 Adjusted Probability of Being a Problem Drinker for Selected Independent Variables

	Probability of Problem Drinking	95% Confidence Limits		N
Gender**				
Male	.039	.026	.058	792
Female	.010	.006	.018	1,306
Age				
Younger (18-34)	.017	.010	.029	857
Older (35-54)	.018	.010	.030	1,238
Residence**				
Urban	.023	.017	.033	1,658
Rural	.006	.002	.015	440
Education*				
Less (0-11 years)	.026	.016	.040	913
More (12+ years)	.012	.007	.021	1,165
Marital status				
Married	.022	.013	.035	875
Not married	.012	.007	.023	752
Never married	.020	.010	.039	465
Family income				
Low (< $10,000)	.019	.001	.031	926
High (> $10,000)	.016	.009	.028	902
Neighborhood perception*				
Good	.016	.008	.022	1,860
Bad	.023	.015	.035	230
Employment status				
Working	.013	.008	.021	1,194
Not working	.027	.017	.043	904
Religiosity*				
Attend often	.010	.005	.020	768
Don't attend often	.029	.017	.048	1,320
Smoking problems**				
Yes	.089	.050	.154	129
No	.016	.010	.023	1,965
Region				
Northeast	.018	.009	.035	390
North central	.021	.001	.038	465
South	.018	.011	.029	1,119
West	.017	.012	.026	124

$* p < .05; ** p < .01.$

Table 4.4 Problem Drinking and Chronic Health Problems

| | Problem Drinking (%) | | χ^2 (1) | N |
	Yes	No		
Arthritis	37.0	23.6	6.87**	505
Ulcers	26.0	8.1	28.29***	183
Cancer	8.2	1.8	14.82***	42
Hypertension	50.7	31.0	12.32***	663
Liver problems	9.6	1.8	21.32***	202
Kidney problems	17.8	9.4	5.77*	43
Stroke	1.4	2.2	0.23	46
Nervous conditions	41.1	21.1	16.54***	455
Circulation problems	13.9	8.5	2.58	181

$*p < .05; **p < .01; ***p < .001.$

12 years of education, living in a neighborhood described as "fairly or very bad," having a smoking problem, and not being active in religious activities are all significantly related to problem drinking among African Americans.

Problem Drinking and Chronic Health Problems

Table 4.4 shows results of bivariate analyses that examine the relationship of problem drinking to the prevalence of specific, doctor-diagnosed health problems. Specifically, the table shows how the percentage of respondents with a particular health problem varies as a function of their drinking. Thus, looking at the first row in Table 4.4, it can be seen that 37% of the problem drinkers had arthritis. In general, the prevalence of health problems was higher among problem drinkers than among those who did not have a drinking problem. Problem drinkers were more likely to have been diagnosed as having arthritis, ulcers, cancer, hypertension, liver problems, kidney problems, and "nervous condition." Specifically, the prevalence of hypertension was 51% among problem drinkers but only 31% among those without a drinking problem. Similarly, whereas 41% of the problem drinkers had a nervous condition, only 21% of the nondrinkers had been so diagnosed. No significant differences in the distribution of stroke and circulation problems were found between problem drinkers and others.

Table 4.5 Problem Drinking and Recent Life Problems

| Psychosocial Problems | Problem Drinking (%) | | χ^2 (1) | N |
	Yes	No		
Money	53.4	51.3	12	1,082
Job	24.7	18.5	1.75	391
Family	23.3	16.3	2.5	346
People	28.2	16.2	8.04**	348
Children	16.4	11.4	1.39	244
Crime victim	16.4	6.3	11.72***	139
Police	9.7	3.0	9.94**	69
Love	31.5	17.5	9.41**	376
Health	54.2	26.3	27.14***	574

$**p < .01; ***p < .001.$

Problem Drinking and Recent Life Problems

Responses to the question on psychosocial problems experienced within the past month provided information on recent life problems. Table 4.5 shows bivariate analyses conducted to test the relationship between problem drinking and psychosocial problems, such as problems in the family, on the job, with the law, and in interpersonal relations. Similar to the analysis for health, earlier findings showed that problem drinkers were disproportionately represented among people with problems in these spheres of life (Brunswick, 1977). Table 4.5 shows that there were significant associations of problem drinking with people, police, love and health problems, as well as with being the victim of a crime. In these cases, and even in cases in which no significant associations were established (money, job, family, and children problems), the pattern of responses showed that problem drinkers were more likely to report having these problems. For example, 16% of the problem drinkers reported being the victim of a crime, whereas the victimization rate was only 6% among those without a drinking problem; 31% of the problem drinkers indicated problems with their "love life," whereas only 18% of the nondrinkers were having love life problems. It is also significant that 54% of the problem drinkers, as opposed to only 26% of those without a drinking problem, had health problems.

Because early analyses showed a strong relationship between gender and problem drinking, and because it is possible that gender is also related to some health problems, the relationship of problem drinking to each of the disorders was examined separately for males and females. These analyses were conducted to answer the question of whether the already established relationship between problem drinking and reported health problems was the same for males and females. The analyses on selected problems for both males and females are shown in Table 4.6.

The data show that, among male respondents, problem drinking was significantly associated with arthritis, ulcers, cancer, hypertension, liver problems, and nervous problems. Among female respondents, drinking was associated with ulcers, liver, kidney problems, nervous problems, and circulation problems. Three problems—ulcer, liver, and nervous—were significantly related to problem drinking for both males and females, but in two cases the relationships were stronger for males. Other problems were distinguished between men and women. Significant associations between drinking and arthritis, cancer, and hypertension were obtained for male problem drinkers, whereas significant associations between drinking and kidney and circulation problems were seen for female drinkers only. The central theme of these analyses is that both male and female problem drinkers suffer from a number of debilitating disorders. The differences in the pattern of reported disease conditions might be due to differences in exposure to other etiological factors for specific diseases.

Discussion

The findings of this study support the general contention that drinking has a deleterious effect on health and social welfare. The list of disorders associated with problem drinking is a long one. Both chronic physical conditions and psychiatric disorders have been shown to affect alcohol abusers more than nonabusers. There is a growing body of literature, however, that supports the hypothesis that moderate use of alcohol may not only be harmless but may be beneficial to the consumer. For example, Gordon and Kannel (1984) have reported that in the Framingham study, men and women who drank alcoholic beverages had slightly lower overall mortality than nondrinkers. They also found, however, that the risk of death from cancer due to alcohol abuse was higher among men than among women. Recent evidence shows that the relationship of alcohol consumption with mortality is curvilinear: Morbidity is lowest among light drinkers and highest among heavy drinkers, whereas abstainers fall in between (Poikolainen, 1991; Shaper, 1990).

Table 4.6 Gender, Problem Drinking, and Reported Health Problems

| | Problem Drinking (%) | | | |
	Yes	No	χ^2	N
Arthritis				
Males	36.2	17.1	10.83***	144
Females	38.5	27.4	1.55	361
Ulcers				
Males	27.7	8.5	18.70***	76
Females	23.1	7.9	7.77**	107
Cancer				
Males	8.5	0.5	28.03***	8
Females	7.7	2.5	2.69	34
Hypertension				
Males	51.1	22.0	19.83***	187
Females	50.0	36.2	2.09	476
Liver problems				
Males	6.4	1.6	5.39*	15
Females	15.4	1.9	22.08***	28
Kidney problems				
Males	10.6	6.3	1.34	52
Females	30.8	11.1	9.66**	150
Stroke				
Males	2.1	1.6	0.07	13
Females	0.0	2.6	0.66	33
Nervous conditions				
Males	36.2	11.9	22.64***	105
Females	50.0	26.5	7.16**	350
Circulation problems				
Males	8.5	5.7	0.65	46
Females	24.0	10.1	5.10*	135

*p < .05; **p < .01; ***p < .001.

In this study, problem drinking was associated with cancer among men only. Looking at the sample as a whole, drinking was significantly related to all the health problems included in the survey except stroke and circulation problems. The expected and overwhelming statistical relationship of drinking with reported health problems shown in this study and the inability to establish a positive relationship between drinking and disease or mortality in some other studies (e.g., Cullen, Steinhouse, & Wearne, 1982) may be due to differences in the definition of drinking. In this study, a problem drinker was defined on the basis of a positive response to the question, "Have you been told by a doctor that you have a problem with your health because of drinking?" This means that only those already showing signs of some problem from prolonged or excessive alcohol consumption were included in the group of problem drinkers. Because the particular health problems indicated by the physicians were not specified in the survey, self-reported disorders were used to determine the types of problems associated with drinking.

Several methodological issues were raised in the study. First, the extent of problem drinking among African Americans might have been underestimated because only extreme cases of alcohol abusers were included. The rate of 3.5% problem drinking in this national sample was a conservative estimate. Not every alcohol abuser goes to a physician, and even though alcoholism is relatively easy to diagnose, not all those who went to their physicians might have been informed of the nature of their presenting complaints. Added to this is the problem of concealment, which may appear in the form of underreporting the amount of alcohol consumed regularly or in actual denial of the behavior or problems associated with drinking. Furthermore, an estimate of problem drinking among African Americans in the NSBA sample would be misleading because of a built-in limitation of the sampling method. Although great effort was made to get a representative sample of African Americans, persons in institutions, such as hospitals and prisons, military personnel, and public inebriates were not included. This is a common feature of social epidemiology, but a significant one in studies of drinking, because problem drinkers are overrepresented in jail populations.

A second issue is that almost all the specific disorders reported by the respondents required prior professional diagnosis. Undiagnosed problems due to nonuse of appropriate services would not have been known to the respondents and, therefore, would not be reported by them. In fact, an earlier analysis of the NSBA data has shown that respondents in the sample used more informal than professional help for all problems from economic difficulties to physical health (Neighbors, Jackson, Bowman, & Gurin, 1983).

A related problem is that some of the diseases used in the survey are known to be caused by more than one factor; alcohol sometimes is only a secondary cause or not related at all to the disorder. For example, the role of cigarette smoking in the etiology of cancer is well-known. Disentangling the separate effect of smoking was not easy (Gordon & Kannel, 1984). There was also no differentiation of cancer types, which is a necessary precaution because the relationship of alcohol to cancer is strong only for some types, such as esophageal and stomach cancers (Blot, 1992; Gordon & Kannel, 1984; Higginson, 1966). The effects of nutritional deficits, in the case of liver problems, and hepatitis were not controlled for.

Another set of consequences of excessive or protracted alcohol consumption is psychiatric morbidity. Psychiatric complications include depressive symptomatology and psychotic states. In this study, there was no direct measure of the mental health of problem drinkers. The inclusion of "nervous" conditions in the list of health problems, however, touched on the issue of psychological distress. There was a highly significant statistical relationship between problem drinking and "nervousness." Problem drinkers reported more nervous conditions than nonproblem drinkers. Whether the stress that this item implied was an underlying predisposition, an episodic experience that alcohol was used to alleviate, or a psychological condition resulting from alcohol abuse could not be determined.

Although unequivocal statements about causality cannot be made, one result is nevertheless quite clear from this analysis of the NSBA data—survey respondents diagnosed as problem drinkers were less satisfied with their health and were more prone to chronic disorders, psychological distress, and negative life experiences than respondents without drinking problems.

The implications of these findings for public health and welfare in African American communities are obvious and are captured poignantly in Rev. Jesse Jackson's comment on the role of alcohol in the social advancement of African Americans: "We can march, run or crawl to freedom, but we cannot stagger to freedom" (cited in Herd, 1985, p. 182). The strategy for control of alcohol-related problems must be part of the overall agenda for the freedom and progress of African Americans.

Note

1. Two response categories were used in the analysis for problem drinking. The "don't know" responses were combined with the "no" responses yielding a yes-no categorization of the problem.

5

An Analysis of Stress Denial

Rhoda E. Barge Johnson
Joan E. Crowley

A review of traditional stress research (e.g., Dohrenwend, 1973; Dohrenwend & Dohrenwend, 1969; Faris & Dunham, 1939; Hollingshead & Redlich, 1958) leads to the conclusion that it is virtually impossible for a minority group member to reach adulthood without having experienced at least one stressful life problem. This assumption, however, is not borne out by the results of the National Survey of Black Americans (NSBA) (Jackson, 1991). A sizable percentage (17%) of the NSBA sample reported neither serious problems in the past month nor any lifetime problems that they could not handle. These negative responses raise questions about how a significant minority of African Americans confront stress during their lives. The purpose of this chapter is to examine a curious phenomenon—those adult African Americans who report never having had a serious recent or lifetime personal problem. Specifically, the objective of this chapter is to clarify the meaning of this finding for African Americans by focusing on the concept of denial. In summary, this chapter will (a) identify the characteristics of those who claim not to have experienced any serious personal problems and (b) develop a data-driven model that summarizes the observed patterns of problem reporting.

The denial of problems by minorities presents a number of conceptual, theoretical, and methodological problems. First, those who deny having a problem eliminate themselves from the analysis of coping strategies, even though denial itself may be a coping strategy. Second, if those who deny stressful problems are consistently distinctive, the theories of coping are not representative of the population. Third, if those who deny problems are similar to those who do not, then what the denial means is left to inference.

Although the history of the concept of denial dates back to 1885 (Weinstein & Kahn, 1955), Anna Freud's (1946) use of denial brought it into prominence. Freud described denial as a specific type of defense mechanism. The goal of defenses was to reduce stress and the threat of reality. Breznitz (1983) has referred to denial as "the discrepancies found between the many individual indicators of stress—the verbal, the physiological, the behavioral" (p. 89). Because denial has been loosely defined as the rejection of reality (Lazarus & Folkman, 1984), any discussion of the denial of stress must include information about the nature of what it means to be in touch with reality when one is a member of a minority group. Is the apparent denial in actuality not a denial but simply an indication of the person's reality? Is denial simply another form of coping with stress? Or is it a reconstruction of the person's life history—an assessment that if a problem has been overcome, it is no longer and never was a serious problem?

Background

More than twenty years ago, Barbara Snell Dohrenwend (1973) identified a similar pattern of findings in a study of heads of families from Washington Heights, Manhattan, New York. In Dohrenwend's study, 49% of the African American respondents, compared with 28% of the other ethnic groups, reported that no stressful life events had occurred in the preceding year. Dohrenwend (1973) concluded that the finding was more a "function of interviewing procedures than a true group difference in experience" (p. 233).

We believe that this curious observation may reflect the effects of oppression rather than simply be a function of methodological procedures. Specifically, we view this anomaly as both an individual response to specific questions about stress and as an indicator of coping in the context of social oppression—a context that emphasizes the social realities that continue to circumscribe ethnic minority groups in contemporary society. During the 1980s, mental health officials expressed concern that the socially oppressed would continue to suffer from a disproportionate number of mental health problems in the years to come (Neighbors, 1987). In response to this concern, national directives called for improved mental health research on racial and ethnic minorities (Ralph, 1983). Despite the concern reflected by these directives, research on the mental health of the oppressed remains fragmented (Anderson, 1991).

Some research in the stress literature has attempted to link the greater morbidity and mortality experienced by African Americans to oppressive and hostile social conditions (Anderson, 1991; Barbarin, 1983; Kessler, Price, & Wortman, 1985; Myers, 1982; Smith, 1985). Anderson, however, has argued that questions about how daily exposure to stressful events leads to symptoms of distress (e.g., suffering, misery, and agony) and negative health outcomes remain unanswered. Research needs to be broadened to take into account "the nature, structure, and dynamics of the cultural experiences and sources of stress" (Anderson, 1991, p. 686). Nevertheless, assumptions about the mental health of the oppressed continue to be based on the numbers and types of stressful life events experienced, the amounts of distress these events elicit, the responses to the distress, and the effect these events have on other life experiences (Greene, 1990).

Oppression, Stress, and Coping

According to Frye (1992), the experience of the oppressed can be characterized as a double bind. Options are reduced, and each option exposes the oppressed to some sort of censure or deprivation. If the oppressed are happy-go-lucky, this behavior is a sign of docility and acquiescence to the situation. If they are not cheerful, however, they are perceived as hostile, angry, or dangerous. Is there something about being oppressed that makes it difficult to discuss or report a stressful life experience? Frye has equated the experience of oppression to being in a bird cage:

> It is now possible to grasp one of the reasons why oppression can be hard to see and recognize: one can study the elements of an oppressive structure with great care and some good will without seeing the structure as a whole, and hence without seeing or being able to understand that one is looking at a cage and that there are people there who are caged, whose motion and mobility are restricted, whose lives are shaped and reduced. (p. 56)

The results of oppression can be seen most clearly in aggregate indices of well-being. Relative to the nonoppressed, the oppressed suffer persistently higher levels of chronic disease, poverty, crime, incarceration, and unemployment. The oppressed have less access to physical and mental health care, education, and financial resources. In the current jargon, oppressed people are a high-risk group (Billingsley, 1992; Locke, 1992).

Notwithstanding these findings, it is much harder to see the results of oppression at the individual level. Any individual problem can result from personal shortcomings and misfortunes rather than being a function of social forces that place individual members of oppressed groups at risk for disaster. Frye (1992) has argued that oppression cannot be seen at the microsocial level of analysis because oppression is a "network of forces and barriers which are systematically related which conspire to immobilize, reduce, and mold the lives we lead" (p. 57).

A few studies, however, suggest that African Americans tend to have more psychological disorders than European Americans, but when class is controlled, the differences become insignificant (Neighbors, 1984a; Warheit, Holzer, & Arey, 1975; Williams, Takeuchi, & Adair, 1992b). When race and class were controlled, however, African Americans were found to be exposed to more stressors than other ethnic groups (Dohrenwend & Dohrenwend, 1969, 1981; Kessler, 1979b; Ulbrich, Warheit, & Zimmerman, 1989). Smith (1985) concluded that African Americans tend to experience more stress related to being members of a highly visible, isolated, and marginalized minority group. Recent studies (Hacker, 1992; Locke, 1992) have tended to suggest that being oppressed is stressful and harmful to African Americans. Nevertheless, racism and oppression, as they relate to contemporary views of stress, have not received systematic study (Anderson, 1991; Boyd-Franklin, 1989; Outlaw, 1993).

How African Americans cope with this visibility has been the subject of some study, but the data have yielded conflicting results (Dressler, 1985b). Rahe (1979) pointed out in his overview of research on life events and symptoms of distress that investigators have not yet reached a consensus on the meaning of life-change events to an individual's life. The numerous studies of the lists of life-change events (e.g., Dohrenwend & Dohrenwend, 1978; Myers, Lindenthal, & Pepper, 1971; Rahe, 1978; Rahe, Meyer, Smith, Kjaer, & Holmes, 1964) have suggested that the meaning of the events is subject to various interpretations.

Generally, the coping with stress hypotheses fall into two types of models (Dohrenwend & Dohrenwend, 1981; Smith, 1985): (a) those focused on individual responses to victimization and (b) those incorporating both external and internal sources that mediate reactions to stressful events. The victimization model views the individual as having little control over exposure to stressful life experiences. Major support for this model comes from epidemiologic studies (e.g., Dohrenwend, 1973; Dohrenwend & Dohrenwend, 1969; Faris & Dunham, 1939; Hollingshead & Redlich, 1958) that link lower socioeconomic status with higher rates of exposure to stress-producing events. Essentially, this model proposes that membership in a disadvantaged category tends to lead to greater exposure to stress because of discrimination or poorer quality of life.

In the second model, internal and external sources are viewed as mediators between exposure and response to stress. This model suggests that stressful life events per se are not important; it is the impact of mediating factors on stress that is central. Because a person belongs to a particular socioeconomic class, he or she may have class-related differences in coping resources or social support mechanisms that may affect levels of stress (Kessler, 1979a; Smith, 1985). Both conceptual and methodological studies of stressful life events and the appearance of symptomatology have tended to focus on the individual's present social environment as a source of stress. Despite the magnitude of this research, no clear picture has been formed of the specific demographic subgroups most likely to report exposure to stressful life events among African Americans.

Denial and Stress

Theoretically, the denial of problems should have negative consequences if the denial prevents the individual from engaging in needed actions. A careful examination of the coping process by Lazarus (1981) suggests that denial of stress can have both positive and negative consequences depending on the type of stress. For example, denial of illness, especially myocardial infarctions in a coronary care unit, had a positive impact on survival (Hackett & Cassem, 1970). The research on coping suggests that the denial of stress could be self-denial, nondisclosure, or something else. Neither self-denial nor nondisclosure is viewed as a form of coping, but rather they are viewed as independent variables that affect coping styles in a number of life areas, such as marriage, family, finances, and work (Carver, Scheier, & Weintraub, 1989). Individuals who are high in nondisclosure are not necessarily high in denial.

One may recognize the problem but not disclose that knowledge to others. The tendency to deny or minimize problems to oneself must be distinguished from the tendency to minimize them to others. The tendency to minimize to self is associated with denial, but the tendency to minimize to others may be associated with a sense of control and independence.

Nondisclosure of information about stress appears to affect the tendency to seek help. In selected situations, such as stress in work and marriage, the more one avoids admitting problems to others, the less likely one is to take direct action or engage in negotiation and emotional release to relieve the stress. In general, the characteristic of nondisclosure of stress affects coping behaviors that involve dealing with other people (Fleishman, 1984). Unfortunately, much of the literature on denial seems to stress the costs or benefits or both of denial-like coping processes rather than the characteristics of those who tend to deny stress (Lazarus, 1981). Despite this tendency, there is some information about the characteristics of stress deniers and acknowledgers. Vulnerability to anxiety and tolerance of ambiguity seem to be related to the tendency to deny or not to deny (Breznitz, 1983). Harburg, Erfurt, Chape, Schull, and Schork (1973) stressed that for African Americans "degree of skin color in American society is another strong social status indicator" (p. 285). Results suggest that the darker the skin color, the higher the blood pressure for African American males. Harburg and associates reasoned that darker-skinned males are more likely to suppress stress-related hostility than lighter-skinned males. This suppression of stress then affects blood pressure levels.

Dressler's (1985a) research on a southern community implies that being reared in a traditional social environment (e.g., in rural, southern United States) may also have an effect on the denial of stress. Other studies by Rahe (1974), Theorell (1974), and Eysenck (1983) all conclude that respondents' recent reports of problems may be affected by past experiences and characteristics such as gender and age. Older persons, for instance, are more likely to report having fewer or no stressful life events (Markush & Favero, 1974). The theory is that they have either forgotten problems long since solved or, at this stage of life, stressful situations are seen as less problematic. In other words, the older the person, the more likely the denial of stress. Interestingly, despite study results that point to differences in the tendency to deny, Breznitz (1983) has noted that the "one overriding difference between individuals which should be noted is their tendency to engage in denial-like coping in the first place" (p. 274).

Measures

Stress Denial

Two sets of questions on the NSBA asked the respondents to report experiences of problems. The first question stated, "Next I am going to read you a list of things which may have happened to you during the past month or so. Please tell me whether or not these things have happened to you in the past month or so." The list of problems included health, money, job, family, love life or marriage problems, problems with people outside of the family, problems with children, being the victim of a crime, problems with the police, and being treated badly because of race.

The second question asked whether the respondents had ever in their lifetimes experienced a problem that caused them serious emotional distress. Probes were used that allowed the reporting of problems beginning with those that created the most emotional response (to the point of nervous breakdown) and ending with those that created the least response.[1]

A composite variable was created by cross-classifying these two questions. Three hundred and forty-five people reported experiencing no problems either over the past month or ever, 434 reported having problems in the past month or so, 206 said that they had experienced a serious lifetime problem, and 1,112 acknowledged having had both recent and serious lifetime problems. A dichotomous variable was created by combining all respondents who had experienced a problem (a lifetime problem, recent problem, or both) and contrasting them to those who reported never having experienced a problem. This dichotomous variable served as the dependent variable for the analyses to follow.

Predictors

Three categories of variables were used to explore the question of denial of life problems: social status, social roles, and group identification. Education, family income, and skin color were used as indicators of social status. Marital status, having children under age 18 at home, rural upbringing, sex, and age were the indicators of social roles. Group identification was measured using a racial identification scale developed by Gurin, Miller, and Gurin (1980).

Education was dichotomized into those who had not graduated from high school and those respondents with high school diplomas and above. For purposes of description, income was collapsed into quartiles. For the multivariate analyses, a 17-category income variable was used representing income in thousands, from no income to $30,000 or more. Interviewers also rated respondents on a number of characteristics, including skin color. This 5-point rating was dichotomized for the analysis into medium-to-light and dark-to-very-dark categories. Dichotomies were developed to measure whether respondents had a spouse or a partner, had children under age 18 living at home, and whether they had a rural upbringing. Age was divided into four categories for descriptive purposes and into a dichotomized variable for the multivariate analysis.

Group identification was measured using these instructions:

> Now I'm going to read you a list of different types of black people. For each one, tell me how close you feel to them in your ideals or feelings about things: poor, religious, young, middle class, working class, older, elected officials, and professional people.

A group identification index was constructed following the procedures employed by Broman, Neighbors, and Jackson (1988). The mean score was 3.35 and the coefficient alpha was .818 (Broman et al., 1988). For this analysis, the scale scores were dichotomized: Low identification was defined as below the mean, and high identification was defined as equal to the mean or greater.

Results

Seventeen percent of the sample (n = 345) reported never having had a problem. Fifty-three percent reported having both recent and lifetime, 21% indicated problems in the past month but not serious lifetime problems, and 10% reported serious lifetime problems but no recent ones. When the characteristics of deniers and acknowledgers of stress were analyzed, the two categories of respondents differed in a number of ways. Table 5.1 shows the relationship of stress denial to the selected independent variables. Individuals without children under age 18 at home were more likely to report no problems than those with children under age 18—21% and 13%, respectively. Age was also related to the denial of problems—those 65 years old or older (33%) were the most likely to report never having had a problem, whereas the two younger age groups (18-24 and 25-44) were least likely to report never having had a problem (10% and 11%). Those respondents raised in a rural environment were more likely than those raised in cities to report no problems. Finally, men (21%) were more likely than women (14%) to indicate no problems, but the relationship of sex to stress denial was dependent on education. Men and women did not differ among high school graduates, but men (29%) were significantly more likely than women (14%) to report no problems among those who had not graduated from high school.

Multivariate Analysis

Table 5.2 presents the results of a logit regression, which estimates the odds that a case with a given set of characteristics would deny having problems. The analysis used a sequential strategy to explore the denial of life problems. Initially, all main effects were entered. Then, in sequence, interaction terms were constructed for each predictor with the remaining variables. The interaction between sex and education was the only interaction that was significant. Model 1 includes all of the individual predictors, Model 2 adds the sex by education interaction, Model 3 includes only the significant main effects, and Model 4 adds the interaction term. All models show significance, but the simplified models (Models 3 and 4) provide the most parsimonious prediction of whether an individual is likely to deny stress. In large part, these results confirm the picture shown in the bivariate cross-classifications in Table 5.1. People who deny problems are more likely to be male, high income, older, and to have a rural upbringing. Family roles, marital status, skin color, racial identification, and education are not related statistically to denial. The interaction between sex and education is highly significant. The direction of the interaction is clearly shown in the dropout by sex variable of Table 5.2. Among those who finished high school, there is no difference between males and females in frequency of denial. The main effect for gender is entirely due to the elevated levels of denial among males who did not finish high school.

Discussion

The goals of this chapter were (a) to examine the characteristics of those who deny and those who acknowledge stress and (b) to develop a multivariate model to summarize the observed patterns of stress denial. People who admit

Table 5.1 Characteristics of Deniers

Characteristic	Serious Lifetime Distress (Deny)	
	%	N
Children under 18**		
Yes	13	1,077
No	21	1,019
Gender**		
Male	21	797
Female	14	1,310
Age**		
18-24	10	328
25-44	11	881
45-64	20	556
65 or older	33	342
Education**		
Dropout	18	919
High school graduate or more	14	1,168
Rural upbringing**		
No	12	1,118
Yes	22	950
Family income		
under $5,000	14	461
$5,000-$10,000	18	469
$10,000-$20,000	15	492
$20,000+	17	413
Married or with partner		
Yes	17	1,357
No	16	792
Skin color		
Light to medium	17	1,274
Dark to very dark	16	792
Identification with blacks		
Low	18	1,016
High	15	1,058
Interaction: Education and Gender		
Dropouts**		
Male	29	346
Female	14	573
High school graduates		
Male	14	444
Female	14	724

** $p < .01$.

Table 5.2 Logit Regression of Denial on Personal Characteristics and Status Indicators

Variable	Beta Coefficient			
	Model 1	Model 2	Model 3	Model 4
Intercept	−2.46**	−2.98**	−2.62	−3.20**
Children < 18	.02	.02		
Sex	−.47**	−.11	−.46**	−.11
Income	.05**	.05**	.05**	.05**
Age	.03**	.03**	.03**	.03**
Married	−.02	−.06		
Upbringing	.47**	.48**	.46**	.47**
Skin color	−.21	−.21		
Identification	−.08	−.08		
Education	.05	1.19**	.05	1.16**
Dropout by sex		−.75**		−.73**
Model χ^2	114.1	125.0	115.6	122.3
df	9	10	5	6
R	.250	.257	.258	.263

$**p < .01.$

to having had one or more serious life problems are more likely to have higher levels of education, a factor we expect to be associated with higher levels of introspection and the ability to articulate problems. Acknowledgers also tended to be younger and had an urban upbringing. This makes sense in that cities have both more resources and more chances of mishap, especially crime. Younger people may be at a stage in which they are more vulnerable to problems. They are still trying to establish themselves in their careers, and they are raising families under the pressures of marital disruption. Problems encountered in the past also, no doubt, look smaller than they do when they are being encountered on a daily basis.

The most provocative finding, however, was that a substantial portion (17%) of the NSBA reported not having experienced any problems. The profile of the "denier" is that of an older, rural, higher income male who did not finish high school. On the surface, it would appear reasonable that such a person might be less likely to experience stress compared to those in other categories. The underlying, ultimate question, however, is whether these people actually never experienced a serious problem or whether they are merely glossing over their negative experiences. One could argue that blacks growing up outside the high-risk areas of the cities, who are relatively affluent despite never having completed high school, and who have survived to at least middle age might, in fact, never have encountered a serious problem. The interpretation that we favor, however, is that men with this profile might be less inclined to acknowledge and verbalize that they have had problems that they could not handle. This leads us to conclude that they may have had problems that they are not willing to divulge rather than that they led charmed lives.

The underlying question remains whether these "stress deniers" were reflecting the reality of their situation. The benign interpretation of stress denial is that some people just manage to cope with life as it comes without encountering challenges beyond their resources. They may not "sweat the small stuff" or dwell on problems. Rather, they look for solutions. Some of the problem deniers are probably both good at coping and just plain lucky. In an effort to explore these interesting questions, additional analyses of the relationship between the experience of problems and indicators of quality of life were performed. Specifically, we crossed the problem variable with life happiness, life satisfaction, family satisfaction, and health satisfaction.

It is the group that reported not experiencing a recent or lifetime problem that is so intriguing and has been the focus of our speculation. If these people are in reality under much stress but denying its existence, they should not differ from the other groups with respect to quality of life. If, on the other hand, these people are truly not experiencing problems, or coping so effectively that they "barely notice" the problems they do have, we might expect this group to exhibit significantly higher rates of happiness and satisfaction than the other groups.

Table 5.3 shows the results of these analyses. Interestingly, the proportion of respondents who designate themselves as "very happy" drops with the experience of problems. Specifically, 54% of those who never had a problem reported feeling very happy in comparison to 35% with either a lifetime or a recent (past month) problem and 19% for those with both a lifetime and a recent problem. A similar trend is seen when inspecting the percentages of respondents reporting feeling "not too happy." Although 24% of those who experienced both serious lifetime and recent problems reported feeling not too happy, only 4% of those with no problems felt this way.

Looking at general life satisfaction, 52% of the no problems group said they felt "very satisfied" with their lives. This compares to 21% of those who experienced both types of problems. A similar trend can be seen for family satisfaction—72% of the no problems group reported feeling very satisfied with their family life, whereas only 42% of the group that experienced both

Table 5.3 Relationship Between Stress-Denial and Quality of Life

	Very happy (%)	Pretty happy (%)	Not too happy (%)	N
Life happiness[a]				
No problems	54	42	4	341
Lifetime or recent problem	35	55	10	623
Lifetime and recent problem	19	58	24	1,107
	Very satisfied (%)	Somewhat satisfied (%)	Somewhat to very dissatisfied (%)	N
Life satisfaction[b]				
No problems	52	41	7	340
Lifetime or recent problem	36	47	17	623
Lifetime and recent problem	21	50	29	1,109
Family life satisfaction[c]				
No problems	72	25	3	338
Lifetime or recent problem	61	30	9	618
Lifetime and recent problem	42	43	15	1,105
Health satisfaction[d]				
No problems	64	30	6	341
Lifetime or recent problem	61	28	11	624
Lifetime and recent problem	43	36	22	1,111

a. $\chi^2 (4) = 215.17, p < .001.$
b. $\chi^2 (4) = 163.50, p < .001.$
c. $\chi^2 (4) = 123.10, p < .001.$
d. $\chi^2 (4) = 109.02, p < .001.$

types of problems indicated feeling very satisfied. Table 5.3 also shows that the differences are not as dramatic for health satisfaction. The group with no problems is not very different from the group that experienced either a recent or a lifetime problem. For example, 64% of the no-problem group reported being very satisfied with their health, whereas 61% of those with a lifetime or recent problem felt that way. Only 43% of those who had experienced both a recent and a lifetime problem, however, were very satisfied with their health. Although these results are admittedly exploratory and preliminary, they are nevertheless consistent with the notion that some African Americans are either extremely effective at coping with problems or are lucky enough not to be exposed to the stresses and strains most blacks must endure. These results cannot, however, rule out the notion of stress denial. If these respondents are stress deniers, denial may not be a totally ineffective coping strategy. Longitudinal follow-up of the mental health of the no problems group would help unravel these competing interpretations.

Determining the effectiveness of denial as a coping strategy is problematic because the very act of coping assumes either the existence of an acknowledged problem or that an experienced event has the potential to be problematic whether acknowledged or not. If denial is a coping strategy that can be advantageous and insulate the individual from the insidious effects of stress, then longitudinal follow-up of the mental health and lifestyles of the no problems group would help unravel these competing interpretations. If, on the other hand, an experienced event is problematic to most people, but is denied by the no problems group and ultimately leads to an unhealthy suppression of feelings such as anger and hostility, we are left to speculate as to whether it is the failure of denial as a coping strategy or the experience itself that creates the problem. In this latter case, a change in the way stress and coping are conceptualized and measured might prove as useful as having more data on the long-term experiences of the no problems group.

Conclusions

Despite these findings, the general health status literature is consistent with the view that African Americans, especially urban males, are more likely to suppress their anger and to die from heart attacks or strokes (e.g., Harburg, Erfurt, Hauenstein, et al., 1973). African American stress deniers might be socialized in the mode of the traditional African American folk hero "John Henry." John Henry was the prototype that stimulated the thinking of Sherman James (1993), who originated and developed the personality construct of John Henryism. Although James refers to males in the definition, he indicated that there was no reason that the concept could not apply to females as well. Essentially, people with high John Henryism are more likely to view themselves as capable of overcoming all obstacles through determination and hard work (James, Hartnett, & Kalsbeek, 1983, p. 263). High levels of John Henryism increase diastolic blood pressure levels among lower socioeconomic status African Americans (James et al., 1983; James, Keenan, Strogatz, Browning, & Garrett, 1992). These findings suggest that denying the existence of real problems that may be insurmountable can lead to detrimental health outcomes. Perhaps backing away from such problems is the only way to effectively deal with them—a coping response that persons with high John

Henryism would undoubtedly find difficult to implement. John Henry worked himself to death to show that he could outwork a machine. The price for John Henry was extreme but represents the potential price of denial.

There are two major implications for future research. The first is methodological. Measures of coping styles based on problem-focused reports omit an important segment of the population—namely, those individuals who cope with problems by denying or at least downplaying them. We recommend alternative approaches to measuring coping styles. Alternative measures, such as responding to hypothetical vignettes, may suffer from their own validity problems because people's hypothetical reactions may be entirely different from their actual reactions. The apparent greater validity of requesting descriptions of responses to actual situations, however, seems to be outweighed by the hazards of eliminating the deniers from the sample.

The second recommendation is that more research is needed on the relationship between the concept of denial and the John Henryism construct. James (1993, 1994) theorizes that John Henryism has a cultural and economic base for African Americans. The origins are rooted in a rural, postslavery past. These people are in part the products of an environment that is fading and being replaced with a more dangerous, urbanized culture. Although we have expressed concern that denying problems may lead to ineffective coping, we must not overlook the possibility that, on a day-to-day level, refusing to let problems be "serious" may in fact be a good approach to living in an oppressive society.

Note

1. The exact wording of the question is as follows: "Problems often come up in life. Sometimes they are personal problems. When problems like this have come up, has there ever been a time when you felt you were about at the point of a nervous breakdown?" Follow-up questions included the following: If the answer was no, "Has there ever been a time when you had a personal problem where you felt so nervous you couldn't do much of anything?" If that answer was no, "Has there ever been a time when you felt down and depressed, so low that you felt like you just couldn't get along?" If no, "Have you ever had a personal problem you couldn't handle by yourself?" If no, "Have you ever had what you thought was a serious personal problem that you tried to handle by yourself?"

6

Marital Status and Mental Health

Diane R. Brown

One of the most consistent findings in the mental health research literature is that married persons have better mental health than people who are not married. This finding has been reported across different indicators of mental health such as happiness (Bradburn & Caplovitz, 1965; Campbell, Converse, & Rodgers, 1976; Glenn, 1975), life satisfaction (Andrews & Withey, 1976; Campbell et al., 1976), depression and distress (Brown, Ahmed, Gary, & Milburn, 1995; Weissman, 1987), and other forms of psychopathology (Eaton, 1975). Persons who are widowed, separated, divorced, or never married have higher rates of mental hospitalization (Kramer, Brown, Skinner, Anthony, & German, 1986) and a higher rate of outpatient mental health services use (Rosenstein & Milazzo-Sayre, 1981). Moreover, they tend to have higher use rates for general hospital services for a range of conditions—not just for mental disorders (Kramer et al., 1986).

Although the relationship between marital status and mental health has been firmly established in the literature (Ensel, 1982; Glenn, 1975; Glenn & Weaver, 1981; Gove, 1972; Gove, Hughes, & Style, 1983; Weissman, 1987), few studies have examined findings for African American respondents. Most of the research findings on marital status and mental health have focused

AUTHOR'S NOTE: The author acknowledges Dr. Harold W. Neighbors and Dr. James S. Jackson for their assistance in the acquisition of data from the National Survey of Black Americans. Also, appreciation is extended to Mrs. Geraldine Davis and Mrs. Annette Dawson for typing the manuscript and to Graduate Research Assistant Ms. Angela Dungee Greene for her invaluable help.

largely on white samples with little consideration for differences by race even though marital patterns among African Americans differ from those of the general population (Reskin & Coverman, 1985; Tucker & Mitchell-Kernan, 1995; Williams, Takeuchi, & Adair, 1992a). Even in major mental health studies that have included African American respondents (Campbell et al., 1976; Eaton et al., 1984; Gurin, Veroff, & Feld, 1960; Srole, Langner, Michael, Opler, & Rennie, 1962; Veroff, Douvan, & Kulka, 1981), not much has been published on within-group differences. Consequently, data are meager in the area of relationships between marital status and mental health among African Americans.

Explaining Marriage and Mental Health

Several hypotheses explain the greater well-being of married persons. The social support hypothesis contends that being married serves as a buffer against the deleterious effects of stress. It is suggested that having a spouse affords the opportunity to engage in an intimate and trusting relationship wherein problems and tasks can be shared and emotional assurance obtained (Burke & Weir, 1977). In addition, marriage constitutes the major societal vehicle for maintaining a primary group relationship for adult males and females. As a primary source of social support for psychological and emotional needs, marriage enables individuals to maintain personal equilibrium and at the same time facilitates the performance of their social roles (Hahn, 1993; Rosen, Goldsmith, & Redlick, 1979).

Little is known about the extent to which marriage is viewed as being socially supportive for African Americans. Brown and Gary (1985) report that a marital partner was viewed as a source of emotional support for less than one third of the married African American females in their study. The major sources of social support for African American females, irrespective of marital status, were family members and extended kin. On the other hand, analyses of the *General Social Surveys* from 1972 to 1984 by Zollar and Williams (1987) indicate that marriage provides greater mental health benefits to African American females than to males. They report that marital happiness makes a larger contribution to the overall happiness of African American wives than it does to husbands. African American males, however, are more likely to report being happy with their marriages than are African American females. Although these findings indicate gender differences on one measure of mental health, they are not direct indicators of the extent to which marriage is socially supportive for African American adult males and females.

The preexisting "pathology" or social selection hypothesis offers another explanation for the association between marital status and mental health. This hypothesis suggests that persons who enter marriage and are able to remain married are mentally healthy individuals. Individuals with psychopathology are apt not to get married or, if they do, their marriages are likely to be disrupted through separation or divorce. Based primarily on data from white respondents, this hypothesis does not consider other factors that affect one's eligibility for marriage nor one's decision to remain married. Particularly for African Americans, economic factors strongly influence marriageability and the stability of marriage (Williams et al., 1992a). Also, the demographics of the African American population affect the number of potentially eligible marriage partners, rendering fewer eligible males than females (Guttentag & Secord, 1983; Staples, 1981b; Tucker & Taylor, 1989).

Gender, Marriage, and Mental Health

Although married persons tend to have better mental health than those who are not married, previous studies also indicate that there are gender differences in the relationship between marital status and mental health. Moreover, there has been considerable controversy in the literature on whether marriage is of greater benefit to males or to females (Bernard, 1972). Different measures of mental health in these studies make it difficult to generalize findings for African American males or for African American females.

Among married individuals, numerous studies consistently report that females have higher rates of psychiatric symptoms than males (Gove, 1972; Weissman, 1987). Veroff, Douvan, and Kulka (1981) suggest that females find marriage less satisfying than males. On the other hand, Gove (1972) attributes the higher rate of psychiatric symptoms among married females to differences in the social roles of married persons. Specifically, the traditional roles of wife and homemaker occupied by married females are often frustrating and stressful. At the same time, married males tend to occupy major social roles, namely breadwinner and household head, that are less restricting and more fulfilling than traditional wife and homemaker roles. Accordingly, married females tend to report higher levels of depression than married males. Moreover, when married females do work outside the home, they usually have to undertake both family and employment responsibilities. This "role overload" may further increase stress, contributing to even higher levels of depression among married women. Not surprisingly, females who are unhappily married tend to be the most severely depressed (Weissman, 1987).

The findings are not consistent with regard to gender differences in depression among nonmarried persons. In general, widowed females are apt to be happier and to have less distress than widowed males. On the other hand, separated, divorced, and never-married females report more distress than similarly situated males (Campbell, 1980; Eaton & Kessler, 1981). The extent to which these findings are applicable to African Americans is not clear. According to Ball and Robbins (1986), the relationship between marital status and mental well-being among African Americans does differ by gender. In contrast to patterns found among whites, however, Ball and Robbins found that widowed African American females had the highest mean level of well-being, followed by those who were divorced, and then by those who were married. Separated and never-married African American females had significantly lower levels of well-being. Warheit, Holzer, Bell, and Arey (1976) found that divorced African American females had lower distress than African American females in any other marital status category. Adding age to the equation, however, Brown, Milburn, Ahmed, Gary, and Booth (1990) found no significant difference in depressive symptoms among married and nonmarried African American females who were 45 years of age or less.

The relationship between well-being and marital status among African American males differs slightly from that of females. From research on a select population of African American males, Gary (1985) found the previously married (divorced, separated, or widowed) to be the least distressed, followed by those who had never married, and then by those who were married. Similar findings have been reported by Ball and Robbins (1986). In their study, widowed African American males expressed the highest level of well-being, followed by those who were divorced or separated, and then by those who had never married. Married men reported the lowest mean level of satisfaction among males. Again, it should be pointed out that the use of different measures of mental health in these studies makes it difficult to generalize findings.

Other research findings indicate that the well-being of married African American males is linked to their ability to undertake the traditional family breadwinner role (Tucker & Taylor, 1989). Specifically, socioeconomic factors appear strongly related to marital adjustment and happiness (Albrecht,

1979; Glenn & Weaver, 1978). Furthermore, according to Ball and Robbins (1986), well-being is greater among married African American males with higher levels of family financial adequacy, whether or not it stems from their own individual financial contribution. Marriage and family life appear to be stressful for African American males who experience economic difficulties.

Trends in Marital Status

The relationship between marital status and mental health among African American adults is particularly important to consider in light of the data that indicate that the relative percentage of currently married African Americans has been declining over the past 25 years and continues to remain below that of the general population (Tucker & Mitchell-Kernan, 1995; U.S. Department of Commerce, 1994). This trend stems from increases in the number of never-married, divorced, and separated African American adults. In addition, the rate of remarriage following divorce, in particular for African American females, has continued to decline in recent years. Consequently, many African American adults spend a significant portion of their life—in some cases, all of their adult life—in a nonmarried status. The ramifications of these trends for the mental health of African American adults need further exploration. Thus, this chapter addresses the following questions: Is being married associated with better mental health than being unmarried? If so, are there differences in mental health among married males and females? Are there gender differences in mental health among those who are not married? Do alternatives to marriage have an association with mental health that is similar to that between mental health and marriage?

Method

The data for these analyses come from the National Survey of Black Americans (NSBA) (Jackson, 1991). The present analysis focused on the 1,322 respondents who reported experiencing a personal problem that had caused them a significant amount of distress. Respondents were asked how they responded to this stressful circumstance. Developed specifically for the NSBA, the dependent measure of psychological distress consisted of an eight-item symptom checklist. The following items are included in this index:

Table 6.1 Percentages of Respondents' Marital Status and Gender

	Females		Males	
	%	N	%	N
Married	34.5	300	47.7	208
Widowed	16.7	145	11.5	26
Separated	13.8	120	6.4	28
Divorced	15.3	133	6.0	50
Never married	19.7	171	28.4	124
Total		869		436

Pearson χ^2 (4) = 65.3, $p < .001$.

feeling lonely, being depressed, feeling jumpy or jittery, having crying spells, not being able to get along, having a poor appetite, having trouble sleeping, and feeling physically sick. This psychological distress measure encompasses the number of symptoms experienced and the frequency of each symptom. Each symptom endorsed by the respondent was probed regarding its subjective severity with the following item: "During that time [when the respondent was experiencing the problem], how often did you feel [lonely, depressed, jumpy, etc.]? Would you say very often, fairly often, not too often, hardly ever, or never?" The more often the respondent indicated experiencing that particular symptom, the more serious that symptom was assumed to be.[1] The index has a mean of 4.08 and a standard deviation of 2.41. The alpha is .83. As anticipated, males reported significantly lower levels of distress than did females. This corroborates the findings of numerous previous studies reported in the literature about gender differences in levels of distress (Eaton & Kessler, 1981).

Results

Marital status consisted of five categories: married, separated, divorced, widowed, and never married. Individuals involved in commonlaw marriages were grouped with those who were married. As expected, there was a significant difference in marital status by gender, with African American males more likely to be married than females (Table 6.1). Nearly one half (48%) of the African American males were married, in contrast to a little over a third (35%) of the African American females. These gender differences are probably due

Table 6.2 Mean Levels of Psychological Distress by Marital Status and Gender

	Females (F Ratio = 1.67, F p = .15)			Males (F Ratio = 4.04, F p < .01)		
	$\overline{X}$	SD	N	$\overline{X}$	SD	N
Married	4.35	2.44	300	3.00	2.35	208
Widowed	4.67	2.57	145	4.58	2.37	26
Separated	5.01	2.35	120	3.29	2.40	28
Divorced	4.48	2.57	133	3.68	2.27	50
Never married	4.53	2.37	171	2.84	2.15	124
Total	4.55	2.46	869	3.14	2.32	436

to the smaller number of African American males who are considered "marriageable" in the U.S. population and the higher rates of remarriage among African American males. In addition, not all African American males are married to African American females.

Although males were more likely to be married, they were also more likely than females never to have married (28% vs. 20%). Conversely, African American females were more apt to be divorced, separated, or widowed. Specifically, 15% of the African American women were divorced compared to 6% of the African American males. Among married males and females, there was no significant difference in the length of time married—an average of 17.9 years for males and 18.2 years for females (not shown in Table 6.1).

Is Marriage Better for Mental Health?

Table 6.2 presents the distribution of psychological distress scores by marital status and gender. An assessment of the data separated by gender indicates that distress varied by marital status for both males and females. For African American males, the never married and married showed the lowest symptomatology with mean levels of distress of 2.84 and 3.00, respectively. (There was no statistically significant difference in distress between married and never-married African American males experiencing a serious personal problem.) The highest level of distress was reported by widowed African American males (4.58) followed by those who were divorced or separated (3.68 and 3.29, respectively).

Table 6.3 Psychological Distress Regressed on Marital Status Separately by Gender (Unstandardized Coefficients)

	Females		Males	
	b	SE	b	SE
Widowed	0.284	.301	1.411**	.544
Separated	0.500*	.279	0.225	.507
Divorced	0.111	.270	0.598	.412
Never married	−0.051	.277	−0.290	.342
Constant	7.480		4.321	
Adjusted R^2	3.97%		3.38%	
F ratio	3.94***		2.23*	

$*p < .05; **p < .01; ***p < .001.$

Unlike the findings for African American males, distress was not significantly related to marital status for black women ($p < .15$). Married women did report the lowest level of distress (4.35), but this did not differ markedly from mean levels of distress reported by never-married African American females (4.53) or divorced women (4.48). Widowed black women showed a somewhat higher level of distress (4.67), whereas those who were separated showed the highest symptom rate (5.01). It should be noted, however, that no particular marital status stands out as more or less distressed than any of the other marriage groups for African American females experiencing a serious personal problem.

A multiple regression analysis was performed to conduct a more rigorous examination of the relationship of gender and marital status to psychological distress. Table 6.3 shows the relationship between marital status and psychological distress while controlling for time[2] and type[3] of problem, as well as age, poverty status, education, employment status, and the presence of children age 17 or under in the home. Regression analyses were conducted separately for men and women. Marital status is represented as a series of dummy variables with married as the excluded category.

These findings indicate that psychological distress does vary significantly by marital status for both African American males and females. Consistent with the results presented in Table 6.2, it is evident that, for African American females, being separated is associated with higher levels of distress as compared to those married. In contrast, among African American males, those who were widowed had higher levels of distress than those married. These findings hold even when a number of sociodemographic factors are controlled. In general, marriage appears to be associated with having better mental health when one is faced with a serious personal problem to the extent that married persons, irrespective of gender, have levels of psychological distress that are lower than those of persons who are separated, divorced, or widowed. Married persons, however, do not appear to have better mental health than those who have never been married. Instead, the level of psychological distress among married persons is similar to that of persons who have never married. These findings differ from those of prior studies of African American populations and from those of the general population. In an analysis of data from a regional sample of African American adults, Brown and colleagues (1990) found that never-married African American females were significantly more depressed than married females. Furthermore, in an epidemiological study of the general population, Eaton and Kessler (1981) reported fewer depressive symptoms among those who were married than among those who had never married.

The fact that the levels of psychological distress of married and never-married African American adults in this analysis do not differ greatly challenges the social selection hypothesis. As stated previously, the social selection hypothesis contends that one reason never-married persons do not marry is that they have greater psychopathology than married persons. Contrary to this hypothesis, data from this analysis do not show that never-married African American adults have greater psychological distress than married persons—at least for those faced with a serious problem. There are undoubtedly factors other than psychopathology that influence why a significant number of African American adults never marry. There are perhaps some who perceive that the psychological distress in their lives can be minimized by never marrying. For others, being married may not be viewed as socially supportive or as enhancing the quality of their lives; this is evidenced in the ongoing dialogue in African American communities regarding African American male-female relationships. Specifically, for some persons it may be a mentally healthier choice never to marry than to enter marriage and risk facing marital disruption. At the same time, other African American adults may never marry for the lack of eligible marriage partners or because of their own personal economic or social characteristics that reduce their marriage-ability.

Gender Differences in Psychological Distress Among the Married

Although these data do not show that marriage among African American adults is necessarily better for one's mental health than never having been married, it is also evident that married persons have lower rates of distress than previously married persons—marriage is clearly associated with lower levels of psychological distress when faced with a serious personal problem when compared to those who are separated, divorced, or widowed. Although marriage has its mental health benefits in terms of lower levels of psychological distress, the literature suggests that the impact of marriage on mental well-being varies by gender.

As mentioned previously, there is considerable controversy focusing on gender differences in the benefits of being married. According to Bernard (1972), marriage provides more benefits to husbands than to wives. This suggests that psychological distress should be lower among those receiving the greater benefits. To examine this hypothesis, data on psychological distress were examined solely for married African American males and females. Using the means in Table 6.2, statistically significant differences in distress were found between males and females who were married. Married females reported greater distress when experiencing a personal problem than did married males. At first glance, these data for married African American males and females appear to support Bernard's hypothesis. The fact that married African American males report less psychological distress than married females is consistent with receiving greater benefits. This conclusion is drawn cautiously, however, because it is difficult from these analyses to attribute the gender differences in distress to differential marriage benefits or to the overall higher psychological distress reported by females across nearly all marital statuses. Several other indicators were examined to test whether marriage is of greater benefit to husbands or to wives. For example, in their responses to the question, "Who do you think gets more out of the relationship, you or your [husband-wife-partner]," there was no significant difference between males and females. The majority of both males (57%) and females (54%) stated that benefits were about equal.

To further examine how marriage relates to gender differences in the levels of psychological distress, an analysis was conducted around perceptions of the importance of having a partner in the house relative to a number of aspects of relationships and family life, such as raising children, obtaining financial security, getting jobs done around the house, having a good love life, and

Table 6.4 Responses by Gender on Importance of Having a Partner in the House

	Very Important (%)	Fairly Important (%)	Not Too Important (%)	Not Important at All (%)	χ^2 (3)
Raising children					
Males	76.3	8.5	6.0	9.2	19.7***
Females	64.3	12.9	7.8	15.0	
Financial security					
Males	35.2	22.9	21.3	20.6	44.9***
Females	53.3	20.9	13.4	12.4	
Jobs around house					
Males	50.7	21.1	15.5	12.7	1.4
Females	47.3	23.1	16.2	13.5	
Good love life					
Males	77.0	13.4	4.8	4.8	89.8***
Females	50.8	20.6	14.7	14.0	
Companionship					
Males	80.3	12.8	4.1	2.7	58.4***
Females	59.5	23.4	8.2	8.8	

***$p < .001$.

having companionship. The results are shown in Table 6.4 separated by gender.

There was a significant gender difference for four of these items. On three of the four items, males felt more strongly than females. Having a partner in the house for raising children, a good love life, and companionship were considerably more important to African American males than to African American females. The gender differences for a good love life and companionship were particularly striking. Seventy-seven percent of the men but only 51% of the women felt that it was very important to "have a [man-woman] live in the house for a good love life." Similarly, 80% of the men but only 60% of the women felt that it was very important to "have a [man-woman] live in the house for companionship." These gender differences support the findings of Staples (1981a), who indicated that companionship is a deeply valued aspect of a marital relationship for African American males. Although males look to a relationship for emotional assurance and nurturing support, they traditionally have not been socialized to provide this type of support to their partner. At the same time, African American females rely on their network of female family members and friends for companionship and emotional support (Brown & Gary, 1985).

These data also indicate that having a partner in the house for financial security was significantly more important to African American females than it was to African American males. Although 53% of the women felt men were very important for financial security, only 35% of the men felt this way about women. There were no significant differences by gender concerning the importance of living with someone to get jobs done around the house. About half of both men and women—51% and 47%, respectively—felt that it was very important to have the opposite sex around "for jobs that need to be done around the house."

When asked what was the most important aspect of having someone live in the house, similar differences were also evident by gender. Although these analyses are not shown, African American males were most apt to say "companionship" or "raising children" were the most important reasons for having a partner in the household. African American females also said having a partner in the house was most important for raising children but believed partners were most important for financial security as well. On the other hand, having a partner in the house for financial security was least important to males (12%). This suggests that both married males and females tend to hold traditional perspectives regarding the major breadwinning role for African American males. For African American females, the least important reason for having a partner in the house was for getting jobs done.[4]

In summary, with regard to gender differences in psychological distress among married African American adults facing a serious personal problem, females reported higher levels of psychological distress than males. Although previous studies suggest that this gender difference is due to the frustrating traditional social roles occupied by married females (Gove, 1972), this explanation is questionable in its applicability to the African American population (Thomas, 1986). Although these analyses did not directly examine this explanation, other studies have indicated that African American females have historically been more likely than married white females to work outside the home while being a wife and mother. There are likely to be other factors contributing to the higher psychological distress reported among married African American females compared to African American males.

The data in this analysis suggest that the gender differences in psychological distress among married African American adults may in part stem from the greater importance that married African American females place on having a partner in the house for financial security—given the economic problems faced by many African American families. The higher levels of psychological distress reported by married African American females may emanate from worries or strains related to the difficulties their male partners experience in maintaining meaningful employment and fulfilling their bread-winning capacity in the American economy. On the other hand, the differences in psychological distress reported among married males and females facing stressful circumstances may reflect the general trend in gender differences in psychiatric symptomatology. Despite these gender differences in psychological distress among married persons, however, males and females do not differ regarding the perceived benefits. Married African American males and females feel that they and their partners share equally in the benefits of the marriage.

Gender Differences in Psychological Distress Among the Unmarried

Gender comparisons in psychological distress were also made across the other marital status groups. Among the separated, divorced, and never married, females reported higher levels of distress than their male counterparts. Only among the widowed were the levels of distress relatively similar for males and females. This occurred because widowed African American males were significantly more distressed than males in the other marital status categories, thus making them more comparable to females.

Separated and divorced respondents were asked to indicate if they thought being separated-divorced was better or worse than being married. The responses from females differed significantly from those of males. About half (51%) of the female respondents stated that being divorced or separated was better, whereas one third (33%) of the African American males felt this way. Twenty-eight percent of both males and females expressed mixed feelings. Although experiencing a marital disruption through separation or divorce tended to increase the levels of psychological distress for African American females facing a serious personal problem, they still preferred their present status to marriage. This suggests that being married was less conducive to the mental well-being of the majority of African American females who were separated and divorced. Of course, their perceptions may have been influenced by the recency of the marital dissolution or factors that were not incorporated into this analysis. Nonetheless, a significantly greater percentage of divorced and separated males were more likely to find marriage preferable to their current status than their female counterparts.

Along with divorced and separated persons, never-married and widowed persons were queried about their perceptions of their current marital status. Specifically, they were asked, "What is the one thing you dislike or like most about being single or unattached?" Unmarried males and females (47% and 40%, respectively) indicated that they disliked the loneliness—that is, the absence of companionship—someone with whom to share and talk. On the other hand, the majority of unmarried African American males and females (67% and 69%, respectively) liked the freedom from responsibility and the independence associated with not being married. Slightly more never-married or widowed males (13%) than females (8%) indicated that there was "nothing" that they liked about being single or unattached, which suggests that marriage is associated with greater well-being for males than for females, although this finding may pertain primarily to widowed men and not to those who have never been married.

Main Romantic Involvement, Marriage, and Psychological Distress

In light of demographic data that indicate that substantial proportions of African American adults are not married at any given point in time (Smith & Johns, 1995), additional analyses were conducted to assess the association between having "a main romantic involvement" (MRI) and psychological distress. Divorced, separated, widowed, and never-married persons were asked, "Do you have a main romantic involvement at this time?" Of the unmarried females responding to the question, 42% indicated that they did compared to 49% of the males. Males and females did not vary significantly in the length of time with a main romantic involvement (4.3 years for males and 5.3 years for females). Males were slightly more likely than females to live with their main romantic involvement (15% and 12%, respectively), but the difference was not statistically significant. Among those without a main romantic involvement, men were significantly more likely than women to desire one—only 36% of the African American females in comparison to 49%

Table 6.5 Mean Levels of Psychological Distress by Main Romantic Involvement and Gender

	Females (F Ratio = 1.94, F p = .12)			Males (F Ratio = 3.67, F p = .01)		
	$\overline{X}$	SD	N	$\overline{X}$	SD	N
Married	4.35	2.44	300	3.00	2.34	208
Main romantic involvement	4.49	2.44	229	2.93	2.24	108
No MRI; desire one	4.96	2.47	115	4.07	2.31	54
No MRI; no desire	4.67	2.47	207	3.31	2.18	59
Total	4.55	2.46	851	3.16	2.31	429

of the African American males stated that they "would like to have a main romantic involvement at this time."

Table 6.5 examines the relationship of psychological distress to marital status taking the availability of a main romantic involvement into account. There is a significant relationship among males but not among females; women display higher mean levels of distress than men whether they are married or involved romantically with someone. There is, however, some indication that distress is highest among those women who do not have a main romantic involvement but would desire one. Among both males and females, distress was lowest for those who were married or those with a main romantic involvement. There was little difference in distress between those who were married and those who had a main romantic involvement for either males or females.[5] Not surprisingly, psychological distress was highest for both unmarried males and females who desired a main romantic involvement but who did not have one. People who did not have a main romantic involvement (MRI) and did not want one had lower levels of psychological distress than those who wanted but did not have a main romantic involvement. This was true for both men and women. Their rates were not, however, as low as those for respondents who were married or for those who did indeed have a main romantic involvement. In summary, unmarried persons without a main romantic involvement who were not desirous of having one had slightly lower levels of psychological distress than those who desired a main romantic involvement, and single African Americans with a main romantic involvement were no more distressed than married African Americans when encountering a stressful circumstance.

Summary and Conclusions

The major objective of this analysis was to assess the associations between marital status and psychological distress among adult African American males and females. In the past, few studies have examined data solely on African American populations despite other research that has indicated that associations among African Americans, particularly those involving family and marriage factors, may not conform to findings reported for white populations (Reskin & Coverman, 1985).

Data from this analysis only partially support those from previous studies of the general population. As demonstrated in prior research, being married appears to have a positive influence on psychological distress. Married African American adults do not experience as much psychological distress when faced with a serious personal problem as those who are separated or divorced. Although marriage may be better for one's mental health than being separated or divorced, being married is not significantly better than having never married. Never-married persons are similar to those who are married in terms of having levels of distress that are lower than those who have separated and divorced. Apparently, the lives of many African American adults are psychologically healthier in terms of minimizing the impact of stressful problems when they marry and stay married or if they never marry.

Understandably, separated and divorced persons suffer the highest levels of distress when faced with a serious personal problem. Nonetheless, despite increased levels of psychological distress, the majority of separated and divorced African American females preferred their current marital status to being married. Separated and divorced African American males, however, preferred being married. That separated and divorced males prefer marriage to being single supports the conclusion that marriage appears to have greater psychological benefits for males than for females. Additional support for gender differences in the benefits of marriage is suggested from findings indicating that African American males, more so than females, perceived that marriage was important for a good love life and companionship. Females were less likely to endorse these aspects. Future research is needed to explore whether these gender differences prevail across socioeconomic status and across other sociodemographic and cultural characteristics.

These findings underscore the viability of marriage among African Americans. In circumstances in which marital relationships can endure, there are positive psychological benefits to be gained. At the same time, however, not marrying seems to be a viable alternative. There is a higher proportion of never-married African American adults when compared to whites, which may stem from the greater acceptance of being single in the African American community. Historically, factors such as poverty, unemployment, and a low male-female sex ratio have, at times, made it difficult, and perhaps stressful, for African Americans to maintain stable marriage and family relationships. For many, never marrying represented the most psychologically beneficial choice. The viability of being never married is also evident when examining the influence of having a main romantic involvement on psychological distress. Never-married males and females who have a main romantic involvement report levels of distress that are similar to those of married African American adults. In other words, having a main romantic involvement can be as protective of one's mental health as being married.

These findings suggest that sociocultural adaptations have emerged in African American communities that provide alternatives that are as conducive to low levels of psychological distress as marriage. These findings are important to consider given the demographic trends and social and economic factors that affect marriage and family decisions for African American males and females. The circumstances in which alternatives to marriage are associated with low levels of psychological distress warrant further investigation, especially given the wide-ranging implications for the numbers of African American adults who are not married at any specific point in time. In particular, additional longitudinal quantitative and qualitative studies are needed that explore how factors such as gender, age, education, income, the presence of children, and the existence of social support networks influence levels of distress among unmarried African American adults. Research is needed most on the factors that facilitate and promote emotional well-being among unmarried African American adults. Future research also needs to include a variety of indicators of well-being, including those focusing on life satisfaction and overall life quality, as well as psychological distress, depression, and other forms of psychopathology. Most important, future studies need to include instruments that are sensitive to the sociocultural context of African American communities.

Although these findings offer insight into associations between marital status and mental health, a note of caution is offered. These findings are based solely on data regarding those persons experiencing a personal problem that had caused them a significant amount of distress. Consequently, the analysis did not encompass data from the entire NSBA sample and cannot be generalized to the entire population. Furthermore, this analysis did not examine differences by marital status in the number or type of personal problems or the available psychological and social resources for dealing with the stressful circumstance.

Notes

1. The psychological distress scale has been compared with other checklists, and there is some overlap between it and the psychological subscales extracted from the Langner (1962) and Gurin et al. (1960) indices. Scores were calculated by assigning the respondent a value of 1 solely for symptoms experienced "very often" or "fairly often." Thus, the range on the measure is from 0 to 8. For example, a respondent who experienced three symptoms, one "not too often," one "fairly often," and one "very often," would receive a score of 2. Responses were required on at least six of the eight symptoms in the index to be included in the analysis.

2. To measure the time of the problem, respondents were asked, "About how long ago did that happen?" Respondents answered this question in terms of days, weeks, years, or by making statements such as "it's happening now," "a while ago," and so on. These responses were recoded to construct a dichotomous variable, with up to 2 years ago considered as a "recent" event (coded 1 in the dummy regression) and more than 2 years ago considered a "nonrecent" problem (the excluded category in the regression dummy variable).

3. The type of personal problem experienced was assessed by asking respondents to describe what happened at the time they were seriously upset. Specifically, the item read, "Thinking about the last time you felt this way, what was the problem about?" Responses to this item were coded as physical health, interpersonal, emotional, death, and economic problems.

4. These aspects of marriage and family life were also examined according to levels of psychological distress reported when facing a serious personal problem. The findings (not shown) indicate that distress varied significantly according to the reason considered most important for having a partner in the house. Distress was greatest among those who felt a partner in the house was most important for financial security and companionship.

5. Regression analyses were run analyzing distress levels of married respondents compared to those of unmarried people with and without MRI as well as to those without a romantic involvement but wanting one. There were no differences in distress among these groups. Neither was there a Gender × MRI interaction.

7

The Association Between Anger-Hostility and Hypertension

Ernest H. Johnson
Larry M. Gant

Hypertension, or chronically elevated blood pressure, is generally recognized as a major health problem afflicting a large percentage of African Americans (Gillum, 1979; Taylor & Fant, 1975). This condition can be caused by disorders such as arteriosclerosis and kidney disease. These secondary causes of hypertension, however, are found in only a small percentage of the African American adults who have chronically elevated blood pressure. In more than 85% of all cases of hypertension in African Americans, the etiology is unknown; such cases are classified as "essential hypertension" (Cruickshank & Beevers, 1982; Stamler, Stamler, & Pullman, 1967; Taylor & Fant, 1975; Thompson, 1981).

A number of diverse factors have been proposed to account for the etiology of essential hypertension in African Americans, including organic factors, diets rich in salt, socioenvironmental stress, and, in more recent publications, psychological-emotional factors (Harburg, Erfurt, Chape, Schull, & Schork, 1973; Johnson, 1984, 1987, 1989a, 1990; Thompson, 1981; Weiner, 1977). It is interesting to note, however, that little research has examined these factors in African Americans, even though it has been established that hypertension is more common among African Americans than among whites in the United

States. Moreover, there is also a growing body of evidence that suggests that essential hypertension may have its onset at earlier ages for African Americans than for whites (Loggie, 1971; Londe, Bourgoignie, Robson, & Goldring, 1971; Londe & Goldring, 1976).

Several studies have indicated that approximately 20% to 30% of the adult African American population is affected by chronically elevated blood pressure, which is well above the 13% to 15% prevalence rates among whites (Boyle, 1979; Comstock, 1957; Hypertension Detection and Follow-Up Cooperative Group, 1977, 1979; McDonough, Garrison, & Hames, 1964; Roberts & Rowland, 1981). Because African Americans have limited access to and may never be seen by the health care delivery system, reported figures for African Americans may be substantially below the true prevalence rate for hypertension (Johnson, 1987; Taylor & Fant, 1975).

Not only are elevated blood pressures and hypertension more prevalent in African Americans, but hypertension mortality rates are also disproportionately higher (Cruickshank & Beevers, 1982; National Center for Health Statistics, 1967). In the United States, the mortality rate for hypertensive heart disease for African Americans is 3 times greater than that for whites (Cooper, 1984; Meriyama, Krueger, & Stamler, 1971; Myers, 1986). Furthermore, the mortality rate for African Americans between the ages of 35 and 54 years is 6 to 10 times greater than that for whites (Hypertension Detection and Follow-Up Cooperative Group, 1977, 1979; Nichaman, Boyle, Lesne, & Sauer, 1962).

It has been observed that African Americans with hypertension have a higher incidence of stroke (Cassel, Heyden, & Bartel, 1971; Tyroler et al., 1971; U.S. Department of Health, Education, and Welfare, 1979). For example, the annual incidence of strokes in the United States for white men and women after age adjustments was 4.7 and 1.2 per 1,000, respectively, compared with 5.8 per 1,000 per year among both African American women and men (Heyman, Karp, & Heyden, 1971).

Research on the role of physiological and environmental variables, such as high use of salt, social-psychological stress, and anger, in the etiology of essential hypertension among African Americans is very limited. Explanations of how these variables contribute to observed differences in the prevalence and pathophysiology of hypertension among African Americans and whites are largely based on speculation, although some definitive work is beginning to emerge, particularly with regard to anger (Brunswick & Collette,

1972; Gentry, 1972; Gentry, Chesney, Gary, Hall, & Harburg, 1982; Harburg, Erfurt, Hauenstein, et al., 1973; Harburg & Hauenstein, 1980; Johnson, 1984, 1987; Johnson, Spielberger, Worden, & Jacobs, 1987; Mattson, 1975).

Research relating essential hypertension to anger is an outgrowth of interest in empirical evaluation of Alexander's (1939, 1939/1948) "specificity hypothesis" regarding the etiology of hypertension. Alexander (1939, 1939/1948) proposed that the inhibition of anger leads to increased elevations in blood pressure and that prolonged blood pressure elevations associated with the inhibition of anger ultimately lead to essential hypertension. In tests of Alexander's specificity hypothesis, anger has been identified as an important factor in studies of hypertension (Baer, Collins, Bourianoff, & Ketchel, 1979; Cochrane, 1973; Crane, 1982; Esler et al., 1977; Gentry, Chesney, Hall, & Harburg, 1981; Harburg, Erfurt, Hauenstein, et al., 1973; Harburg & Hauenstein, 1980; Mattson, 1975; Robinson, 1962; Schneider, Egan, Johnson, Drobney, & Julius, 1986; Whitehead, Blackwell, DeSilva, & Robinson, 1977). It is quite possible that anger and hostility resulting from racial prejudices, injustices, and low socioeconomic status experienced by African Americans may operate to initiate the rise in blood pressure. Moreover, anger may interact with environmental and familial factors to cause the early emergence of elevated blood pressure and hypertension in African Americans.

Studies of the association between anger and hypertension in African Americans have provided strong support for Alexander's (1939, 1939/1948) hypothesis (Gentry et al., 1982; Harburg, Erfurt, Hauenstein, et al., 1973; Harburg & Hauenstein, 1980; Johnson, 1984, 1987; Mattson, 1975; Miller, Stein, & Grim, 1979). These studies also support historical and social analyses that assert that African Americans are forced into social positions in which they experience anger-hostility as a result of verbal and physical attack, yet suppress their expression of anger and hostility (Clark, 1965; Gentry, 1985; Grier & Cobbs, 1969).

This chapter reviews studies examining the association between the expression of anger and elevated blood pressure. The chapter then describes the relative prevalence of hypertension for the sample of African American adult males and females who participated in the National Survey of Black Americans (NSBA). Finally, the chapter concludes with future directions for research on the role of anger-hostility in hypertension.

Studies of Essential Hypertension Using Objective Tests

Studies of the role of anger, hostility, and aggression in essential hypertension have used objective personality measures (Gentry, Julius, & Johnson, 1992; Spielberger et al., 1991). In fact, a large number of studies have reported a relationship between hypertension and anger-hostility using a wide variety of psychological scales (Cochrane, 1973; Harburg, Julius, McGinn, McLeod, & Hoobler, 1964; Lee, Carstairs, & Pickersgill, 1971; Pilowsky, Spalding, Shaw, & Komer, 1973; Robinson, 1962; Sainsburg, 1960; Schonecke, Schuffel, Schafer, & Winter, 1972).

In one of the few studies investigating the relationship between hostility and hypertension in African Americans (Mattson, 1975), four groups of patients (hypertensives, diabetics, diabetic hypertensives, and general medical controls) were compared on the Foulds and Caine measures of hostility and aggression. It was hypothesized that the hypertensives would exhibit greater "inward hostility" and less "outward anger" than patients in the other groups. In addition, it was predicted that within the hypertensive group, measures of inward hostility would correlate positively with blood pressure, whereas measures of outward aggression would correlate negatively with blood pressure.

The results indicated that there were differences among the groups in the amount of hostility or anger that they experienced. For the hypertensive and control groups, negative correlations were found between measures of outward hostility and blood pressure. For the diabetic and diabetic hypertensive subjects, positive correlations were found between outward anger and blood pressure. Miller et al. (1979) compared African American hypertensives with an African American normotensive control group and found that the hypertensives could be described as being humble, docile, sober, serious, astute, controlled, and exerting willpower, compulsions, and precision.

Gentry (1972) examined the relationship between anger and aggression and vascular arousal (blood pressure) in a biracial situation. The subjects were 28 male and female African American college students, half of whom were subjected to insults from a white peer experimenter of the same sex. The results indicated that there was greater self-reported anger, direct and indirect verbal aggression, and elevated diastolic blood pressure (DBP) in the group that was verbally attacked compared to the group that was not insulted.

Brunswick and Collette (1972) examined the relationship between psychological variables and elevated blood pressure in a sample of African American adolescents. Included in this study were a number of indicators of "psychological well-being" that included questions concerning feelings of depression, hostility, anxiety, loneliness, and the physicians' and subjects' reports of the presence of a nervous or emotional problem. The results of this study indicated that African American adolescents with elevated DBP scored in the "less well" direction when compared to the normals.

Spielberger, Jacobs, Russell, and Crane (1983) defined *state anger* as a transitory emotional condition that consists of subjective feelings of tension, annoyance, irritation, fury, and rage, as well as by arousal of the autonomic nervous system. State anger may vary in intensity and fluctuate over time as a function of the amount of frustration and annoyance that results from perceived injustices or the blocking of goal-directed behavior. *Trait anger* refers to relatively stable individual differences among people in the disposition to perceive a wide range of situations as annoying or frustrating and in the tendency to respond to such situations with marked elevations in state anger. Persons high in trait anger are more likely to experience more intense elevations in state anger whenever annoying or frustrating conditions are encountered.

Because few investigations of the relationship between hypertension and anger have been clear in their conceptualization and measurement of the various dimensions of anger, it is difficult to determine in the research literature which specific aspect of anger (frequency of experience, intensity of experience, or direction of expression) is related to hypertension. Crane (1982) conducted one of the few studies comparing hypertensive and normotensive patients in which the dimensions of anger were clearly conceptualized and measured. The two groups were compared on measures of state anger (intensity of anger experienced) and trait anger (frequency of experienced anger) that form the state-trait personality inventory (STPI) (Spielberger et al., 1991). Results of this study indicated that hypertensives scored higher on the trait and state anger scales of the STPI. Hypertensives also scored higher on measures of state and trait anxiety, as well as the irritability and resentment scales of the Buss Durkee Hostility Inventory (BDHI). Further analyses of the individual BDHI items indicated that the hypertensive patients were more irritable than the controls and that they tended to suppress hostility and aggressiveness in interpersonal situations.

The study by Crane (1982) is important because the results clearly indicate that hypertensive patients experience a greater frequency and intensity of anger and anxiety when compared to normotensive controls. It is difficult, however, to interpret the findings with regard to differences between hypertensives and controls in the expression of hostility. The results of factor analysis of the instrument (BDHI) used to assess the expression of hostility have indicated that the factor structure of this scale does not correspond with the a priori definitions of the subscales. There is also relatively little evidence of the construct validity of the BDHI (Russell, 1981).

Another study, also using the state-trait anger and anxiety scales of the STPI, was conducted by Johnson (1984, 1989b). In his study, African American and white male and African American female adolescents with elevated blood pressure experienced a greater intensity of anger and anxiety (state) than their counterparts with normal blood pressures. African American male and female adolescents with elevated blood pressure also experienced anger (trait) more frequently than their normotensive counterparts. There were no differences in the frequency in which anger (trait) was expressed for white adolescents in the high and normal blood pressure groups.

Studies of Anger Expression and Hypertension

Funkenstein, King, and Drolette (1957) hypothesized that the physiological component of anger is mediated by the direction of anger expressed (i.e., inward toward self or outward toward others). Building on the work of Ax (1953), which indicated that anger was related to elevated blood pressure and other psychophysiological measures, Funkenstein et al. classified subjects according to their mode of expression of anger and anxiety. In their study, male university students were harassed and criticized in several stress-inducing "problem" situations. On the basis of post-experiment interviews that focused on the emotional reactions experienced by the subjects during the problem situation, students were classified as "anger-out," "anger-in," "mixed anger-anxiety," or "anxiety reactions." Results for the stressful situation in which the students were harassed while solving math problems indicated that the anger-out students exhibited a large increase in DBP with little systolic blood pressure (SBP) or heart rate (HR) change and marked peripheral resistance. The "anxiety" students manifested larger increases in SBP and HR and relatively little change in DBP, whereas the anger-in students fell in the intermediate range between the anger-out and anxiety students on all measures except SBP, which was similar to the anger-out group.

Harburg, Erfurt, Hauenstein, et al. (1973) followed up the work of Funkenstein et al. (1957). They systematically investigated the relationship between anger-in and anger-out coping styles and black-white blood pressure differences. The subjects were 1,000 African American and white males and females, ages 25 to 60, residing in high- and low-socioeconomic stress areas of a large midwestern city. Socio-ecological stress was defined in terms of crime rates, population density, residential mobility, degree of marital breakdown, and economic factors. Suppressed anger was defined in terms of ratings of anger directed inward in response to vignettes concerning injustice from police and homeowners. The four response categories were (a) expressed anger-no guilt, (b) expressed anger-guilt, (c) suppressed anger-no guilt, and (d) suppressed anger-guilt. Before the vignettes were presented, SBP and DBP readings were obtained.

Results of the first report indicated that the SBP and DBP for African American males living in high-stress areas were significantly higher than the blood pressures of the other groups (Harburg, Erfurt, Hauenstein, et al., 1973). Suppressed anger was associated with higher DBP levels for African American males living in high-stress areas and white males living in low-stress areas. The African American men with hypertension living in low-stress areas tended to keep their anger in and to deny feeling guilty, whereas white men with hypertension living in high-stress areas felt guilty after expressing their anger. The percentage of diagnosed hypertensives was 12.25% for respondents classified as using the anger-out coping style compared to 19% for respondents using the anger-in coping style.

The finding that white males living in high-stress areas had lower blood pressure levels than African American males living in high-stress areas suggested that racial factors play at least some role in hypertension. The fact that the BP of African American males living in high- and low-stress areas differed from each other, however, suggests that racial factors alone do not account for the observed blood pressure differences. Syme et al. (1974) also found that African American males in high-stress living situations had higher blood pressure than African American males living in low-stress areas and white males living in high- and low-stress areas.

Other epidemiologic studies have found evidence of an association between hypertension and socio-ecological stress as defined by area (urban vs. rural) of residence (Gentry, Harburg, & Hauenstein, 1973; James & Kleinbaum, 1976). In general, these studies have indicated that the prevalence of hypertension for African Americans residing in rural areas is significantly higher than that of their socioeconomic peers in urban places. Although the outcome of these studies appears to be inconsistent with the belief that urban life is more "stressful" than rural life, the results consistently indicated that the prevalence of hypertension is greater for rural residents. It is not clear why rural residents have a greater prevalence of hypertension. One explanation is that the association between hypertension and place of residence is mediated by socioeconomic status, social stress/instability, anger expression, or other environmental variables.

In a study reported by James and Kleinbaum (1976), the association between hypertension-related mortality rates and socio-ecological stress was examined in a sample of African Americans and whites residing in North Carolina. Their results indicated that the average hypertension-related mortality rate for nonwhite males (96% African American) in high-stress counties in North Carolina was nearly twice that for white males in low-stress counties. The hypertension-related death rate was higher for whites and nonwhites with low socioeconomic status (SES) and high social instability scores (SIS). The magnitude of the difference attributable to the SES and SIS factors, however, strongly suggested that for nonwhites SIS was a more important mediator of hypertension-related deaths than SES, whereas SES was more important among whites. Given the urban-rural lifestyle differences between Detroit and North Carolina, the convergence of results supports the hypothesis for an association between socio-ecological stress and hypertension-related morbidity and mortality.

In a second report by Harburg and his associates (Gentry et al., 1973), the effects of anger expression and guilt on diastolic blood pressure for African American and white females residing in high- and low-socio-ecological stress areas was examined. The women in this study were classified in terms of their habitual anger-coping pattern in the same manner as the males in the first report. The hypothetical situations described in the vignettes involved an angry boss, a policeman, and housing discrimination. For the African American females residing in high-stress areas, an anger-in coping response to the angry boss or housing discrimination vignettes was associated with higher diastolic blood pressure than was an anger-out coping response. White females who resided in low-stress areas and used the anger-in coping response to the angry boss or policeman also had higher DBPs than white females using the anger-out coping response. There were no significant differences in DBP between African American women with anger-in and anger-out coping styles who lived in the low-stress areas or for white women with these coping styles who resided in high-stress areas.

In a third report based on a different analysis of the original data, Harburg, Blakelock, and Roeper (1979) examined the relationship between elevated BP and anger-coping styles that they labeled "resentment" (i.e., keeping anger in or expressing it through overt aggressive behavior) and "reflective" (i.e., bypassing anger and focusing on a problem-solving approach to the anger-provoking situation). The subjects who responded to the "angry boss" vignettes with resentment had significantly higher blood pressures than those who used the reflective coping response. The reflective anger-coping style was also associated with lower mean pressures than resentment for the normal, borderline, and hypertensive subjects. Approximately 15% of the individuals using the resentment coping style were hypertensive compared to only 9% of those using the reflective coping style.

A fourth report, based on the Harburg, Erfurt, Hauenstein, et al.'s (1973) and Harburg, Erfurt, Chape, et al.'s (1973) original data, examined the effects of race, sex, sociological stress, and habitual anger-coping styles on SBP, DBP, and the risk of being classified as hypertensive (Gentry et al., 1982). Subjects were classified as high, medium, or low in expressed anger, which was determined by summing their responses to all five vignettes describing anger-provoking situations. After adjusting for age and weight, the results indicated that (a) African Americans and low-anger expressers were higher in DBP; (b) African Americans and males were higher in SBP; (c) anger expression was inversely related to SBP for females only; (d) all four behavioral factors were independently related to the relative risk of being labeled hypertensive; and (e) the odds of being diagnosed as hypertensive were higher for African Americans, males, persons who suppressed their anger (low-anger expressers), and those residing in high-stress areas. Moreover, an individual's odds of being diagnosed as hypertensive increased with the addition of each behavioral risk factor.

The findings of Harburg, Erfurt, Hauenstein, et al. (1973); Harburg, Erfurt, Chape, et al. (1973); and Gentry (1985) clearly demonstrate the importance of the anger-in distinction and show that hypertension is associated with holding anger in rather than expressing it in anger-provoking situations. Due to a number of problems in the procedures employed in the assessment of anger expression, however, it is difficult to interpret their findings, which limits the extension of their procedures to other populations. For example, the hypothetical anger-provoking situations that composed Harburg and colleagues' questionnaire were designed to assess anger expression in adults residing in a large city and may not be appropriate for other populations. They also inquired about subjects' reactions to hypothetical situations that many had never actually experienced, and they failed to take into account the frequency of occurrence of reactions to the same or similar situations.

Another major limitation of the assessment procedure of Harburg, Erfurt, Hauenstein, et al. (1973) and Harburg, Erfurt, Chape, et al. (1973) is that the subjects are classified into dichotomous groups on the basis of their responses to only two hypothetical situations. A much larger number of situations would be needed to establish the ecological validity of this classification, and it would be desirable to have a continuous measure of the degree of anger-in and anger-out expression. Although the procedures employed by Gentry (1985) are based on five hypothetical anger-provoking situations, and subjects are classified into low, medium, and high anger-out groups, the ecological validity of their situations is still questionable, and there are only three categories, rather than a continuous measure, of anger expression.

Building on the work carried out by Harburg, Erfurt, Chape, et al. (1973) and Harburg, Erfurt, Hauenstein, et al. (1973), Johnson (1984) and Spielberger et al. (1985) initiated research to clarify the association between hypertension and anger expression. To begin this process a continuous (frequency) measure of anger expression was developed. To our surprise, the results of the factor analysis of the anger-expression measure revealed two factors (anger-in and anger-out) that were orthogonal and empirically independent. Similar results were found by Pollans (1983) for college students.

In a study of the relationship between anger expression and blood pressure, Johnson (1984) found that the systolic and diastolic blood pressures of African American and white male and female adolescents who had higher anger-in scores were significantly higher than those of their counterparts with lower anger-in scores. On the other hand, adolescents with higher anger-out scores had significantly lower blood pressures than adolescents with lower anger-out scores. These findings indicated that the concept of "anger expression" is not unidimensional and bipolar as suggested by Funkenstein et al. (1957); Harburg, Erfurt, Chape, et al. (1973); Harburg, Erfurt, Hauenstein, et al. (1973); and Gentry et al. (1982). In other words, anger expression is not a single bipolar dimension for which behaviors range from inhibition or suppression (anger-in) of angry feelings to the extreme expression of anger (anger-out) toward other persons or the environment.

A second study using the anger expression scale was conducted by Schneider et al. (1986). In this study, higher anger-in scores discriminated borderline hypertensives whose blood pressures were elevated at the time they were evaluated in the hypertensive clinic and at their home from those whose blood pressures were normal at home (subjects measured their own blood pressures twice a day for 7 days). There was no significant difference in the frequency that anger was expressed (anger-out) for the two groups of border-line hypertensives. Hypertensives whose blood pressures were elevated both in the clinic and at home, however, reported experiencing a greater intensity of anger in response to frustrating time-pressured social situations.

In another study (Johnson, 1989b, 1990), African American male students with and without a parental history of essential hypertension (EH) participated in a laboratory session during which two mental challenge tasks (anagrams and mental arithmetic) were presented. The rationale behind the study was that differences in cardiovascular responses to mental stress, psychological factors, and self-determined home blood pressure between African American individuals with and without a family history of EH may suggest mechanisms responsible for the high incidence of EH in African Americans. Following the laboratory session, all subjects made daily recordings of their morning and evening blood pressure for 4 weeks (28 days). The results showed that sons of hypertensive parents had higher systolic and diastolic blood pressures than sons of normotensive parents at rest and during mental challenge; no reliable differences in heart rate were observed. Sons of hypertensive parents also had higher self-determined home blood pressure (SBP and DBP) and scored significantly higher on psychological measures of trait-anger/temperament, anger-out, and submissiveness. There was no significant change in SBP or DBP over the 4 weeks prior to final examinations in either of the groups. Although the resting BP level, weight, and family history predicted a large proportion of the variance in home SBP and DBP, the amount of explained variance, particularly for DBP, was significantly increased by the inclusion of psychological variables and the level of cardiovascular responses (and not the amount of change) to mental challenge in the regression equation. These findings indicate that the degree to which self-determined home blood pressures can be predicted is enhanced significantly by considering both the level of cardiovascular responses to stress and the psychological measures of the experience and expression of anger. The implications of these results are discussed in light of current research demonstrating that average home blood pressures are a better predictor of cardiac complications than office blood pressures. In other words, individuals who remain hypertensive outside the office are believed to be a higher risk for hypertension and its vascular and cardiac complications.

In conclusion, the studies reported by Johnson (1984), Spielberger et al. (1985, 1991), Johnson et al. (1987), and Schneider et al. (1986) clearly indicated that anger-in and anger-out are independent dimensions of anger expression, and the results of these studies indicated that both modes of anger expression have an independent influence on blood pressure.

Methodology

The present investigation examined the relationship between the prevalence of hypertension and the frequency that anger is expressed outwardly toward people and objects in one's environment. It was predicted that the prevalence of hypertension would be greater for African American males and females who scored low on the anger-out scales in comparison to African American respondents who scored high on the anger-out scales. In addition, it was predicted that the prevalence of hypertension would be higher for (a) respondents who live in highly stressful environments, (b) older subjects, (c) males, (d) respondents with low incomes, (e) respondents with low education levels, and (f) previously married African American respondents (i.e., divorced or widowed).

The measure of anger expression was obtained only for those respondents who reported experiencing a serious personal problem. Sixty-three percent, or 1,323 of the respondents, reported having experienced such a problem. All 1,323 subjects were asked a 15-item symptom checklist, which required them to indicate how often (very often, fairly often, not too often, hardly ever, or never) they had experienced a particular emotion during the time of the personal problem. Three of the items in this checklist assessed anger expression. The anger measure consisted of three items: "Did you lose your temper?" "Did you fight and argue with other people?" "Did it [the personal problem] cause problems in your family?" These three items loaded together on the same factor (.73 to −.93) and correlated highly with each other ($\alpha = .65$). These items are identical to items on the anger-out subscale of the anger expression scale that was developed by Johnson (1984) and Spielberger et al. (1985).

These items were combined to create the anger expression scale used in this chapter. Respondents had to have valid data on at least two of the three items to be included in the scale. As a result, 22 cases were lost due to missing data ($N = 1,301$). The frequency distribution for the anger expression scale was then used to divide the sample into quartiles that were labeled low, moderate, moderate-high, and high.

The environmental stress measure required respondents to indicate their degree of satisfaction regarding four community services: police protection, garbage collection, schools, and public transportation. Three additional items, which assessed the degree that problems with crimes, drugs, and police-resident interactions were present in the neighborhoods, were also included in the measure ($\alpha = .65$).

Results

The results of the present study are presented in three sections. In the first section, the association between key demographic factors and the prevalence of hypertension are examined. In the second section, the association between anger, socio-environmental stress and the prevalence of hypertension are described, and in the third section, the relative risk of being diagnosed hypertensive for the anger/socio-environmental stress and demographic factors are described.

Approximately 32% ($n = 664$) of the 2,107 African American male and female respondents who took part in the NSBA reported that they had been told by a doctor that they had hypertension or "high blood pressure" (Jackson, 1991).

Demographic Factors

Gender. Twenty-four percent of the African American males and 36% of the African American females reported being told by a physician that they had hypertension. Table 7.1 presents the prevalence of hypertension for each of the demographic factors (age, income level, employment status, marital status, education, and urbanicity) for the total sample and separately for males and females. The results of the chi-square analysis revealed that the percentage of African American females with hypertension was significantly greater than that for African American males.

Table 7.1 Prevalence of Hypertension by Demographic Factors for Males and Females in the National Survey of Black Americans

Demographics	Black Males (%)	Black Females (%)	Total Sample (%)
Age			
18-34	8	16	13
35-54	26	42	36
55+	46	60	55
χ^2	106.4***	190.80***	295.11***
1978 Income			
< $5,000	33	46	43
$5,000-$10,000	27	35	32
$10,000-$20,000	17	33	26
> $20,000	23	32	23
χ^2	11.32**	31.00***	49.19***
Employment status			
Unemployed	33	46	42
Working	20	28	24
Never worked	0	37	32
χ^2	20.50***	45.96***	75.61***
Marital status			
Previously married	31	47	43
Married	26	34	30
Never married	13	19	7
χ^2	18.98***	62.08***	95.04***
Education			
< 11 years	32	50	43 (43.9)[a]
High school graduate	17	28	24 (29.9-34.2)
Some college	16	23	20 (27.1)
College graduation	22	20	21 (27.7)
χ^2	22.05***	99.95***	105.18***
Urbanicity			
Urban	24	35	29
Rural	24	42	38
χ^2	0.36	4.89*	12.20**

a. The numbers in parentheses represent the prevalence of elevated diastolic blood pressure ($\geq$ 95 mmHg) for blacks at home screening by education from the Hypertension Detection Follow-up Program, 1973-1974.
$*p < .05$; $**p < .01$; $***p < .001$.

Age. Age was also associated with the prevalence of hypertension (Table 7.1). Approximately 13% of the respondents in the 18- to 34-years-old age group reported having hypertension in comparison to 36% for the 35- to 54-year-old group and 55% for the 55-years-old or older group. An analysis of the association between age and prevalence of hypertension taking gender into account was carried out, and it revealed the same pattern for both men and women—reported hypertension increases with age. Although there was a higher percentage of females with hypertension in each age group, the percentage of males and females with hypertension in the 55-years-old or older age group was significantly higher than that in the younger age groups.

Income. Income level was significantly related to having hypertension. Individuals in the lowest income level (under $5,000) had the highest rate of hypertension (43%). The prevalence rate for hypertension was highest for both males (33%) and females (46%) at the lowest income level. For females, the prevalence of hypertension decreased in a linear fashion as the income level increased. The highest income group had the lowest prevalence of hypertension. The prevalence of hypertension for males also exhibited a linear decrease but only up to the second highest income level ($10,000-$20,000); the prevalence of hypertension increased from 17% to 23% for the highest ($20,000 or more) income group.

Employment Status. As predicted, the prevalence of hypertension for African American adults who were unemployed (42%) was significantly higher than that for African Americans who had never worked (32%) and that for African Americans who were currently employed (24%). This relationship held for both men and women. The prevalence of hypertension for unemployed African American men (33%) was significantly higher than that for males currently employed (20%); there were no males in the sample who had never worked. The results for females also indicated that the prevalence of hypertension was higher for the unemployed (46%) than for women who had never worked (37%) and for women who were currently employed (28%).

Marital Status. Table 7.1 also shows that marital status was significantly related to the prevalence of hypertension. The prevalence rate for the previously married (43%) was higher than the rate for respondents who were currently married (30%) and the rate for those who were never married (7%). Similar patterns were observed when the analyses were conducted separately for males and females.

Education. The education level of respondents was also significantly associated with the prevalence of hypertension. African American respondents at the lowest educational level (no school up to grade 11) had a higher prevalence rate of hypertension (43%) than respondents at any of the other educational levels. Education was significantly related to the prevalence of hypertension for males and females. The prevalence of hypertension for males and females at the lowest education level (32% and 50%, respectively) was higher than that for their

Table 7.2 Prevalence of Hypertension by Anger Expression and Environmental Stress for Males and Females in the National Survey of Black Americans

Variable	Black Males (%)	Black Females (%)	Total Sample (%)
Anger expression			
Low	27	43	38
Moderate	20	35	30
Moderate-high	19	38	32
High	20^a	29^a	26^a
χ^2	3.56	10.77**	11.93**
Environmental stress			
Low	24	43	36
Moderate	27	34	31
Moderate-high	25	36	32
High	19	32	27
χ^2	3.47	11.24**	0.92**
N	793	1,308	2,101

a. The sample size was restricted to respondents who reported that they responded to having a serious personal problem by experiencing and expressing anger.
**$p < .01$.

counterparts at each of the higher education levels, and the prevalence rate was higher for females than for males at most education levels. Approximately 17% of the males who graduated from high school reported having hypertension compared to 16% who had some college and 22% who graduated from college. For females, approximately 28% of those who graduated from high school had hypertension compared to 23% for women with some college and 20% for women who graduated from college.

Urbanicity. The prevalence of hypertension for rural residents (38%) was significantly greater than that for urban residents (29%). The difference, however, is only among females; there were no urban-rural differences in the prevalence of hypertension for African American males. The prevalence of hypertension for females who resided in rural areas (42%) was significantly greater than the prevalence rate for women residing in urban areas (35%).

Anger Expression

Data regarding the frequency that anger is expressed were available for 1,301 subjects. The relationship between anger expression and reported hypertension is reported in Table 7.2. The prevalence of hypertension for respondents in the low anger-expression group (38%) was higher than that for respondents in the high anger-out group (26%). The prevalence of hypertension for the low anger-expression group was also higher than that for the moderate (30%) and moderate-high (32%) groups. The results of the chi-square analysis comparing these percentages indicated that a significantly greater number of hypertensives scored low on anger expression. Table 7.2 also indicates that although the relationship between anger expression and the prevalence of hypertension followed a similar pattern for males and females, the relationship was significant for females only. Approximately 43% of the African American females in the low anger-out group had hypertension compared to 29% of African American women in the high anger-expression group. The prevalence of hypertension for African American women in the moderate group was 35% compared to 38% for African American women in the moderate-high group. Although there was no significant difference in the percentage of African American males in the anger-out groups with hypertension, there was a tendency for the prevalence to be lower among higher anger-out groups.

Environmental Stress

The prevalence of hypertension for the four levels of environmental stress (low, moderate, moderate-high, and high) are also reported in Table 7.2. The chi-square analysis revealed a significant relationship between environmental stress and reported hypertension. Approximately 36% of the respondents with low stress scores had hypertension compared to 27% of the respondents with high stress scores. Although there was no difference in the prevalence of hypertension for respondents with moderate (31%) and moderate-high (32%) stress scores, these prevalence rates were higher than those for respondents with high stress scores, but lower than those for respondents with low scores (36%).

There was no significant association between hypertension and environmental stress for men. There was, however, a trend indicating that the prevalence of hypertension was lower for the high-stress males (19%). The prevalence rates for the low-, moderate-, and moderate-high-stress groups were nearly equal—24%, 27%, 25%, respectively. In contrast, environmental stress was significantly related to hypertension among women. The prevalence of hypertension for African American females exposed to high stress (32%) was significantly lower than the rate for African American females in the low- (43%), moderate- (34%), or moderate-high-stress (36%) areas.

Differential Risk of Being Classified Hypertensive

In the present sample, the risk of being classified hypertensive versus normotensive was independently associated with each of the variables described in the previous analyses. Table 7.3 shows that the unadjusted and adjusted odds of being diagnosed hypertensive were highest for the older respondents. A closer look at the unadjusted odds values shows that the odds of being diagnosed hypertensive were also higher for respondents who were (a) low on anger expression, (b) low in environmental stress, (c) residents of rural areas, (d) low income, (e) unemployed, (f) previously married, (g) low education, and (h) females. The unadjusted odds ratio was greater than 1.0 for each of the variables. Adjusting the odds values leads to a reduction in the odds ratio (less than 1.0) for anger-out, environmental stress, urbanicity, and income.

Summary and Directions for Future Research

The goal of this chapter was to review the research literature on the role of anger-hostility in hypertension and to describe the relationship between anger and hypertension for the sample of African American adults who participated in the NSBA. Although a vast amount of research has been directed at establishing whether anger is related to essential hypertension in general, notably little work has been conducted to understand how anger operates among African American hypertensives in particular. Essential hypertension, unfortunately, is a case in which the group most at risk has been least studied. Research conducted thus far is highly suggestive of a role of anger, particularly suppressed anger, in the evaluation and etiology of hypertension among African Americans.

Data presented in this chapter revealed some evidence in support of the relationship between hypertension and anger. Overall, the findings were consistently stronger for women than for men. This could be a reflection of the higher prevalence of hypertension for women in the NSBA or differences between men and women in how they responded to the anger expression scale. It should also be noted that the measure of anger expression used in the NSBA measures the frequency that feelings of anger are expressed outwardly, whereas most previous research shows that hypertension is related to the suppression of anger. This may explain why anger expression was not related

Table 7.3 Differential Risk (Odds) of Being Classified Hypertensive Associated With the Presence of Psychosocial Factors

	Unadjusted		Adjusted	
Factor	*Odds*[a]	*Odds Ratio*	*Odds*[a]	*Odds Ratio*
Anger-out				
Low	.597	1.428	.355	0.965
High	.418		.368	
Environmental stress				
Low	.515	1.232	.309	0.732
High	.418		.422	
Urbanicity				
Rural	.550	1.361	.355	0.981
Urban	.404		.362	
Age				
Older	.577	17.920	.779	4.69
Younger	.088		.166	
Income				
Low	.869	4.061	.337	0.871
High	.214		.287	
Employment status				
Unemployed	.730	2.645	.504	1.768
Employed	.276		.285	
Marital status				
Married	.395	2.079	.350	1.074
Previously	.683	3.595	.384	1.178
Never	.190		.326	
Education				
Low	.789	3.000	.475	1.522
High	.263		.312	
Gender				
Female	.527	1.945	.447	1.878
Male	.271	0.238		

a. The odds for each variable are adjusted for each of the other variables in the column.

to hypertension in the multivariate analysis. It may also be the case that hidden within the multivariate analyses is a significant gender-hypertension interaction that is parallel to the univariate analyses showing significant relationships only for women. In any event, the finding that the prevalence of hypertension was higher among women than men merits further investigation because it goes against the grain of other studies.

It should be noted that the bulk of the previous research has shown a greater prevalence of hypertension among men using the actual measure of blood pressure to determine the diagnosis of hypertension. This was not the case for the NSBA sample, which defined hypertension based on whether the participants reported that they had been diagnosed by a physician or health care professional. Although there is no empirical evidence showing that women are more accurate in reporting diagnosed health problems than men, it is quite possible that the lower rates of hypertension for men might be associated with a lesser awareness of the problem. This lack of awareness of blood pressure status might be attributable to the tendency for men to delay and not seek medical care as regularly as do women. In this regard, it is quite possible that some men simply do not know whether they have hypertension. This is relatively easy to comprehend when one considers that hypertension has no obvious or overt symptoms. Given the high rates of chronic disease and mortality from hypertension and heart disease among African Americans, it will be important for future research to investigate the health care-monitoring behaviors of African American men and women. Results of this nature might shed some new insights on gender differences in hypertension and other health problems for African Americans.

Although the measure of environmental stress was somewhat unusual (i.e., a measure of the degree of satisfaction regarding community services and problems in participants' neighborhoods), the results were consistent with what was predicted. This, however, was not the case with respect to the association between hypertension and urbanicity. The basic finding shows that the odds of hypertension are higher for residents of rural than of urban areas. This is opposite of what was expected in that it was assumed that life for rural African Americans would be less stressful and more easygoing. The findings of this inquiry suggest that this may not be the case, at least with respect to the impact that life in rural America has on the health of African Americans.

Life for rural Americans is usually associated with a sedentary and relaxed way of dealing with challenges and demands. If a person has the resources (i.e., economic, personal, psychological, etc.) necessary to cope with the problem, it seems reasonable to assume that both the problems and the process for coping with them would be less troublesome for individuals living in rural rather than in urban America. The major difficulty with this assertion is that African Americans tend not to have easy access to the resources necessary to successfully prevent or eliminate exposure to harsh and stressful living circumstances. Given the rapidly increasing rates of unemployment, poverty, and racism in rural America, it is highly possible that African Americans in rural America have a more difficult time handling stressful life events than do African Americans living in urban areas of the United States. Although there may not actually be any differences in the prevalence of stressful events for African Americans living in rural and urban regions, access to the resources for coping may be greatly restricted for those residing in rural areas. Consequently, rates of hypertension and chronic diseases may be higher for rural Americans. It is also quite possible that the sedentary lifestyle of rural Americans contributes to overweight and obesity, which in turn raise the blood pressure through neurohormonal mechanisms. The higher rates of hypertension for rural African Americans could also be accounted for by dietary factors. Unfortunately, neither of these factors was assessed by the NSBA. Future research needs to determine whether these lifestyle factors can help to explain the higher prevalence of hypertension for rural African Americans.

There is a great need for future research aimed at clearer identification of the links between well-defined measures of anger and important pathophysiological factors that are etiologically linked to hypertension. For example, it would be of great interest to conduct laboratory studies of physiological, biochemical, and hormonal responses to emotional states and various laboratory stressors. There is also a pressing need to determine whether measures of anger are related to blood pressure obtained in natural settings outside of the clinic. The rationale behind such investigation is the fact that ambulatory blood pressures recorded at work have been shown to be a better predictor of cardiovascular morbidity than doctors' office blood pressures. Finally, a well-organized line of research examining the influence of anger management training on blood pressure would be of great interest and provide additional types of information concerning the role of anger in the pathogenesis of essential hypertension.

Hypertension is multifactorially determined. Age, sex, diet, family history, and psychosocial and environmental factors all play some role in determining whether hypertension will develop in a given individual. This multifactorial perspective assumes that different patterns of variables operating in each individual express themselves through common pathways, which lead to hypertension. In light of our willingness to regard hypertension as multifactorial in origin, it is curious that standard measurement and treatment procedures have been lacking in breadth and variety. Current research is needed to determine whether African Americans with hypertension would benefit from psychological intervention projects that provide coping skills (e.g., ways of dealing with racism) that emphasize the true nature of our struggles. Without such efforts, African Americans will continue to suffer needlessly from hypertension and the excessive morbidity directly related to the "silent killer."

8

Coping With Personal Problems

Clifford L. Broman

Research in mental health has documented that although African Americans are more exposed to stressful conditions, they generally evidence similar levels of psychological distress as do whites (Mirowsky & Ross, 1980). Coping is argued to be a factor that may significantly alter the response to stress of African Americans, yet there have been few investigations of coping strategies. Using the National Survey of Black Americans (Jackson, 1991), this chapter examines the different coping strategies that African Americans use to deal with personal problems. These results show that African Americans most frequently use active behavioral strategies, such as seeking outside help. They also show that the characteristics of the problem and social status have strong effects on the use of coping strategies. These results differ from those of previous research, and the chapter explores the possibility that these differences are due to the unique conditions of African American culture. These results show clearly the necessity of further race-comparative studies of coping.

The use of coping strategies in response to life stress is an important issue in the study of mental health. The study of coping has increased in importance as investigators have learned that exposure to stressors alone does not account for patterns of psychiatric morbidity (Kessler, 1979b; Kessler & Cleary, 1980). Coping strategies are argued to be an important intervening mechanism that mediates the relationship between life stress and psychiatric morbidity

(Menaghan, 1983; Pearlin, Lieberman, Menaghan, & Mullen, 1981). The strategies used by African Americans to cope with stress still are not well understood. This is unfortunate because such studies would aid researchers in understanding race differences in psychiatric morbidity in the United States. The puzzling fact is that although African Americans are more exposed to stressful social conditions than are whites (Health Resources Administration, 1980; Kessler, 1979b), they evidence similar levels of psychiatric morbidity (Autunes, Gordon, Gaitz, & Scott, 1974; Markush & Favero, 1974; Mirowsky & Ross, 1980; Roberts, Stevenson, & Breslow, 1981; Warheit, Holzer, & Arey, 1975; Warheit, Holzer, & Schwab, 1973; Yancey, Rigsby, & McCarthy, 1972). There are, however, important exceptions to this finding (Hamilton, Broman, Hoffman, & Renner, 1990; Kessler & Neighbors, 1986; Ulbrich, Warheit, & Zimmerman, 1989). These previous studies have documented that in more fine-grained analyses, there are instances in which levels of psychiatric morbidity among African Americans exceed those of whites. However, even in these studies the levels of distress are not what we might expect given the pervasiveness and severity of the plethora of stressors to which African Americans are exposed. We currently do not understand why African Americans do not evidence higher levels of psychiatric morbidity than do whites, given their greater level of exposure to stressful conditions (Broman, 1989). The clarification of this issue, we believe, requires the study of intervening mechanisms in the stress process that affect mental health-related outcomes. Our approach is to examine coping. Coping patterns and strategies may be an important reason for lower than expected levels of distress among blacks.

Dimensions of Coping Strategies

The term *coping* is used very broadly and often without recognition of the need to be precise. Lazarus and Folkman (1984) have attempted such precision in their discussions of coping. They define it as the constantly changing cognitive and behavioral efforts to manage specific external or internal demands or both that are appraised as taxing or exceeding the resources of the person. A central notion is that people attempt to cope when demands (which may be external or internal) exceed the resources available to meet those demands. Several different coping patterns might apply to various types of problems or excessive demands. These can be categorized into cognitive, behavioral, and resigned.

Cognitive coping involves an attempt to handle problems through rational, cognitive means. There are several dimensions of cognitive strategies. In using selective comparison processes, people may attempt to assure themselves that things could be worse or that they are better off than some other people. This strategy may be thought of as downward comparison. People also attempt to convince themselves that the problem is not worth getting upset about or that the problem will not last long (minimization). People might also attempt to reinterpret the situation so that it is perceived as nonproblematic, or they may attempt distraction as a way of handling the problem.

Behavioral coping involves active attempts to make a decision and change the problem situation. Strategies such as problem solving are used, which involves gathering information relevant to the problem, evaluating alternative courses of action, and making the decision to pursue one or another course of action. Direct action involves an attempt to change the problem situation. Withdrawal involves leaving the problem situation, such as quitting a job with an overly demanding supervisor. Avoidance is also a behavioral coping strategy, wherein people attempt to avoid problem situations altogether. People might also engage in indirect action, which might change the problem situation or change the way they feel about the problem situation. Indirect actions involve relaxation or active attempts to provide alternatives to a stressful situation. Indirect actions may lead to the use of cognitive coping strategies. Use of medications, alcohol, and other drugs are examples of indirect action.

Last, some people simply become resigned to the problem situation. This is based on an individual's belief that nothing can or should be done about the problem and that the problem must simply be accepted and endured. Prayer may be a means of resigned coping. Some may accept that there are problems that cannot be changed and use prayer as a way of attempting to accept the problem situation. (For more information on these various strategies, see Billings & Moos, 1981; Lazarus & Folkman, 1984; Menaghan & Merves, 1984.)

These various strategies overlap and may be continually used by people attempting to cope with a single problematic event. The strategies listed above constitute a repertoire of various strategies that people may draw on. The actual strategies people use have been found to be heavily dependent on the type of problem situation people face (Lazarus & Folkman, 1984). Strategies that attempt to directly deal with the problem tend to be used when people feel there is something they can do about the problem, whereas coping attempts to change the way one feels about the problematic situation are used when people feel the stressor is something that cannot be changed and must be endured (Lazarus & Folkman, 1984).

Factors in Coping

Almost no research explicitly examines coping in the African American population. Because of this, much of the research reviewed here does not focus on coping among African Americans. For this reason, the relationships between factors related to coping must be taken as suggestive. The factors identified by previous research on non-African American populations as influential in handling life stress may be different within the African American community.

Despite this limitation, two factors identified as most predictive of coping are problem type and social status factors, such as age, sex, education, and income. Most research has found that problem type has an important influence on the coping strategy used (Broman, 1987; Lazarus & Folkman, 1984). People tend to use behavioral strategies, such as seeking professional help or talking with informal associates, to cope with physical health problems (Billings & Moos, 1981). Cognitive coping strategies, such as prayer, use of optimistic comparisons, and consideration of other alternatives, are used by people handling economic problems (Billings & Moos, 1981; Menaghan & Merves, 1984). Similar strategies are used to cope with marital problems (Menaghan, 1982).

Social status characteristics are also important predictors of the use of coping strategies. A most important factor is socioeconomic status. People of lower socioeconomic status tend to use more avoidance coping strategies, such as drinking, smoking, or eating more (Billings & Moos, 1981; Cronkite & Moos, 1984). Gender is also important; women tend to use both more behavioral and avoidance strategies (Billings & Moos, 1981). The results for age vary strongly by problem type. Older people tend to use optimistic comparisons and restricted expectations to cope with marital problems (Menaghan & Merves, 1984; Pearlin & Schooler, 1978) but are less likely to use these strategies to deal with economic problems (Pearlin & Schooler, 1978). Social status and problem type factors have been identified as important correlates of coping strategies in studies of the general population, but their significance among African Americans has not been shown. The goal of this chapter is to examine both the strategies used by African Americans to cope with stress and the significance of social status and problem type as correlates of those coping strategies.

Measures

The mental health-related measures to be used in this study come from a section of the National Survey of Black Americans ($N = 2,107$) that was organized around the concept of a stressful episode. Respondents were asked questions about a personal problem they experienced that caused them considerable distress. Respondents experiencing a stressful personal problem ($n = 1,322$) were then asked about the specific nature of the problem, the level of distress at that time, and how they handled the problem. Every respondent who said he or she had experienced a problem was asked, "Thinking about the last time you felt this way, what was the problem about?" For this analysis, these problems were collapsed into five types: (a) physical health problems, (b) interpersonal (involving marital or family problems), (c) emotional adjustment problems (mood disturbances, personal adjustment issues), (d) problems involving the death of a significant other, and (e) economic problems.

Coping was assessed from this statement: "I'm going to read you some things a person might do to deal with a personal problem. As I read each one, please tell me if you did any of these things to make your problem easier to bear." The response options were (a) relax, (b) try to forget the problem, (c) pray, (d) drink liquor or get high, (e) take pills or medicine, (f) keep busy by doing other things, and (g) face the problem and do something about it. Respondents answered yes or no to each option; thus, all respondents could choose any strategy. Whether the respondent sought help from informal associates regarding this personal problem was also assessed in the interview and is included as a coping strategy.[1]

The sociodemographic measures used were age (measured in years), years of education completed, gender, and family income. Family income was measured with a 17-level ordinal variable that ranged from $0 to over $30,000. Respondents with missing values on family income were coded at the mean value of family income for respondents of their educational level ($n = 113$). Due to missing values for coping or problem type items, this analysis is based on 1,101 respondents for whom complete information is available. Most of the missing 221 respondents failed to answer the question regarding

Table 8.1 Social Characteristics of the Study Sample (N = 1,136)

	%	N
Age		
18-29	31.3	355
30-44	31.4	357
45-64	25.9	294
65+	11.4	130
Gender		
Male	32.7	371
Female	67.3	765
Educational level		
No high school diploma	40.2	457
High school diploma	32.4	368
Some college	27.4	311
Family income		
Less than $10,000	49.1	558
$10,000-$20,000	29.2	331
$20,000 or more	21.7	247

problem type. Presented in Table 8.1 are the social characteristics of the study sample.

Results

Table 8.2 presents the percentage of respondents using various coping strategies. Most respondents use all coping strategies frequently, with the exception of taking drugs or medicine and drinking or getting high. The most frequently used strategies were those that involve active behavior on the part of the respondent. These strategies were seeking outside help and doing something about the problem. Prayer was the next most frequent, whereas escapist strategies (drinking or getting high, taking drugs or medicine) were the most infrequent. It is clear from these data that most respondents engaged in activities designed to deal directly with personal problems rather than attempting to escape from them.

Table 8.3 presents the distribution of coping strategies by problem type. Each cell in Table 8.3 represents the percentage of people who said they used the particular coping strategy by type of problem. For example, we see that

Table 8.2 Percentage Using Coping Strategy (N = 1,136)

	%	N
Relax	69.7	792
Try to forget	68.8	781
Pray	80.5	915
Drink or get high	19.8	225
Take drugs or medicine	22.0	250
Keep busy	77.2	877
Face problem/do something	87.4	993
Seek informal help	88.3	1,003

Table 8.3 Percentage Using Coping Strategy, by Problem Type

	Physical Health	Inter-personl	Emotional	Death	Economic	χ^2 (df = 4)
Relax	68.0	68.2	69.2	67.6	75.0	4.18
Try to forget	61.6	71.0	63.9	74.5	70.1	8.69+
Pray	91.4	78.6	72.9	85.3	78.3+	22.11***
Drink or get high	11.9	20.6	18.0	21.6	24.6	11.44*
Take drugs or medicine	40.5	18.4	21.8	23.5	14.3	49.03***
Keep busy	70.3	82.2	69.9	67.6	80.7	22.78***
Face problem/do something	87.0	88.3	85.0	83.3	88.9	3.18
Seek informal help	87.0	91.7	74.4	91.2	88.9	31.33***
N	185	472	133	102	244	1,136

$+p < .10; *p < .05; **p < .01; ***p < .001.$

68% of the people with physical health problems said they tried to relax. The other 32% indicated that they did not use this strategy. Table 8.3 shows that the coping strategies used vary depending on the type of problem. The dominant strategies for coping with physical health problems are active behavioral strategies and prayer. A similar pattern is observed for death and economic problems. The dominant mode of coping with interpersonal problems is to face the problem or do something and to seek outside help. Respondents tend to deal with emotional problems in a similar manner. Although escapist strategies are used relatively rarely overall, drinking or getting high is most commonly used by people facing economic problems.

Taking drugs or medicine is most often used by people with physical health problems.[2] Although there are significant differences by problem type in the use of coping strategies, overall, behavioral strategies are used most often regardless of problem type.

Table 8.4 presents the summary results of 40 multiple regressions of coping strategies on sociodemographic factors, by problem type. Each coping strategy is regressed on age, sex, education, and family income within types of problem. Significant predictors and the direction of significance are indicated by the label given. For example, note that males are significantly more likely than females to use the strategy of relaxation to cope with problems involving death. Sociodemographic factors are not significant predictors of using the relaxation strategy for related economic problems. This is indicated by the dashed lines.

In general, sociodemographic factors are important in the use of coping strategies. Age is significant for coping with physical health, interpersonal, and economic problems. Older African Americans use prayer and taking drugs or medicine as coping strategies for physical health problems and prayer to cope with interpersonal problems. Younger African Americans seek help from informal associates to cope with interpersonal and economic problems. Gender was found to be highly significant. Men were significantly more likely to cope by drinking or getting high for all problems except health problems. African American women used prayer to cope with all problems except economic problems. For economic problems, African American women tended to try to forget or seek informal help. A key finding in this study was that the socioeconomic factors, education and family income, were of limited significance in the use of coping strategies. There were a few exceptions. Less educated African Americans used relaxing and trying to forget to cope with emotional problems and used forgetting to handle economic problems. Lower-income African Americans used taking drugs or medicine to cope with interpersonal problems, whereas prayer and facing the problem or doing something were used to handle economic problems.

Discussion

The first key finding from this research is that there is significant variation in the use of coping strategies among African Americans. Most strategies for handling personal problems are used quite frequently, with the exception of

Table 8.4 Summary of Regression Analysis of Coping Strategies on Age, Gender, Education, and Income, by Problem Type

	Physical Health	*Interpersonal*	*Emotional*	*Death*	*Economic*
Relax					
Age	—	—	—	—	—
Gender	Female	Female	—	Male	—
Education	Lower	—	Lower	—	—
Income	—	—	—	—	—
Try to forget					
Age	—	—	—	—	—
Gender	—	—	—	—	Female
Education	—	—	Lower	—	Lower
Income	—	—	—	—	—
Pray					
Age	Older	Older	—	—	—
Gender	Female	Female	Female	Female	—
Education	—	—	—	—	—
Income	—	—	—	—	Lower
Drink or get high					
Age	—	—	—	—	—
Gender	—	Male	Male	Male	Male
Education	—	—	—	—	—
Income	—	—	—	—	—
Take drugs or medicine					
Age	Older	—	—	—	—
Gender	—	Female	—	—	—
Education	—	—	—	—	—
Income	—	Lower	—	—	—
Keep busy					
Age	—	—	—	—	—
Gender	—	—	—	—	—
Education	—	—	—	—	—
Income	—	—	—	—	—
Face problem/do something					
Age	—	—	—	—	—
Gender	—	—	—	—	—
Education	—	—	—	—	Higher
Income	—	—	—	—	Lower
Seek informal help					
Age	—	Younger	—	—	Younger
Gender	—	—	—	—	Female
Education	—	Higher	—	—	—
Income	—	—	—	—	Higher

NOTE: Predictors are significant at $p < .05$ in the direction specified.

drinking or getting high and taking drugs or medicine. It is clear that African Americans are using strategies to confront their personal problems, as opposed to using escapist strategies such as drinking or getting high and taking drugs or medicine.

The use of escapist types of coping strategies does not attempt to solve the problem and has been shown to be associated with higher levels of psychological distress (Billings & Moos, 1981). On the other hand, strategies such as facing the problem or doing something, seeking informal help, and praying have been found to be associated with decreasing psychological distress (Billings & Moos, 1981; Veroff, Douvan, & Kulka, 1981). This research has shown that African Americans are most likely to use the coping strategies associated with reduced levels of psychological distress. The fact that African Americans tend to use these strategies frequently has positive implications for their mental health.

Problem type was found to be an important correlate of the use of coping strategies. For the most part, findings of the present investigation are similar to those of previous research on whites. The one key difference involves the use of escapist strategies. Other investigations have found that these strategies are more likely to be used by people with interpersonal problems (Billings & Moos, 1981), whereas the present results show that these strategies are more commonly used to cope with economic problems. One reason for this disparate finding is that other studies have not explicitly examined the strategy of drinking or getting high as is done here. Our results suggest that the omission of this strategy may be critical, particularly in the study of race and coping. Another reason for the different finding may be that previous studies have not focused exclusively on African Americans. It may be that African Americans are more likely than whites to use drinking or getting high as a strategy for coping with economic problems, whereas whites use these types of strategies to cope with interpersonal problems. This speculation awaits further research for possible confirmation.

Another key finding of this research is that sociodemographic characteristics predict the use of coping strategies. That is, not all African Americans use the same strategy to cope with similar problems. Women are more likely to use prayer as a strategy, whereas men are more likely to use drinking or getting high as a strategy. This is perhaps the most important finding of this research. These patterns reflect the fact that men tend not to express their feelings (Balswick & Peek, 1971). Alcohol and drugs may be used to mask feelings of distress associated with a personal problem. The finding that

African American men are more likely than African American women to use escapist coping strategies is, however, opposite of findings from the general population. Other studies have shown that women are more likely than men to use coping strategies such as drinking or getting high, taking drugs or medicine, eating, and smoking (Billings & Moos, 1981). This contradictory finding illustrates the need for more studies of race differences in the use of coping strategies. It may be that the relationship between gender and the use of escapist strategies differs by race, or these results could reflect different measurement strategies.

The finding that African American women are more likely than African American men to use prayer as a coping strategy also bears on previous findings from research on race and mental health. Veroff, Douvan, and Kulka (1981) found that African Americans were more likely to use prayer as a coping strategy for coping with personal problems than are whites. However, due to the small number of African Americans in their data, they were unable to elaborate on this finding. Our analyses show that it is not African Americans in general who use prayer but African American women who pray in response to physical health, interpersonal, emotional, and death problems. The importance of a large African American sample is thus illustrated, because we are able to focus on the response of different members of the African American community to different problems and pay closer attention to the heterogeneity among African Americans in the use of coping strategies.

The results for age show that older African Americans used prayer to cope with physical health and interpersonal problems and that younger African Americans were more likely to seek help from informal associates to cope with interpersonal and economic problems. These results were consistent with research on the general population. Veroff, Douvan, and Kulka (1981) found that older people were more likely to use prayer as a coping strategy and that young people were more likely to seek informal help.

In contrast to the findings for age, the findings for socioeconomic factors were not consistent with previous research. Our results showed that socioeconomic factors were generally of limited significance. These results are different from previous studies that reported that people of lower socioeconomic status are more likely to use escapist strategies (Billings & Moos, 1981). We find no such effect here. Among African Americans, people of low education tended to try to forget, whereas low-income African Americans prayed and faced the problem, if it was an economic one. African Americans of low education used the strategies of relaxation and trying to forget for emotional problems. Note that African Americans with more education and lower incomes used the same strategy to cope with economic problems. Overall, however, our results for socioeconomic status differed greatly from previous research on whites. Again, there is a need for more research to clarify these discrepant findings.

The response of lower socioeconomic status African Americans to emotional problems may have implications for their mental health. Their limited use of behavioral strategies may have increased their risk of psychological distress resulting from having a personal problem. Strategies of relaxation and trying to forget were used, whereas active behavioral strategies, such as facing problems and seeking outside help were not. The strategies used may exacerbate the problem, bringing about a more serious psychological disturbance. Longitudinal investigations of coping have clearly shown that the use of strategies such as relaxation and forgetting are associated with higher levels of subsequent psychological distress and more problems (Cronkite & Moos, 1984; Menaghan & Merves, 1984). The use of these strategies rather than seeking outside help, for example, may reflect attempts by these people to hide their emotional problems due to the possible stigma of mental distress. Whatever the reason, these are likely to be ineffective ways of handling personal problems.

Research in mental health has clearly documented that although African Americans are more exposed to stressful conditions, they evidence levels of psychological distress similar to whites. Coping is argued to be a factor that may significantly alter African American's response to stress. This chapter addressed this issue. We found that African Americans frequently used coping strategies that attempted to solve their problems and that there was significant variation in the use of coping strategies. This research has also pointed out the need for more research that examines race differences in coping. Our study has indicated results that vary from studies of whites. Only through race-comparative studies can these conflicting findings be adequately examined. There is also a need for longitudinal investigations to examine the effectiveness of using a particular coping strategy in reducing psychological distress and problem levels (see Broman, Hoffman, & Hamilton, 1994). This study has identified an important area for research on race and mental health, and it is hoped that such investigations will be forthcoming in the near future.

Notes

1. Other analyses with these data (Broman, 1987; Neighbors, 1984b, 1985; Neighbors, Caldwell, Thompson, & Jackson, 1994; Neighbors & Howard, 1987; Neighbors & Jackson, 1984) have explored professional help seeking in response to personal problems, and for this reason, only the use of informal help is examined here.

2. It is of course possible that some people with physical health problems who take drugs or medicine do so at the direction of a physician. There is no way to ascertain which respondents are included in this group, and this must be noted as a limitation of these data.

9

Kin and Nonkin as Sources of Informal Assistance

Robert Joseph Taylor
Cheryl Burns Hardison
Linda M. Chatters

The onset of serious personal problems often compels individuals to actively solicit assistance from both formal and informal sources. Among African Americans, informal support networks provide significant amounts of aid during such crises (Chatters, Taylor, & Neighbors, 1989). Informal networks play an important role in defining the complexity and significance of a personal problem, moderating the effects of stress, and providing referrals to professional service providers (Doherty, 1992; Steinglass, 1992). Although families represent the major source of informal assistance, nonkin associates—such as friends, neighbors, coworkers, and church members—also play a critical role in the informal support networks of African Americans (Billingsley, 1992; Chatters, Taylor, & Jackson, 1985; Chatters et al., 1989; Dilworth-Anderson, Burton, & Johnson, 1993; Hatch, 1991; McAdoo, 1980; Staples & Johnson, 1993).

The significance of both kin and nonkin sources of assistance in coping with the physical and mental health problems of African Americans has been well documented (Aschenbrenner, 1975; McAdoo, 1980; Stack, 1974). These studies describe an elaborate and complex system of exchange involving both emotional and instrumental assistance provided by extended family members and close friends. McAdoo found that African American mothers relied on their friends for assistance with child care, financial problems, and emotional support. Taylor and Chatters (1986) found that in a study of elderly African Americans 8 of 10 people received support from either a best or a close friend, 6 of 10 received support from church members, and more than 5 of 10 received support from extended family members. A small minority of respondents was "socially isolated" in the sense that they did not have a best or a close friend and did not receive support from either their family or church members.

The present study continues this line of research on the informal help-seeking behavior of African Americans. In particular, this analysis examines predictors of the use of kin and nonkin helpers in response to a serious personal problem. Sociodemographic characteristics, levels of social contact, and type and degree of seriousness of the personal problem are used as independent variables. In addition to providing information on the impact of demographic factors on help-seeking behavior, this investigation provides insight into the specific social and personal circumstances in which kin, as opposed to nonkin, are used in response to a personal problem.

Kin and Nonkin Networks

Research on patterns of use of kin and nonkin helper networks views the two types of resources as functioning in a complementary (Litwak, 1970) and compensatory (Cantor, 1979) manner. Litwak argues that primary group structures and the nature of the support task itself are critical for determining the specific roles that each group will perform. Family members are predominant in providing instrumental assistance (e.g., financial aid, cleaning, and grooming), whereas friends provide mainly interpersonal and emotional support (Litwak & Szelenyi, 1969). In contrast, Cantor's hierarchical-compensatory model suggests that use of kin or nonkin networks for assistance is determined by the primacy of the relationship that exists between the support provider and the recipient. In the absence of kin resources for assistance, nonkin networks are employed as replacements.

In the gerontology literature, a popular perspective suggests that involvement with kin is competitive with interaction with nonkin (Jonas, 1979). This view suggests that there is an inverse relationship between time spent with family and time spent with nonkin. Assuming that the family is the primary relationship, increased participation with family limits the amount of involvement with nonkin (Jonas, 1979). Others argue, however, that the quality of the relationship, whether it involves family or nonkin, is more important (Liang, Dvorkin, Kahana, & Mazian, 1980; Shanas, 1979). Chappell (1983) argues that the kin versus nonkin distinction is important and useful. Furthermore, her work identifies age peer (i.e., intragenerational) versus intergenerational differences as important for understanding interaction patterns. An investigation of social support satisfaction among older adults found that age peers were more desirable support providers regardless of whether the age peers belonged to family or nonkin networks.

Research on older African Americans indicates that kin and nonkin function in both complementary and compensatory roles. With respect to the complementary roles of kin and nonkin, Taylor and Chatters (1986) found that elderly African Americans were more likely to receive companionship and other socioemotional support from friends, whereas financial assistance and goods and services were provided mainly by family members. Similarly, during periods of illness, elderly African Americans reported receiving complementary support from both family and church members. Family members provided extensive primary care, whereas church members provided encouragement and companionship (Taylor & Chatters, 1986). In contrast, research involving unmarried and childless elderly African Americans illustrates the manner in which kin and nonkin resources compensate for one another. Specifically, in the absence of primary kin (i.e., spouse or children), older adults substituted nonkin in their support networks (Chatters, Taylor, & Jackson, 1986).

Friendship Networks

Friendship and other nonkin relationships are governed by different sets of values, expectations, and norms from those that pertain to the family. Whereas kin relationships are socially defined and closely regulated, individuals may exercise considerable freedom to initiate, maintain, and discontinue friendships. Because friendships are voluntarily based, these bonds can be easily broken. Friends are thought to be more flexible and compromising in their interpersonal relations than family and more likely to respect personal boundaries and the need for personal space (Rubin, 1985). Litwak and Szelenyi (1969) note that in kinship structures, "people are related in semipermanent biological or legal ways" (p. 467). Friendship ties are held together by affectivity. Friends are best suited to handle matters in which there is continuous fluctuation, whereas kin are more equipped to handle issues that are long term (Litwak & Szelenyi, 1969).

Even in circumstances in which supportive and adequate family ties exist, friends are still important to personal well-being (Rubin, 1985). Crohan and Antonucci (1989) suggest that friends usually have a positive impact on well-being, whereas family may have either positive or negative effects. One valuable function of friendships is that they provide a source of self-confirmation by influencing perceptions of self-identity and social worth (Allan, 1989; Bell, 1981). Friends are frequently peers who share common characteristics (i.e., age, gender, ethnicity, and life experiences) (Verbrugge, 1977). Consequently, they can provide feedback and support that influences self-identity in a manner that is different from that of family members. For example, friends were found to be uniquely helpful in adjusting to widowhood (Bankoff, 1983; Wood & Robertson, 1978).

Research on the role of friends and other nonkin in the supportive networks of African Americans is somewhat limited. Overall, however, this literature suggests that friends are an integral part of African Americans' supportive networks. Although friends generally provide companionship and other types of emotional support, they may also provide child care, monetary loans, and other goods and services. Several researchers, however, argue that compared to kin, nonkin assistance lacks resilience (Liebow, 1967), is inconsistent (Liebow, 1967), and is characterized as exploitive (Rainwater, 1970). Dressler (1985a) concludes that nonkin contribute very little to the support networks of African American adults. These apparent differences in the primacy and resiliency of nonkin assistance resources may be attributable to differences in the social context within which support occurs or the structural and functional characteristics of the networks themselves (i.e., size, density, composition, and reciprocity) or both.

Informal and Formal Help Seeking

A considerable amount of research from the National Survey of Black Americans (NSBA; Jackson, 1991) has examined formal and informal help seeking in response to a serious personal problem. As is evident in Figure 9.1, for the most part this work has focused on the use of formal, professional helpers. For the purpose of the present analysis, we will limit our review to those articles that include analyses of informal helpers.

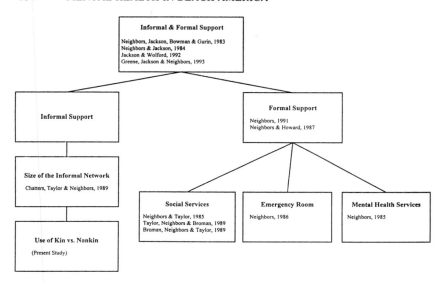

Figure 9.1. Research on Informal and Formal Help Seeking Using Data From the National Survey of Black Americans

Neighbors and Jackson (1984) examined patterns of informal and professional assistance in response to an identified personal problem. The majority of respondents used informal help only (43%) or a combination of both informal and professional help (44%). Four percent of the respondents used professional support only, whereas 8.7% did not receive any outside assistance for their problems. Gender, age, income, and problem type were related to four patterns of informal and professional help seeking: (a) Women were more likely than men to seek both informal and professional help; (b) older respondents were less likely than younger respondents to seek informal help only; (c) persons with physical health problems were more likely than persons with other types of problems to seek both informal and professional assistance; and (d) respondents with emotional problems were least likely to seek help from either source.

Taylor, Neighbors, and Broman (1989) found that informal helpers functioned as a critical link to social service agencies. Almost half of respondents who sought help from social service agencies indicated that they initially heard about the agency from a friend or a relative. Similarly, a large percentage of respondents indicated that a friend or relative was instrumental in facilitating their use of the social service agency. Chatters et al. (1989)

examined several characteristics of the informal helper networks that are used during a serious personal problem. Overall, kin were more prevalent than nonkin in informal helper networks. There were gender differences in the composition of informal networks—men were more likely to seek assistance from brothers and fathers, whereas women were more likely to consult sisters. No gender differences, however, were found in the use of mothers as helpers. Information as to the number of informal helpers used indicated that 13.1% of respondents stated they had no helpers, 20.4% reported one, 20.3% stated two, 18.5% indicated three, 13.3% stated four, and 14.4% reported using five (or more) informal helpers. Multivariate analysis revealed that women and higher-income respondents had larger helper networks than their counterparts, and that respondents with interpersonal, emotional, and economic problems all had smaller networks than those with physical health problems. The data also showed that increases in the frequency of family contact and having a best friend were associated with larger informal networks.

Recognizing that older African American adults may employ unique patterns of formal and informal help seeking, Greene, Jackson, and Neighbors (1993) conducted a detailed analysis of help-seeking patterns focusing on possible age differences. Similar to rates of formal assistance that are reported by younger adults, half of the older African American adults who experienced a serious personal problem indicated they had sought formal assistance. There was, however, a slight age difference among respondents who reported seeking informal support from family and friends—9 of 10 respondents aged 18 to 54 years old sought informal assistance, whereas 8 of 10 adults 55 years of age or older indicated seeking such assistance.

An analysis of age differences among these older adults revealed that 85% of respondents 55 to 64 years old, 79% of respondents 65 to 74 years old, and 53% of respondents 75 years or older sought assistance from their informal support networks. Furthermore, among respondents who were 75 years of age or older, men (47%) were less likely to seek assistance than were women (58%). Persons who were 75 years old or older were also less likely to use formal assistance. Whereas more than half of respondents in the age groups of 55 to 64 years old and 64 to 74 years old used formal help, only 33% of respondents who were 75 years old or older sought formal assistance. Gender differences in rates of seeking formal support among persons 75 years old or older indicated that only half as many men used formal services compared to women (21% and 42%, respectively). Overall, 36% of respondents 75 years old or older did not use either formal or informal assistance when confronted with a serious personal problem (Greene et al., 1993).

Jackson and Wolford (1992) examined changes in patterns of formal and informal help seeking using data from the 1979-1980 NSBA and the 1987 Panel Study of Black Americans. During this period, there was a significant decrease in rates of seeking assistance for serious personal problems. Overall, three times as many African Americans in 1987 as in 1980 reported that they did not receive either form of help (8.7% in 1980 vs. 24.5% in 1987). The percentage of respondents receiving only formal help and both formal and informal help was relatively stable over the 7-year period. Consistent with earlier work by Neighbors and Jackson (1984), elderly respondents were the most likely to report that they did not use either formal or informal help for serious personal problems.

In summary, a variety of research approaches have addressed the question of informal assistance in response to personal difficulties among African Americans. This literature review has highlighted a number of salient issues in relation to that work: (a) the participation of family, friends, and other nonkin in the informal support network; (b) the presence of sociodemographic variability (e.g., age and gender) in both the composition and the functioning of informal support networks; and (c) differences in patterns of help seeking (i.e., formal and informal) for personal problems. Although information continues to accumulate with regard to informal assistance networks among African Americans, this review of the literature underscores the gaps in the knowledge base that remain. The present study addresses the specific question of the use of kin and nonkin assistance in response to a personal problem.

Methods

Sample and Variables

The data for this analysis come from the NSBA. The present analysis focuses on respondents who used informal sources for help with a personal problem. The section of the NSBA questionnaire designed to examine help-seeking issues focuses on the concept of a serious personal problem. Respondents were asked to report a personal problem they had experienced in their lives that had caused them a significant amount of distress. A total of 1,322 respondents reported experiencing a serious personal problem. They were then asked to describe the nature of the problem and how they adapted to the stressful episode. In particular, they were presented a list of informal helpers and asked if they had talked to any of the persons listed about their problem. The informal helper list included spouse, son, daughter, father, mother, brother, sister, other relative, friend, neighbor, and coworker. In the present analysis, the dependent variable is whether respondents used kin versus nonkin (only first-mention responses were used) as informal helpers (0 = kin, 1 = nonkin). Several sociodemographic and social support variables are included in the analysis as independent variables; they are described in Table 9.1.

Descriptive Statistics and Analysis

Table 9.2 presents the univariate profile of informal helpers who were used in response to a serious personal problem.[1] Overall, 8 of 10 (82.5%) respondents indicated that they sought assistance from kin as opposed to nonkin sources. The most frequently mentioned kin helpers were spouses (28%) followed by mothers (16%) and sisters (9.5%). For the nonkin categories, the largest percentage of respondents reported assistance from friends (15%), whereas relatively few respondents mentioned neighbors, coworkers, or other nonrelatives as informal helpers. Table 9.3 presents logistic regression models for the use of nonkin (as opposed to kin), controlling for the influence of family, personal problem, sociodemographic, and network availability factors. Models 1 and 2 are identical except that Model 2 also controls for the effects of an interaction term (i.e., Age × Child interaction), combining respondent's age and parental status (i.e., whether or not they have a child). Several studies using the NSBA data demonstrate the importance of including an interaction term combining respondents' age and the presence of a child (i.e., parental status) for predicting the size of informal helper networks (Chatters et al., 1989) and the receipt of assistance from family members (Taylor, 1986b).

Both Models 1 and 2 show that several independent variables are significantly related to the use of nonkin. In particular, marital status, education, region, family contact, problem type, and having a best friend all have significant relationships with the dependent variable. With respect to marital status, all unmarried respondents (i.e., divorced, separated, widowed, and never married) are significantly more likely to use nonkin helpers than are married respondents. Respondents with lower levels of formal education are more likely than their counterparts to use nonkin helpers. Regional differences

Table 9.1 Description of Independent Variables

Variable	Description
Age	Range 18 to 101 years of age
Gender	Dummy variable, females = 0, males = 1
Marital status	Dummy variable, married category excluded
Education	Years of education; range = 0-17
Income	Family income
Urbanicity	Dummy variable, rural = 0, urban = 1
Region	Dummy variable, the excluded category is the South
Family closeness (subjective)	"How close are your family members in their feelings toward each other?" (1) not close at all . . . (4) very close
Family contact	"How often do you see, write or talk on the telephone with family or relatives who do not live with you?" (1) hardly ever . . . (6) nearly every day
Problem severity	Severity of serious personal problem 1. A problem you wouldn't handle by yourself? 2. Felt down and depressed, so low you just couldn't get going? 3. Felt so nervous you couldn't get going? 4. Ever felt at the point of a nervous breakdown?
Problem type	Type of serious personal problem: physical (poor health, accident), interpersonal (loneliness, trouble with family or friends, divorce), emotional (depression, unhappiness, self-doubt, fear), death (death of loved one), economic (poor or declining financial status, loss of assets), dummy variable, physical = 0
Have best friend	0 = No best friend, 1 = Have a best friend
Have parents	0 = No parents, 1 = Have parents
Have children	0 = No children, 1 = Have children
Age × Child	Age and children interaction

indicate that respondents who reside in the Northeast are more likely to use nonkin helpers than are Southerners.

Family contact is negatively associated with the dependent variable, indicating that persons reporting less frequent contact with their family are more likely to use nonkin helpers. Findings for problem type indicate that persons with an interpersonal problem are more likely than respondents with a physi-

Table 9.2 Univariate Descriptions of Informal Helpers Used in Response to a Serious Personal Problem

	Percentage Informal Helpers	*N*
Nonkin helpers		
Friend	15.27	173
Neighbor	.79	9
Coworker	.97	11
Other nonrelative	.44	5
Kin helpers		
Spouse	27.80	315
Son	6.88	78
Daughter	6.70	76
Father	5.38	61
Mother	16.33	185
Brother	5.38	61
Sister	9.53	108
Other relative	4.50	51
Total	100	1,133

cal health problem to select nonkin helpers as informal helpers. Finally, respondents who have a best friend have a greater likelihood of seeking assistance from nonkin helpers. Model 2 includes the interaction between respondent's age and parental status. This interaction borders on significance (Model 2), indicating that the relationship between respondent's age and informal helper choice varies as a function of parental status. Specifically, older African American adults with children are more likely to seek assistance from kin, whereas those elderly without children are more likely to seek assistance from nonkin helpers.

Discussion

The results from this analysis indicate that among African Americans, both kin and nonkin helpers represent important sources of informal assistance during a serious personal problem. These findings were consistent with work that demonstrates the importance of family and friends in the informal social support networks of African Americans (e.g., Taylor & Chatters, 1986). The predominance of family members as informal helpers in this analysis was also

Table 9.3 Logistic Regression Models of Use of Nonkin as a Source of Assistance

	Model 1		Model 2	
	b	*SE*	*b*	*SE*
Intercept	−2.188	.895	−1.361	.991
Age	.017	.009	.046*	.018
Gender (male)	−.371	.214	−.404	.215
Marital status				
Divorced	.853**	.269	.853**	.270
Separated	1.070***	.292	1.085***	.293
Widowed	1.165***	.306	1.129***	.307
Never married	1.268***	.300	1.146***	.310
Education	−.066*	.033	−.068*	.033
Income	.016	.025	.012	.025
Urbanicity (urban)	−.025	.249	−.016	.250
Region				
Northeast	.540*	.246	.550*	.247
North Central	.195	.231	.208	.232
West	.528	.369	.524	.370
Family closeness	−.226	.130	−.246	.131
Family contact	−.133*	.061	−.137*	.061
Problem severity	−.050	.082	−.040	.082
Problem type				
Interpersonal	.676***	.257	.707*	.259
Emotional	.617	.399	.579	.401
Death	−.054	.353	−.037	.355
Economic	.271	.300	.279	.300
Have best friend	1.162***	.341	1.114**	.340
Have parents	−.419	.251	−.382	.252
Have children	.231	.239	−.767	.570
Age × Child			−.023[†]	.012
χ^2	102.040***		1,025.700***	
N	863		863	

[†]$p < .10$; *$p < .05$; **$p < .01$; ***$p < .001$.

consistent with work on the composition of informal helper networks (Chatters et al., 1985, 1986). Similar to several other studies (Allan & Adams, 1989;

Stoller & Earl, 1983), the present analysis found that nonmarried persons were more likely to use nonkin than were married respondents. Unmarried elderly African American adults substituted nonkin as informal helpers in the absence of a spouse. Brown and Gary (1985) found that never-married African American women rely on nonkin helpers for emotional support. A study of assistance during an emergency, however, failed to find any marital status differences in the use of nonkin among African American adults (Taylor, Chatters, & Mays, 1988).

Education had a significant negative association with the use of nonkin helpers. African American adults who had fewer years of formal education were more likely to use friends as a source of assistance. Previous research findings for educational differences in the use of kin versus nonkin helpers are equivocal. Fischer (1982) found that college graduates had a higher percentage of nonkin in their networks than did persons with lower educational attainment. Our findings suggest, however, that friends may be of greater significance as informal helpers for persons with lower educational levels. Similar to the low-income women in Carol Stack's research (1974), less educated respondents in this analysis tended to select friends when confronted with a serious personal problem.

Regional differences in the receipt of informal social support and the composition of informal support networks is an area that has rarely been addressed in research among both African American and white Americans. Some of our work in this area has revealed significant regional differences (Chatters & Taylor, 1993; Chatters et al., 1985, 1986; Taylor, 1985; Taylor & Chatters, 1991), whereas other work has shown that regional differences are not significant (Chatters, Taylor, & Neighbors, 1989; Taylor et al., 1988). Our work has found that in comparison to other regions, older African American Southerners live closer to their relatives (Taylor & Chatters, 1991), receive support from extended families on a more frequent basis (Taylor, 1985), and have larger helper networks composed of both family and friends (Chatters et al., 1985, 1986). Chatters and Taylor (1993) found that among African American men, those who resided in the North Central region provided support to their parents less frequently than those who resided in the South. In the present analysis, respondents who resided in the Northeast were more likely than southerners to use nonfamily members for help.

Taken together, findings from a variety of studies (e.g., Chatters & Taylor, 1993; Taylor, 1985; Taylor & Chatters, 1991) suggest that Southerners may have a family support advantage in comparison to African American adults who reside in other regions of the country. To the extent that family members are more reliable and consistent members of informal support networks (compared to friends), the present analysis corroborates the previous findings of a potential family support advantage for African Americans who reside in the South. Explicit, regionally based cultural values among African Americans may promote helping relationships in the South (Chatters & Taylor, 1993). Clearly, further survey and ethnographic work is needed to clarify the nature and extent of regional variation in supportive relationships among this group.

With respect to family contact, respondents who maintained frequent contact with family were more likely to use kin, whereas those reporting infrequent contact were more likely to use nonkin helpers. These results for family contact corroborate earlier findings based on the NSBA data set. Taylor (1986b) found that frequency of interaction with family was positively associated with receiving support from kin. The present findings suggest that nonkin assistance may be particularly important for persons who have minimal contact with family. Furthermore, African Americans who are without family members or who are estranged from their family are likely to substitute friends as members of their informal networks.

Compared to physical health problems, interpersonal problems were more likely to be addressed by the use of nonkin helpers. One possible explanation is that family members themselves may be the source of, or a contributing factor in, the interpersonal problem in question. In coping with the stresses of events such as divorce, marital difficulties, relationship problems, and difficulties with children, close friends and confidants are often valuable sources of advice and companionship. Friendships are often grounded and defined in relation to their role in resolving interpersonal problems. Finally, friends typically share common backgrounds, values, goals, and life experiences (Adams, 1989; Fischer, 1982; Matthews, 1986) and, consequently, are uniquely suited to provide feedback, personal validation, and assistance during personal crises (Lowenthal & Robinson, 1976).

In contrast, nonkin helpers appear to play a less central role in relation to direct care and assistance during a physical illness. To a great extent, physical health conditions are considered family matters. Caregiving during episodes of illness is still primarily provided by family members, and in particular, women. Kin, as distinct from friends, operate under specific obligations and expectations to provide assistance during serious health problems and long-term crises. The role of friends during illness has been characterized as providing moral support or acting as an adviser rather than providing direct care (Allan, 1989). Furthermore, the social isolation that physical illness sometimes creates can result in the restriction of the nonkin network and limit the likelihood of receiving assistance from friends.

As expected, the availability of a best friend was positively related to the use of nonkin as helpers. Conversely, respondents who did not have a best friend were more likely to seek help from family members. This finding suggests that both family and friends are important informal help resources. Other work indicates that the presence of a best friend is related to larger helper networks overall (Chatters et al., 1985, 1989). Clearly, respondents who have both family and friends on which to rely are in an advantageous support position. As indicated by the present findings, however, persons who have relatively infrequent contact with their families, as well as those with a best friend, are more likely to seek assistance from nonkin. For these respondents, nonkin operate in important ways as family surrogates. Previous work indicates that persons without friends or family do not have any informal helpers to assist them during a serious personal problem (Chatters et al., 1989).

Gerontological research has identified two important factors for understanding the informal support networks of elderly adults. First, the significance of age status suggests that older adults generally have smaller support networks compared to their younger counterparts (Antonucci & Depner, 1982). Second, the elderly parent-adult child bond is a primary factor for determining the level of assistance that older adults receive (Cantor, 1979). Research on African Americans indicates that having a child mitigates the negative effects of older age on support resources (Chatters et al., 1985, 1986, 1989; Taylor, 1985, 1986b). Older respondents with children had larger networks than their childless counterparts and were more likely to receive support from their family. In contrast, elderly persons without children were more likely to rely on nonkin (Chatters et al., 1986).

In the present analysis, using a sample of the entire adult age range, the Age × Child interaction only bordered significance. Although not fully supportive of previous work with respect to the centrality of adult children, the present findings suggest that the presence of children, whether minor or adult, may serve as an important link to kin resources. Findings on the role of adult children in elderly parents' support networks have highlighted their potential as both direct support providers and mediators of assistance from family and other groups (e.g., church-based networks). The present analysis, with a sample of respondents representing the entire adult age range, has greater variability with respect to the ages of respondents' children. Consequently, the measure of whether the respondent has a child(ren) refers to both minor and adult children. Presumably, minor children would not fulfill the same types of supportive functions as would adult children. Irrespective of age of the child(ren), however, the presence of offspring apparently offsets the impact of parents' age on the use of kin versus nonkin resources (i.e., older age associated with the use of nonkin) and facilitates the use of kin resources. Conversely, the absence of children relates to the use of nonkin helpers to a greater degree.

Conclusion

The present analysis has helped to describe the conditions and circumstances surrounding the use of kin versus nonkin forms of assistance in response to a serious personal problem. Significant status group differences in the use of informal helpers indicated that marital bonds remain one of the primary ways that individuals define family networks as being an appropriate helping resource. Conversely, lower levels of education, residency in the Northeast region, and being older without children were related to the use of nonkin resources. In addition to sociodemographic variability in the use of kin versus nonkin resources, the circumstances of family contact and having a best-close friend, as well as the nature of the personal problem itself, were significant in determining helper choice. These findings suggest married individuals may be in an advantageous position in relation to support activities. A consideration of the nature of the problem (i.e., physical illness or emotional problem), however, is important in understanding preferences for informal helpers.

Taken together, the findings suggest that in comprehending the ways that kin and nonkin respond to assistance demands, it is important to consider various aspects and characteristics of the particular networks within which persons are embedded. It is often the case that family helpers are the first and only assistance resources that are identified in relation to supportive relationships. The current emphasis on family may result in an increasing dependency on family caregivers to the exclusion of other potential helpers. These findings suggest that a reliance on family resources during physical health problems may be appropriate because families seem most able and willing to provide this form of help. The findings also suggest, however, that family resources may be unduly monopolized to deal with other informal support needs.

Nonkin sources of support may be more integral for assistance with interpersonal and other problems and in the ancillary (e.g., companionship) care of persons with physical health problems. The position of nonkin in relation to interpersonal problems indicates that in addition to being informal helpers, they may represent an important link to formal resource use. The present findings suggest that the use of nonkin may be even more significant for persons who are not married, who reside in the Northeast region, who possess fewer years of education, and who are older adults without children.

A number of benefits accrue from our increasing sophistication in understanding African American kin and nonkin networks. First, there is increased appreciation for how both kin and nonkin networks respond to the support requirements of their members. Of equal importance is understanding the specific conditions under which particular sources can be enlisted for assistance. A comprehensive understanding of available support resources and their strengths and limitations can also provide important information as to when sources may become overburdened by the demands placed on them. Finally, investigations of natural helper networks (kin and nonkin) allow a better understanding of the interface between informal networks of assistance and formal health and social welfare agencies (Israel & Rounds, 1987). Work of this type provides formal agencies with useful information for the design and administration of appropriate and effective assistance programs.

Note

1. It should be noted that 166 respondents with a serious personal problem did not talk to anyone.

10

Predisposing, Enabling, and Need Factors Related to Patterns of Help-Seeking Among African American Women

Cleopatra Howard Caldwell

African American women often experience high levels of economic and psychological distress in America. Given their historical background and structural position within society, they are likely to have low incomes, higher health risks, and multiple role strains (Jackson & Wolford, 1992). These factors subject them to many serious stressors. Despite the high level of stress African American women face, many have exhibited successful coping and adaptation skills. Very little research, however, has focused on the different coping strategies African American women employ to maintain their psychological well-being. One coping strategy, the concept of help-seeking behavior, has received a fair amount of attention in the general literature (Bui & Takeuchi, 1992; Nickerson, Helms, & Terrell, 1994; Scheffler & Miller, 1991; Sue, Fujino, Hu, Takeuchi, & Zane, 1991). Help-seeking has been defined as any communication about a problem or troublesome event that is directed toward obtaining support, advice, or assistance in times of distress (Gourash, 1978). Embedded in this definition is the idea of social interaction, suggesting other people's involvement in one's own coping efforts.

Most research on help-seeking behavior has focused on the use of professional services (Mutchler & Burr, 1991; Sussman, Robins, & Earls, 1987;

146

Veroff, Kulka, & Douvan, 1981). These studies are typically concerned with developing social and demographic profiles of people most likely to use health or social services. As such, utilization research provides insufficient information about individuals deciding not to seek help or those who decide to seek assistance from informal resources. Further, recent studies suggest that there are higher levels of mistrust associated with negative attitudes about using professional services among African Americans than among whites (Bailey, 1987; Biafora et al., 1993; Nickerson et al., 1994). Sue et al. (1991) found that African Americans had less positive mental health treatment outcomes than other ethnic groups, whereas Sussman et al. (1987) identified fear of treatment and of being hospitalized as the main reasons preventing African Americans from seeking professional mental health services. Consequently, the use of informal resources remains an important help-seeking strategy for many African Americans (Taylor & Chatters, 1988).

Family members, friends, neighbors, coworkers, and church members are often the providers of informal social support (Hatchett & Jackson, 1993; Taylor, 1986b; Taylor & Chatters, 1988). These helpers have interpersonal and interdependent relationships with the help seeker. Previous research has indicated that females were more likely than males to be involved in supportive networks and that African Americans used professional services less frequently than whites even when serious mental health problems were evident (Sussman et al., 1987). Furthermore, use of professional services may either be facilitated or hindered depending on the specific helper contacted within the social network (Calnan, 1983; Powell & Eisenstadt, 1983; Procidano & Heller, 1983).

Prior to seeking assistance from professionals, many people rely on social contacts within the community to define and suggest responses to problems. The nature of these contacts has been found to be an important influence in the help-seeking process (Mindel & Wright, 1982; Mindel, Wright, & Starrett, 1986; Procidano & Heller, 1983). Thus, there is a need for more information on what predicts different patterns of help seeking from professionals and from informal sources of assistance. Because it is impossible for the professional system of service delivery to accommodate all people in need, it becomes necessary to distinguish between individuals who require professional help, those who can effectively cope if they receive assistance from informal social supports, and those who can manage on their own (Neighbors & Jackson, 1984). Efforts to augment the professional service delivery system have resulted in attempts to identify informal community-based supports, such as churches, especially for African Americans (Caldwell, Greene, & Billingsley, 1994; Eng, Hatch, & Callan, 1985). More research on the correlates of patterns of help seeking will help to illuminate environmental factors and personal characteristics of individuals who may benefit most by such an approach.

This chapter identifies characteristics of African American women exhibiting different patterns of help-seeking in their problem-solving efforts. It examines specific antecedents for use of informal or professional sources of assistance. Demographic variables related to utilization behavior as well as psychological and environmental factors associated with these two patterns of help seeking are also examined.

Conceptual Framework

The present study adopts a modified version of the Andersen and Newman (1973) theoretical framework for use of health services. Three groups of variables are expected to influence use behavior. These include the following:

1. Predisposing or propensity factors (i.e., social and psychological variables existing before the help-seeking behavior)
2. Enabling variables (i.e., factors that facilitate or hinder the use of services)
3. Need considerations (i.e., perceived or evaluated severity of the problem)

Previous studies have shown that age, gender, and ethnicity represent important predisposing variables for predicting use of specific professional services (Lin, Inui, Kleinman, & Womack, 1982; Mutchler & Burr, 1991; Scheffler & Miller, 1991; Sussman et al., 1987). In addition, marital status and self-esteem have been associated with help-seeking behavior (Hobfoll & Walfisch, 1984; Warren, 1981). The present study controls for race and gender of respondent. Thus, only age, marital status, and self-esteem are included as predisposing factors. A measure of personal efficacy was also included as a predisposing variable because a belief that one can successfully execute the necessary behaviors to produce desired outcomes could influence the selection of a specific helper, particularly for African American women.

Financial resources, insurance coverage, availability of services to the population, knowledge of services, and place of residence are enabling variables that have been found to influence use behavior (Eve, 1984; Wolinsky,

1982). Although predisposing characteristics may be indicative of some individuals' propensity to use services, if barriers to services exist, use of professionals may not occur. Accordingly, family income and geographical area of residence were included in the enabling category.

Social support (in the form of family cohesion) and education were also classified as enabling variables for the purpose of this study. Previous studies have used these items as predisposing factors (Coulton & Frost, 1982; Wolinsky, 1982); for a sample of African American women, however, the availability of social support would be more appropriately listed as an enabling variable. Because most African American women are embedded within social networks and have access to informal support, any lack of support when needed should result in the use of professional services (Greenley, Mechanic, & Cleary, 1988). Education, on the other hand, was included as an enabling variable for pragmatic reasons. The amount of education achieved was used as a proxy for potential knowledge of the service delivery system (Coulton & Frost, 1982).

Consistent with previous studies, the need category included measures of personal problem severity. We assumed that although propensity for service use is high and access is possible, the need for services is also necessary. Individuals who perceive the need for professional services as negligible, whether through their own decision making or through evaluations from informal sources, have no reason to use professional services. Thus, severity of need should contribute significantly to the identification of women who will rely solely on informal support versus those who are likely to use professional helpers.

Methods

Sample. Respondents were a subset of 1,322 African American women (18 years old or older) who participated in the National Survey of Black Americans (NSBA) (Jackson, 1991). Only the 856 women who reported having had a serious personal problem and who went to someone for help were included in this analysis. Demographic distributions for the sample indicated that most women (44%) were between the ages of 18 and 34 years, with 33% in the 35- to 54-year-old age range and 23% aged 55 years or older. Of the sample, 43% had less than a high school education, 32% were high school graduates, and 25% had at least some college-level training. Approximately one third (32%)

of the women had an annual family income of less than $5,000, whereas 25% fell between $5,000 and $9,999, 25% had annual family incomes between $10,000 and $20,000, and 18% had family incomes greater than $20,000. Fifty-one percent of the respondents lived in the southern portion of the United States, whereas the other 49% were scattered among the northeast, north central, and western regions. Most of the women in the sample (45%) were separated, widowed, or divorced at the time of the interview. Thirty-five percent were currently married, whereas 20% had never been married.

Measures. The analyses focus on a subset ($N = 856$) of African American women who reported having had a serious personal problem and went to someone for help. Respondents who had experienced a stressful episode were asked if they had contacted a particular informal helper about the problem. They were also asked a question about contacting professional helpers about the problem. Help-seeking was assessed by a nominal level, dichotomous measure indicating whether the respondent had used informal help only or both informal and professional help.

Women who had contacted informal helpers only were classified as informal help seekers ($N = 353$). Women who used both informal and professional helpers were classified as "both" ($N = 407$). Very few women sought only professional help ($N = 33$) or no help at all ($N = 63$). Thus, analyses were restricted to a comparison of characteristics of women who exhibited patterns reflecting informal only or both informal and professional help-seeking.

Self-esteem, personal efficacy, social support, and problem severity were included as independent variables along with demographic variables. Based on Rosenberg's (1965) self-esteem scale, a measure of self-esteem was used, including four items that represented both a positive (i.e., "I am a useful person to have around," "I feel that I am a person of worth," and "As a person I do a good job these days") and a negative (i.e., "I feel I do not have much to be proud of") sense of self. The internal consistency for the selected items was moderate ($\alpha = .56$). The self-esteem index was constructed by summing across all response categories. Possible scores ranged from 4 to 16, with higher scores representing higher levels of self-esteem. The mean score on this index for the sample was 14.10 (standard deviation [SD] = 1.93). Personal efficacy was measured using a four-item summed index ($\alpha = .58$). Possible scores ranged from 4 to 8 with higher scores representing greater perceptions of efficacy. The mean score was 6.32 ($SD = 1.27$).

Social support was limited to family support. A self-report measure was used: "Would you say your family members are very close in their feelings to each other, fairly close, not too close, or not close at all?" This item was selected over other family support measures because it had emerged as the most significant predictor of help seeking in a previous study (Howard, 1983). The measure represents feelings of closeness or cohesion within the respondent's family. It implies an availability of social support based on the intensity of network relationships: A close family system should allow its members to feel that help is available when needed. Conversely, a family system that is not too close should facilitate the use of professional services.

Of all problems reported, 61% had occurred within a 2-year period before the interview, which allowed for an evaluation of need for help within a recent time frame. Problem severity or the need for help was measured by two items. A dichotomous variable, high versus low need, was used, representing the responses to questions concerning the women's feelings about the problem. High need included only women who felt that they were nearly at the point of a nervous breakdown when they experienced the identified problem; all other levels of difficulty were coded as low.[1] The second measure of need was a self-report of the number of symptoms the respondent had experienced in relation to the identified problem. Symptoms, such as feeling depressed, jumpy or jittery, physically sick, and so on, were included in this measure. This item represented the number of symptoms the women reported ($\alpha = .83$). Possible scores ranged from 0 to 16. The mean score for this measure was 9.15 ($SD = 2.88$).

Analysis Procedure. Chi-square analyses were used to determine the bivariate relationship between patterns of help seeking and selected predisposing, enabling, and need factors. Logistic regression was used at the multivariate level of analysis. This technique uses the log of the odds of one response category of the dependent variable to estimate the effects of the independent variables. This analysis predicts the log odds of using informal help only versus using both informal and formal help.

Results

Table 10.1 presents the results of the bivariate analysis of the predisposing, enabling, and need variables for the two types of help-seeking behavior

Table 10.1 Bivariate Analysis of Predisposing, Enabling, and Need Variables on Patterns of Help-Seeking Behavior

	Informal Only (%)	Informal + Professional (%)	N	χ^2 (df)
Predisposing				
Self-esteem				.08(2)
Low	45.7	54.3	223	
Medium	46.9	53.1	294	
High	46.1	53.9	228	
Personal efficacy				.59(2)
Low	46.6	53.4	378	
Medium	45.1	54.9	293	
High	50.0	50.0	72	
Marital status				2.75(1)[+]
Married	46.5	53.4	269	
Not married	44.3	55.7	490	
Age				3.04(2)
18-34	49.7	50.3	346	
35-54	43.0	57.0	258	
55+	44.1	55.9	152	
Enabling				
Family income				2.04(3)
< $5,000	45.1	54.9	204	
$5,000-$9,999	45.6	54.4	171	
$10,000-$20,000	51.7	48.3	176	
> $20,000	46.0	54.0	126	
Family cohesion				4.68(2)
Not too close	36.8	63.2	87	
Fairly close	45.3	54.7	243	
Very close	49.2	50.8	427	
Region				
South	48.2	51.8	392	
Non-South	44.7	55.3	367	
Education				7.79(3)*
Less than high school	44.9	55.1	301	
High school graduate	52.0	48.0	256	
Some college	46.2	53.8	130	
College graduate	33.8	66.2	68	
Need				
Problem severity				12.09(1)***
High	40.9	59.1	423	
Low	53.6	46.4	336	
Number of symptoms				25.61(2)***
0-7	59.2	40.8	191	
8-10	48.5	51.5	295	
11-15	35.7	64.3	272	

[+]$p < .10$; *$p < .05$; **$p < .01$; ***$p < .001$.

exhibited by women in the sample. None of the predisposing variables included are significantly related to patterns of help seeking. Regarding enabling variables, educational attainment is significantly related to patterns of help seeking ($p < .05$)—with a curvilinear relationship. African American women who are college graduates and those who have less than a high school education are more likely to use both types of assistance, whereas those with some college-level training or a high school diploma are more likely to use only informal help. Although not statistically significant, the results of the analysis with the family cohesion variable suggest a trend in the data. Women who have very close families are more likely to rely solely on informal help than those whose families are not as close.

An analysis of the need category indicates that both problem severity and symptomatology have a significant positive relationship with patterns of help seeking. Women who did not perceive their problem as severe are more likely to rely only on informal assistance, whereas those who indicate that their problem was severe are more likely to use both types of assistance. Similarly, women who express multiple symptoms are much less likely to rely on informal help only.

The results of logistic regression analyses of the relative contribution of various groups of independent variables for predicting type of help-seeking are presented in Tables 10.2 and 10.3. As shown in Table 10.2, the inclusion of enabling factors as a group does not improve the significance of Model 1, the predisposing variables. Age, education, and family cohesion, however, independently emerge as significant factors for distinguishing among patterns of help seeking. Results suggest that older women are more likely than younger women ($p < .01$) to seek help from both informal and professional resources. Furthermore, women with higher levels of education are more likely than those with less education to use both types of helpers ($p < .05$). Findings also indicate that women who reported that their family members are not very close are significantly different from those whose families are closer. Specifically, women who are not part of cohesive family systems have a greater tendency to seek help from both formal and informal sources of assistance.

Table 10.3 presents the results of a logistic regression that analyzes the contribution of need factors beyond the combined effects of the predisposing and enabling factors on patterns of help seeking. Model 2 is significant, suggesting that the incremental contribution of the need variables to the overall model is significant. Clearly, need is an important predictor of patterns and help-seeking behavior. African American women who had experienced

Table 10.2 Logit Analysis of Predisposing and Enabling Factors on Patterns of Help-Seeking Behavior

	Model 1 b^a	Model 2 b
Intercept	.53	−8.60*
Predisposing		
Self-esteem	−.04	−.03
Personal efficacy	−.05	−.05
Marital status		
Not married	.10	.08
Age	.01**	.02**
Enabling		
Family income	—	−.02
Family cohesion[b]		
Not too close	—	.51
Fairly close	—	.02
Region		
Non-South	—	.01
Education	—	.08*

NOTE: Due to Model 1: $\chi^2 = 7.86$, $df = 4$, $p < .10$; due to Model 2: $\chi^2 = 10.30$, $df = 5$, $p < .10$.
a. Unstandardized regression coefficient.
b. "Very close" is the excluded category.
*$p < .05$; **$p < .01$.

a higher number of symptoms as a result of their problems are likely to seek both types of help ($p < .01$). In addition, women who perceived their problems as severe are also likely to seek help from both sources of assistance than those who perceive their problem as less severe ($p < .05$).

Age ($p < .01$) and education ($p < .05$) remain significant after the inclusion of the need variables; family cohesion, however, is eliminated as an important distinguishing factor. This change in influence of family cohesion suggests that this relationship may be mediated by need. To test this proposition, we conducted a hierarchical logistic regression analysis using the dichotomous problem-severity item as the dependent measure.

The influence of predisposing and enabling factors on perceptions of problem severity is presented in Table 10.4. Results show that both models are significant. Enabling factors as a group of variables, however, contribute very little to the predisposing variables for determining the probability of perceiving a problem as severe. Further analysis indicates that the level of

Table 10.3 Logit Analysis of Predisposing, Enabling, and Need Factors on Patterns of Help-Seeking Behavior

	Model 1 b^a	Model 2 b
Intercept	−8.60*	−10.47*
Predisposing		
Self-esteem	−.03	−.00
Personal efficacy	−.05	−.07
Marital status		
Not married	.08	.07
Age	.02**	.02**
Enabling		
Family income	−.02	−.02
Family cohesion		
Not too close	.51*	.38
Fairly close	.02	.01
Region		
Non-South	.01	.02
Education	.08*	.09*
Need		
Problem severity		
Low[b]	—	−.23*
Number of symptoms	—	.10**

NOTE: Full Model 1: $\chi^2(9) = 18.14$, $p < .05$; due to Model 2: $\chi^2(2) = 20.67$, $p < .001$.
a. Unstandardized regression coefficient.
b. High severity is the excluded category.
*$p < .05$; **$p < .01$.

personal efficacy and family cohesion are significant variables for determining need. Findings show that African American women with higher levels of personal efficacy have a greater tendency to report that their problem caused them a great deal of difficulty ($p < .001$). Family cohesion is also related to perception of problem severity ($p < .01$). African American women who are not part of a close family are more likely to perceive their problem as severe than any other group. The results of this analysis lend support to the proposition that the relationship between patterns of help seeking and family cohesion are mediated by perceptions of problem severity.

Table 10.4 Logit Analysis of Predisposing and Enabling Factors on Patterns of Problem Severity

	Model 1 b^a	Model 2 b
Intercept	−1.00	5.68
Predisposing		
Self-esteem	−.07	−.05
Personal efficacy	.30***	.26***
Marital status		
Not married	.03	.01
Age	.01	.00
Enabling		
Family income	.00	−.01
Family cohesion[b]		
Not too close	—	.62**
Fairly close	—	−.06
Region		
Non-South	—	−.03
Education	—	−.06

NOTE: Due to Model 1: $\chi^2(4) = 34.77$, $p < .01$; due to Model 2: $\chi^2(5) = 13.84$, $p < .05$.
a. Unstandardized regression coefficient.
b. Very close is the excluded category.
**$p < .01$; ***$p < .001$.

Discussion

The present study was concerned with identifying factors related to different patterns of help-seeking behavior exhibited during a stressful episode for a sample of African American women. Findings indicated that perceived problem severity and symptoms of distress were the most important predictors for classifying women as either informal-only help seekers or both informal and professional help seekers. Results from general use studies also have shown that the influences of other factors are diminished when need is considered (Coulton & Frost, 1982; Leaf et al., 1988; Mechanic, Cleary, & Greenley, 1982).

Although the contribution of the need factor was substantial beyond the predisposing and enabling factors, age and education consistently emerged as influential variables. Younger women used their informal network as the sole source of help more frequently than older women who relied on both informal and professional help. In contrast, previous studies have shown that younger people typically seek help from a variety of resources more frequently than do older people (Gourash, 1978). Eve (1988) found that health status and previous use of services by the elderly were important factors in accounting for use of medical services. Mindel and Wright (1982), on the other hand, identified need as the most influential causal variable for use of social services by the elderly. Thus, age alone is less informative when accounting for differing use patterns of older people than it is when put in the context of their lives.

Clearly, the older women in this sample were not isolated and frequently engaged in help seeking. In addition to contacting professionals, older African American women were part of informal social networks that allowed them to ask for help when needed. Younger women, on the other hand, seemed to limit their help-seeking activities to the informal network. It is plausible that perceived need for help did not differ based on age because age was not a significant predictor of perception of problem severity. If this is true, then these results suggest that variations in problem type at different stages of the life cycle lead to different patterns of help-seeking behavior. An alternative explanation could be that there may be a preference for specific helpers among African American women at different age levels.

The influence of education is the most consistent finding at all levels of analysis. Women with higher levels of education were more likely to use both informal and professional resources than women with less education. One explanation for this relationship is that women with higher levels of education have greater access to professional services than women with less education. This may be due to increased knowledge of service availability and the methods for negotiating formal systems. We did find, however, a curvilinear relationship between education and patterns of help seeking at the bivariate level of analysis. Women with less than a high school education and those with a college degree were more likely to use both types of assistance. Further research is necessary to determine whether the types of services used by each group are similar or different. Different aspects of the formal system could be overused by some groups at a particular educational level, whereas other aspects are less frequently used by that same group. For example, women with less than a high school education may rely on assistance from social services, whereas those with a college education may use preventive health services with more frequency. This speculation is partially supported by Neighbors, Caldwell, Thompson, and Jackson's (1994) finding that African American college graduates contacted doctors more frequently than women at other educational levels. Understanding the differences in types of services used by different groups is important when trying to determine unmet needs.

Surprisingly, family income did not emerge as an important factor in this analysis. Previous findings from the NSBA have found that income is related to the use of specific formal help sources. For example, Neighbors (1986) found that low-income African Americans were significantly more likely to use the hospital emergency room for all types of problems. Neighbors and Taylor (1985) noted an income effect for African Americans who used social service agencies. Specifically, low-income African Americans were more than twice as likely to use social service agencies than any other type of professional help, regardless of education, age, gender, or problem type. These findings lead to the expectation that those with higher incomes have greater access to professional help. Neighbors (1984b) found, however, that income was not related to the decision to seek professional help when need and problem type were taken into account. Similarly, Neighbors and Jackson (1984) found that income was not related to help seeking when all four combinations (no outside help, informal only, formal only, and both informal and formal) of informal and professional help were explored. Thus, perceived need for services appears to be a consistently better predictor of seeking professional help than family income among African Americans, which supports the idea that access alone is not sufficient to encourage professional services use.

The inclusion of need in the multivariate model (Table 10.3) completely eliminated the relationship found between family cohesion and patterns of help seeking in Model 2 of Table 10.2. Through subsequent analysis, we were able to demonstrate that family cohesion may operate through need. Thus, perception of need may be based on the social situation in which a person is embedded. Women who perceive their family systems as close may rely on family members to help them define which events constitute a problem, how severe the problem is, and whether professional intervention is required. Women who are not part of a close family must rely on themselves or other members of their social network to determine problem severity and their approach to problem resolution.

Family members usually offer lay solutions to problems that may delay or negate the need for professional help (Dohrenwend & Dohrenwend, 1974a; Horwitz, 1977). We found that women who perceived their problem as severe were generally not part of close family systems and were much more likely to use both types of assistance. Because this study limited social support to family, we do not know whether those who used both types of assistance chose friends or family members as their informal help source. Other studies have shown that friends referred the help seeker to professionals at a much faster rate than family members (Calnan, 1983; Powell & Eisenstadt, 1983; Procidano & Heller, 1983). Thus, the specific helper contacted within the social network could facilitate or hinder the use of formal services.

The overwhelming majority of African American women in this study relied on informal social support in their problem-solving efforts whether or not they sought professional help. This finding suggests that use of professional services does not negate the need for social support (Mindel et al., 1986). Previous studies have indicated that those who underused professional services generally had stronger network ties than individuals who used professional services (Birkel & Reppucci, 1983; Greenley et al., 1988; Powell & Eisenstadt, 1983; Procidano & Heller, 1983). This broad generalization may not be quite as appropriate for African American women.

Mindel and Wright (1982) found that family support systems were much more important for African Americans than for whites. These family support systems were used to supplement formal services—not as an alternative. Literature on African American extended families has consistently noted the critical role that family support networks play in the survival of African American people (Billingsley, 1992; Hatchett & Jackson, 1993). Because African American women are typically embedded within social networks, the use of professional services may not mean that their social networks are deficient. Thus, it is important to determine under which conditions their social networks are functional and supportive when serious problems arise and under which conditions they are not.

Personal efficacy did not emerge as an important factor for determining patterns of help seeking; its effects, however, are significant for determining perception of problem severity. The fact that women with higher levels of efficacy had a greater likelihood of perceiving their problem as severe can be explained by a vulnerability interpretation. That is, women with a higher sense of personal efficacy are free to interpret problems as more severe than women with lower levels of efficacy because they possess more positive self-conceptions; this allows them to acknowledge severe problems with confidence in their ability to solve them. Admitting to having a serious problem is a challenging first step in deciding what action, if any, is necessary to resolve the conflict.

Conclusions and Implications

A major finding from this study of African American women is that need factors contributed substantially more than predisposing and enabling factors to the kind of help selected. The results indicate that African American women are similar to the general population regarding factors influencing professional services use. Several studies have found that the rate of use of only professional services for African Americans is lower than that of whites (Mindel & Wright, 1982). Indeed, only 4% of our sample relied on professional help alone. This suggests that the pathway to professional services for African American women almost always includes input from their social networks. The effectiveness of this input is still an empirical question.

We were not able to test the causal direction of the relationship between use of social networks and professional helpers—that is, are help seekers more likely to contact professionals before or after contact with informal social networks? Nevertheless, it is clear that, for most African American women, network members are an important influence in the decision to seek professional help. We found that younger African American women, those who are a part of close family systems, and those with less than a college education are at greatest risk for not receiving professional help when needed. These groups may have less knowledge about the availability of and access to professional help. Professional service providers should extend their outreach efforts to specifically target these groups. Moreover, outreach efforts aimed at African American women must consider how they incorporate specific network members into their problem-solving efforts. This information may then be used to encourage more accuracy in determining need for professional assistance as well as increased effectiveness in the quality of services provided.

Note

1. Problem severity was also used as a dependent variable in the logistic regression reported in Table 10.4. The problem-severity variable was created from a series of questions inquiring how much the respondent's personal problem interfered with his or her usual social functioning. All persons indicating that their problem brought them to the point of a nervous breakdown were coded "high" on problem severity. All persons indicating their problem interfered with their social functioning, but did not elicit feelings of breakdown, were coded "low" on problem severity.

11

Mental Health Symptoms and Service Utilization Patterns of Help-Seeking Among African American Women

Vickie M. Mays
Cleopatra Howard Caldwell
James S. Jackson

There has been increasing concern among mental health service professionals about the problems faced by ethnic minorities, particularly African Americans,[1] and their underutilization of traditional mental health services (Comas-Diaz, 1992; Mays, 1995; Mays & Albee, 1992; Neighbors, 1985; Solomon, 1988; Sue, McKinney, Allen, & Hall, 1974; Yamamoto, Dixon, & Bloombaum, 1972). Many of the studies reported in the literature focus on the problems of the use of psychotherapy and mental health services within the context of patient-therapist social class levels, interracial dyads, psychotherapy versus medication (Flaherty, Naidu, Lawton, & Pathak, 1981; Sue, 1977; Yamamoto, James, & Palley, 1968), misdiagnosis of minority patients (Lawson, Hepler, Holladay, & Cuffel, 1994; Mukherjee, Shukla, Woodle, Rosen, & Olarte, 1983; Strakowski et al., 1995; Strakowski, Shelton, &

AUTHORS' NOTE: This research was funded in part though support from the Center for Minority Group Mental Health, National Institute of Aging to the third author and a National Institute of Mental Health Individual Research Award to the first author at the University of Michigan, Institute for Social Research, Program for Research on Black Americans. The authors would like to thank Dr. Barbara Henker for her helpful comments on an earlier draft of this chapter. Reprints of the chapter with references can be obtained from the first author. E-mail: mays@psych.sscnet.ucla.edu

Kolbrener, 1993), and other structural factors in the provision of mental health services to minority populations (Mays, 1985). Few studies are available that inform service providers of the factors influencing the help-seeking and mental health service use process from the perspective of the intended client. Seldom have research questions focused on the types of problems ethnic minorities regard as appropriate for seeking professional services or on the factors that influence their decision to seek professional mental health services. This seems particularly important because studies indicate that some Black Americans are less likely to use outpatient mental health services and more likely to (a) use informal sources of help for their problems (Neighbors, 1985; Vernon & Roberts, 1982), (b) leave treatment prematurely (Acosta, 1980; Sue, 1977; Yamamoto et al., 1968), or (c) benefit less than Whites, Mexican Americans, or Asian Americans from treatment (Sue, Fujino, Hu, Takeuchi, & Zane, 1991). Such findings have raised questions for concerned mental health professionals about the adequacy, cultural appropriateness, and responsiveness of current mental health services to address the unique ethnic/cultural values and life experiences of Black Americans (Mays, 1995; Mays & Comas-Diaz, 1988).

Such questions seem appropriate as we enter an age of managed mental health services whose interest centers on early identification of problems in order to prevent episodes of serious mental illness. In the African American community, where healthy distrust and wariness about psychotherapy continue in the face of studies that document the higher incidence of psychiatric misdiagnosis (Lawson et al., 1994; Mukherjee et al., 1983; Strakowski et al., 1995; Strakowski et al., 1993), substandard assignment in referral practices for treatment and reliance on medication (Lawson et al., 1994; Lewis & Shanok, 1980; Strakowski et al., 1995), and a long, checkered history of racial mistrust between Black and White Americans (Lawson, 1986; Mays & Cochran, 1995, 1996; Neal & Turner, 1991; Worthington, 1992), those African Americans who cross the thresholds of public or private mental health centers have made strong statements regarding their problems and their ability to cope (Block, 1981).

These individuals have acknowledged that their problems are within and have demonstrated a willingness to risk treatment in a historically negative environment (Block, 1981; Worthington, 1992). By seeking help from traditional professional mental health services, they are indicating to some extent that the support mechanisms that Blacks usually rely on for help with personal problems (Neighbors, 1985, 1988), such as ministers, general physicians, medical emergency rooms, and friends, may not be working. The decision to seek mental health services is often not consistent with African American cultural coping styles that emphasize the use of informal systems and the ability to "do it" oneself (Block, 1981; Mays & Comas-Diaz, 1988). Block suggests that help-seeking for environmental needs within the family and through social service agencies is culturally permissible in the Black community. On the other hand, admitting an intrapsychic problem that cannot be solved by oneself or with informal help is often not consistent with images of how ethnically identified Blacks cope with problems. This is particularly true for Black women, for whom the tradition of being self-reliant is synonymous with the role of being an adult Black woman (Mays, 1995; Mays & Comas-Diaz, 1988; Robinson, 1983).

Service Utilization Research

Research on the mental health service use patterns of Black Americans is a mixed picture, with some studies reporting underutilization (Smith, 1981; Sue, 1977) and others reporting overutilization (Bui & Takeuchi, 1992; Dawkins, Dawkins, & Terry, 1979; Flaskerud & Hu, 1992; Smith, 1981; Sue et al., 1991). Cheung and Snowden (1990), in their review of mental health service use patterns, cite several studies reporting an increase in use by African Americans, especially in inpatient and residential care. Critical to the picture is whether the data are based purely on public health facility use or whether patterns of service use with private mental health practitioners and facilities are included. Data on the latter group are often harder to collect in that diagnosis or use of services may never be recorded if a third-party payment system is not used. Further, the lack of accurate reporting of the true nature of psychological problems can occur when there is concern about stigma attached to particular diagnoses.

The picture of use among African American women is no clearer. Some research studies have demonstrated an underutilization of psychotherapy services by Black women (Armstrong, Ishiki, Heiman, Mundt, & Womack, 1984; Smith, 1981; Sue, 1977; Sussman, Robins, & Earls, 1987) with patterns different from those of White women or Black men. Earlier studies based on national statistics revealed that Black women have a higher use rate of public rather than private mental health facilities, whereas the opposite is true of White females (Smith, 1981). Although Blacks as a group use community mental health centers at almost twice the rate of the general population (Rudov & Santangelo, 1978), Black women use these facilities less than do Black men. This is opposite to the pattern for White women and men (Smith, 1981). This tendency of Black women to use community mental health services less when compared to other groups was supported in a study that analyzed the use patterns of ethnic minorities in 17 community mental health centers. Contradictory evidence, however, was found in a study of users of public mental health facilities in Chicago where Black women used services at almost twice the rate of African American men (Dawkins et al., 1979). Interestingly, in a study of the client population of a group of Black psychiatrists, more Black women than men were seen, and for both Black women and men they were more likely to be seen as private clients rather than as patients of mental health facilities (Jones & Gray, 1984).

Other sociodemographic patterns of African American women's use of psychotherapy services indicate that they use public services and private facilities most often during the 25 to 44 age range (Jones & Gray, 1984; Smith, 1981). Women users of both public and private mental health services tend more often to be married (Dawkins et al., 1979; Jones & Gray, 1984). Divorced women comprise the next largest group of private practice patients, which contrasts with the second-largest group of private practice users of Black men, who are more likely to be single.

Data on education and employment status were found only for users of private therapists (Jones & Gray, 1984). Black women, like Black male users of services, were typically in technical or semitechnical professional occupations, with Black women professionals being the second-largest group. The educational level of Black women was a little higher than that of Black men, with more high school or college graduates among the women. The patterns of Black women's use of mental health services are more different from than similar to those of either White women or Black men. In addition, when users of public versus private mental health services are compared, differences are noted among Black women. Other studies support the influence of education on mental health service use rates. Capers (1991) and Flaskerud (1980) found that Black Americans with more education sought psychiatric management of their problems at a higher rate than did those with less education.

Yet using only sociodemographic variables as the criteria for evaluation of mental health service patterns in African American communities has been found to be inadequate (Block, 1981; Dawkins et al., 1979). Not enough attention has been given to the role of culture or lifestyle characteristics as means for identifying mental health needs and for planning mental health services for Black Americans (Dawkins et al., 1979). Attitudes and beliefs regarding what constitutes a psychological problem and when and whom one seeks help from are often mediated by gender, culture, and racial-ethnic factors (Cleary & Mechanic, 1983; Hough et al., 1987; Marsella, Kinzie, & Gordon, 1973; Mays & Comas-Diaz, 1988). Black Americans sometimes seek help for psychological problems from informal sources—friends, relatives, church members (Neighbors & Jackson, 1984; Taylor, 1986c; Taylor & Chatters, 1988). As an example, some Blacks cope with distressing problems by turning to religion, prayer, or church members for support in handling those problems. A study using data from this same data set (National Survey of Black Americans [NSBA]) found that as the seriousness of distressing problems increased, so did the use of prayers as a coping mechanism (Neighbors, Jackson, Bowman, & Gurin, 1983).

Religious participation among African Americans, especially women, has been associated with the use of specific types of informal helpers. For example, Taylor and Chatters (1988) found that church members provided a substantial amount of support, including emotional support, to many older African Americans. In addition, Hatch (1991) found that attending religious social events was predictive of preferences for nonrelative helpers among African American women, but not among White women. A summary of the work by Taylor and Chatters using NSBA data indicates that church attendance, church membership, subjective religiosity, and religious affiliation were all significantly related to the receipt of support from church members among African Americans (Caldwell, Chatters, Billingsley, & Taylor, 1995). The availability and use of informal helpers for emotional problems and the selection of church members and nonrelatives as helpers have implications for pathways into professional mental health services for African American women. The influence of religious beliefs and activities (e.g., prayer) as well as the reliance on religious social networks for fellowship and emotional support may replace or delay the need to seek professional mental health services among religious women. This issue remains an empirical question as surprisingly few studies have investigated the role of religion in the use of professional mental health services.

Another sociocultural factor that might influence the use of mental health services by African American women is mistrust of the system of care (Neal & Turner, 1991). Sussman et al. (1987) identified fear of treatment and of being hospitalized as the main reasons preventing African Americans from seeking professional mental health services. Establishing trusting relationships between professional mental health workers and African American clients can be difficult when feelings of oppression and discrimination are considered (Nickerson, Helms, & Terrell, 1994; Worthington, 1992). The issue of client mistrust of the professional service delivery system is further complicated by evidence that suggests that African American patients are significantly more likely than Whites to be hospitalized or diagnosed with schizophrenia or a psychotic disorder, whereas Whites are likely to be diagnosed with a personality disorder (Solomon, 1988; Strakowski et al., 1995). African Americans have also been found to have fewer sessions with a primary therapist and more treatment with medications than Whites with comparable symptoms (Flaskerud & Hu, 1992). Because much of mental health services are shaped by the values and beliefs of European American culture (Comas-Diaz, 1992; Mays & Albee, 1992), such services may not be perceived as desirable or helpful (Wallen, 1992) by African Americans who identify strongly with an ethnic group on whom society has used a variety of tools of oppression. Some would consider psychotherapy to be such a tool. Thus, the patterns of professional services utilization by African American women may reflect sociocultural barriers based on shared ethnic group beliefs.

Consequently, the purpose of this study is to explore the role of socio-demographics, social support, and sociocultural characteristics in African American women's use of community mental health centers and private psychotherapists. In that regard, this study examines the particular importance of sociocultural factors such as religiosity, ethnic group consciousness, and preference for Black therapists and cultural sources of social support, such as church networks. Knowing the correlates of Black women's mental health service use is necessary for designing delivery systems and research that can effectively meet their needs and expectations.

Method

Sample

Details on the sampling plan for African American women participating in the NSBA can be found in Jackson (1991) and Mays, Coleman, and Jackson (1996). For this particular study, only those women ($N = 455$) who reported using any type of professional helper in their problem-solving efforts were included for analyses.

Measures

The section of the interview designed to study mental health was problem focused. Respondents were asked to report a personal problem they had experienced that caused them a significant amount of distress. If the person had ever experienced a personal problem of this type, she was asked the nature of the problem. Reliability and validity for these questions were established during the pretest phase of the study. Focus groups and back-translation procedures were used as well as face validity established by a panel of mental health experts (Jackson, Tucker, & Bowman, 1982).

Problem Type. Every respondent who said she had experienced a problem was asked the following question: "Thinking about the last time you felt this way, what was the problem?" This question was designed to ascertain how the respondent conceptualized the nature of the distress experienced. The answer to this question represents the specific locus to which the respondent attributed the cause of her personal distress. For analytic purposes, responses to this question were categorized using face validity and interrater reliability. Three clinical psychologists averaging a mean of 3 years post-PhD training achieved a reliability score of .90. The problems were classified into five categories: financial, health, adjustment, emotional problems, and other. Adjustment problems referred to problems that could be characterized as temporary and not of a long-standing nature. In contrast, emotional problems were characterized by their duration and their ability to seriously affect the respondent over a lengthy time period.

Problem Severity. Problem severity was determined by the person's perception of how much the problem interfered with her ability to perform her usual social obligations. Answers to several questions that ranged from feeling at the point of a nervous breakdown to lesser degrees of difficulty were obtained. This measure was then dichotomized to represent those women who felt they were at the point of a nervous breakdown as high severity and those at all other levels of difficulty as lower severity.

Professional Help Use. If the respondent had experienced a problem, she was presented with a list of professional help facilities and asked if she had gone to any of the listed places for help with her personal problem. The list included the following sources: hospital emergency room, medical clinic, social services, community mental health center, private mental health psychotherapists, private physician's office, minister, lawyer, police, school, and employment agency. For purposes of analysis, the women were categorized into three groups: (a) those who went to a community mental health center ($n = 27$); (b) those who sought help from a private psychotherapist ($n = 46$); and (c) those who consulted other professional helpers ($n = 382$) for a total sample of $N = 455$.

Sociodemographic variables included in the analyses were standard items of age, education, income, urbanicity, and region. The social support measures (help from church members, family, and friend networks and involvement in a main romantic relationship) and sociocultural variables (religiosity, desire for a Black helper, and intention to return for further help) were all single-item measures of either social network involvement and the provision of help or ethnic preferences for professional helpers.

Results

In general, the data indicate that African American women typically seek professional help from sources other than private therapists or community mental health centers. However, the type of problems taken to mental health professionals differed by the type of mental health professional used (community mental health vs. private practice). For example, women with adjustment problems used a variety of sources of help. However, women with financial or health problems were more likely to use private therapists or other resources, whereas women with emotional problems relied more on community mental health centers (see Table 11.1) As expected, there was a significant difference in the level of problem severity of users of mental health services versus users of other sources of professional help—$\chi^2(2) = 12.37$, $p < .01$. Black women who perceived the problem as very severe and were moved to seek help were more likely to use private therapists or community mental health centers than those who perceived their problems as less severe (see Table 11.2).

Sociodemographics. Further analyses of the data were conducted to examine the relationships among three categories of variables that previous research suggests might influence utilization behaviors: demographics, social support, and sociocultural factors. Table 11.3 presents the results of the analyses of the sociodemographics variables. In the present sample, only age—$\chi^2(4) = 14.16$, $p < .01$—and region—$\chi^2(2) = 8.91$, $p < .01$—were significantly related to use of a particular type of service. Specifically, older women were less likely to use mental health professionals than any other age

Table 11.1 Black Women's Problem Types, by Services Used

Problem Type	Private Therapist		CMHC[a]		Other		Total
	%	N	%	N	%	N	(%)
Adjustment	17.6	31	9.1	16	73.3	129	100
Financial	10.2	5	6.1	3	83.7	41	100
Emotional	9.8	4	12.2	5	78.0	32	100
Health	9.3	5	5.6	3	85.1	46	100
Total N		45		27		248	

$\chi^2(8) = 20.49, p < .01.$
a. Community mental health center.

Table 11.2 Severity of Black Women's Problems, by Type of Service Used

Level of Severity	Private Therapist		CMHC[a]		Other		Total
	%	N	%	N	%	N	(%)
High	13.3	37	7.6	21	79.1	220	100
Low	5.1	9	3.4	6	91.5	162	100
Total N		46		27		382	

NOTE: $\chi^2(2) = 12.37; p < .01.$
a. Community mental health center.

group. Regarding region, Black women who did not reside in the South used private therapists significantly more than those who did reside in the South.

Social Support. As indicated in Table 11.4, the selected social support items were not important independent factors. However, the relationship variable of main romantic involvement did suggest a possible trend. Black women who had a main romantic involvement were more likely to use mental health professionals than were those who did not have such a romantic involvement—$\chi^2(2) = 4.89, p < .10$).

Sociocultural. Religiosity was the only sociocultural factor related to type of service used—$\chi^2(6) = 13.89, p < .05$. Specifically, Black women who said they were fairly religious were more likely to use a private therapist, whereas those who indicated that they were not religious at all tended to use community mental health centers (see Table 11.4).

Table 11.3 Characteristics of Black Women, by Type of Professional Help Used

Sociodemographics	Private Therapist %	Private Therapist N	CMHC[a] %	CMHC[a] N	Other %	Other N	Total (%)	$\chi^2(df)$	Cramer's V/ϕ
Age								14.16(4)***	.13
18-34	11.5	21	5.5	10	83.0	151	100		
35-54	12.8	21	5.5	15	78.0	128	100		
55+	3.7	4	1.8	2	94.5	103	100		
Total N		46		27		382			
Education								7.08(4)	.09
Less than high school	7.5	15	8.0	16	84.5	169	100		
High school graduate	10.5	14	3.0	4	86.5	115	100		
Some college+	14.3	17	5.9	7	79.8	95	100		
Total N		46		27		379			
Personal income								3.62(4)	.07
Less than $5,000	9.0	19	7.1	15	84.0	174	100		
$5,000-$9,999	8.7	9	3.9	4	87.4	90	100		
$10,000+	14.3	13	6.6	6	79.1	72	100		
Total N		41		25		336			
Family income								1.79(6)	.05
Less than $5,000	9.4	12	7.0	9	83.6	107	100		
$5,000-$9,999	11.0	11	8.0	8	81.0	81	100		
$10,000-$19,999	9.9	9	5.5	5	84.6	77	100		
$20,000+	8.2	6	4.1	3	87.7	64	100		
Total N		38		25		329			
Urbanicity								5.80(2)	.12
Urban	11.7	43	5.4	20	82.9	305	100		
Rural	3.4	3	8.0	7	88.5	77	100		
Total N		46		27		382			
Region								8.90(2)***	.14
South	6.1	14	6.9	16	87.0	201	100		
Non-South	14.3	32	4.9	11	88.5	181	100		
Total N		46		27		382			

***p < .01.
a. Community mental health center.

Discussion

This study attempted to identify those demographic, sociocultural, and social support factors associated with specific types of mental health services used by African American women. The most striking finding in this study was the difference in the level of severity of problems among users of the three types of professional helpers. Women with the most severe problems tended to use community mental health centers. Also, when any type of mental health service was used, the problems were more severe than when other sources of professional help were used. This finding suggests that by the time African American women enter therapy, their problems have escalated to a critical stage.

In another study based on this same data set, it was found that African American women tend to combine informal with formal services to a greater extent than do Black men (Neighbors & Jackson, 1984). The study described in Chapter 10 also found that African American women often sought informal help in addition to formal services. Although this may be true, when problems are viewed as very severe, Black women do seek professional mental health services.

The results of the analyses for the age variable were not unexpected in the Black women in the 35 to 54 age group. They used mental health services proportionately more than did the other age groups. Problems generally associated with the use of mental health professionals must be interpreted in mental health terms before such use occurs. The results of a national replication study on the mental health of the American population by Veroff, Kulka, and Douvan (1981) suggested that younger people are more likely to define problems in mental health terms than are older people.

A finding unique to the present study was that region of the country was significantly related to type of service used. Because data for this study were based on a national probability sample, we were able to analyze the relation between residential region and patterns of service use. African American women who lived in the South were less likely to use private therapists than were women in other parts of the country. This finding is not unexpected in that for Blacks living in the South, indigenous and community-based resources, particularly church-based sources of help, are frequently used to deal with problems rather than traditional mental health services (Jackson, 1981).

The expectation that social support would be related to the type of service used was not confirmed. Degree of religiosity was, however, significantly related to type of service used by Black women. Black women who said that

Table 11.4 Relationship of Informal Resources, by Type of Professional Services Used

Sociocultural	Private Therapist %	N	CMHC[a] %	N	Other %	N	Total (%)	χ^2(df)	Cramer's V/ϕ
Help from church members								4.04(4)	.08
Often	10.1	11	4.6	5	85.3	93	100%		
Sometimes	10.1	16	4.8	6	86.1	136	100%		
Never	8.7	6	10.1	7	81.2	56	100%		
Total N		33		18		285			
Help from family								4.34(4)	.08
Fairly often	9.0	20	5.4	12	85.5	189	100%		
Not too often	12.8	17	4.5	6	82.7	110	100%		
Never	10.3	8	10.3	8	79.5	62	100%		
Total N		45		26		361			
Friendship network								4.75(4)	.07
Some	6.7	6	4.4	4	88.9	89	100%		
A few	11.8	38	5.9	19	82.4	266	100%		
None	4.9	2	9.8	4	86.4	35	100%		
Total N		46		27		381			
Main romantic involvement								4.89(2)[+]	.13
Yes	14.6	18	9.8	12	75.6	93	100%		
No	9.8	18	4.9	9	86.3	157	100%		
Total N		36		21		250			

Sociocultural	Private Therapist		CMHC[a]		Other		Total	$\chi^2(df)$	Cramer's V/ϕ
	%	N	%	N	%	N	(%)		
Religiosity								13.89(6)*	.12
Not at all	0.0	0	16.7	1	83.4	5	100		
Not too religious	8.9	4	13.3	6	77.8	35	100		
Fairly religious	13.8	32	4.3	10	81.9	190	100		
Very religious	5.8	10	5.8	10	88.3	151	100		
Total N		46		27		381			
Racial consciousness								2.21(4)	.05
Low	10.1	20	4.5	9	85.4	170	100		
Medium	10.1	12	5.0	6	84.9	101	100		
High	11.3	9	8.8	7	80.0	64	100		
Total N		41		22		335			
Ethnic preference for helper								3.05(4)	.08
Wanted black	19.5	8	7.3	3	73.2	30	100		
Did not want black	6.9	2	6.9	2	86.2	25	100		
No difference	11.0	15	7.4	10	81.6	111	100		
Total N		25		15		166			
Would go again								2.57(2)	.08
Yes	9.7	37	6.1	23	84.2	320	100		
No	17.0	9	5.7	3	77.4	41	100		
Total N		46		26		361			

a. Community mental health center.
+p < .10; *p < .05.

they were not at all religious tended to use community mental health centers in preference to private therapists or other sources of professional help. These women also had the most severe problems. This suggests that these women may be less likely to have helping networks that include organized resources such as ministers, church organizations, or church members. On the other hand, African American women who were very religious used sources other than mental health professionals. It is possible that religious women rely more on ministers and other resources generated from their church network for help with their problems. The institution of the Black church has always served as a source of strength, mutual aid, and comfort for Black women in their personal struggles (Caldwell, Greene, & Billingsley, 1994; Murray & Harrison, 1981; Taylor, 1986c; Taylor & Chatters, 1988).

An interesting culturally based methodological comment can be made about the lack of significance in the social support variables in the face of finding significance for religiosity. If our study had chosen, as most studies have, to only measure social support, it would have appeared that social support had little to do with the seeking of mental health services. Yet when religiosity is included, which is a different but culturally understandable way to assess sources of support, particularly for African American women for whom the church and its extended network structure are culturally permissible places to seek help for emotional problems, we learn that religion may be a moderator of mental health help seeking.

Learning that those Black women who identify themselves as religious tend not to be the ones seeking services for serious emotional problems may be a clue to successful prevention strategies. In the prevention of serious mental illness in African American women, it may be important to consider the role of community-based resources rather than confining ourselves to individually oriented private or community mental health center treatment strategies. In Comas-Diaz's (1992) prediction of the shape of psychological services for ethnic minorities in the future, coping through reliance on faith and prayer will be encouraged, coupled with a sense that normative self-development includes the spiritual. In a commentary on the future of mental health services for ethnic minorities in the future, Mays and Albee (1992) see the traditional private practice mode as one infrequently used for the delivery of mental health services in favor of work sites, home, schools, churches, and other commonplace everyday settings.

Several factors investigated in this study proved not to be significantly related to the type of mental health services used by Black women. Family or personal income, education, availability of social support, and satisfaction with services received were not associated with the type of professional helper selected by these women. A major limitation of our study was that, although our analyses were based on a national probability sample, less than 75 women had used professional mental health services, thereby restricting our analytic procedures to bivariate analyses. It is not clear whether using a larger sample would result in more significant relationships. It is also not clear from our findings whether the significant relationships found might be explained by socioeconomic factors such as income or education, as other studies have suggested. Multivariate analyses that incorporate sociodemographics as well as sociocultural variables are necessary in future studies to understand adequately the complex relationships among these variables for African American women.

However, one must be cautious about the reliance on sociodemographics alone in predicting patterns of service utilization of Blacks in that studies indicate demographics are less reliable for African American patterns than for Whites (Dawkins et al., 1979; Griffith, 1985). Our study indicated that age, region, and religiosity are better predictors for Black women. These particular variables may yield better prediction because of their cultural-ethnic relevance. Religion has always functioned as an important coping mechanism for Blacks (Neighbors et al., 1983). Furthermore, women living in the South, in contrast to many other regions, may have retained more indigenous health care beliefs that may interfere with their seeking professional help.

One conclusion that can be drawn from our results is that African American women underuse professional mental health services and, therefore, do not seek help for their emotional problems, except when their problems become very severe. This conclusion is often reached erroneously by some health service researchers who overlook other sources of professional or informal help that African American women perceive as appropriate starting points for problem solving.

First, it is important to recognize that patterns of mental health service utilization by African American women are complex. Although we do know several variables, such as education, income, availability of third-party payment sources, age, and others, that are influential in the choices of treatment, the mixed picture in several utilization studies makes it clear that other factors are at work. The results of our study call for the inclusion of culturally based factors such as religion and other well-thought-out measures that take into account the unique life experiences, beliefs, and values of African American women.

Recent studies have turned their attention toward the role that naturally occurring social support networks and self-help activities play in help-seeking patterns and individual well-being (Griffith, 1985; Mays, 1985, 1995). A growing body of data suggests that an individual's social support network buffers stress and provides instrumental support that lessens the need for professional mental health care (for a review, see Mitchell & Trickett, 1980). Self-help and common-concern groups are increasing among Black women as sources of help for coping with personal problems (Mays, 1985, 1995).

Second, mental health services research that will distinguish between events amenable to naturally occurring community support systems or other sources of professional help and those conditions for which Black women are more likely to need professional intervention is greatly needed. Third, research that would clarify the types of problems that Black women define as severe enough to seek professional treatment would greatly enhance the planning of mental health service delivery and aid in training sensitive minority and nonminority mental health service providers. Fourth, mental health services, congruent with the needs and cultural patterns of Black women, are more likely to be successful in their goal of effectively responding to their psychological needs. Comas-Diaz (1992) points out that successful mental health services of the future will need to adapt themselves to the use of integrative and comprehensive frameworks that encompass the realities of the everyday lives of Black women and other minorities. Finally, mental health services that incorporate realities such as the importance of racial-ethnic identity in choosing therapists, the importance of religion, and sensitivity to the relationship between racism and discrimination to ill health (Cochran & Mays, 1994; Comas-Diaz, 1992; Mays, 1995; Mays et al., 1996) will improve help seeking and mental health service use for mental health problems (Campinha-Bacote, 1991) for African American women as well as for other minorities.

Note

1. The terms *African American* and *Black* are used interchangeably throughout this chapter.

12

The Police: A Reluctant Social Service Agency in the African American Community

Patricia A. Washington

The literature on how African Americans view the police contains contradictory results and interpretations. Some studies suggest that African Americans
hold extremely negative attitudes toward law enforcement (Campbell &
Schuman, 1969; Cooper, 1980; Michigan State University, 1967; Radelet,
1973; U.S. Department of Justice, 1979; U.S. National Advisory Committee
on Civil Disorder, 1968; Wallach & Jackson, 1973). Studies on the nonenforcement activities of the police reviewed by Regulus, Taylor, and Jackson
(1986) suggest, however, that African American hostility toward the police
may be overstated (Burnett, Carr, Sinapi, & Taylor, 1976; Carr, 1979; Scott,
1975). In fact, much of the literature on the nonenforcement activities of
police is not consistent with the position that blacks hold negative attitudes
toward law enforcement. Findings from the Regulus et al. (1986) analysis
suggest that the overestimation of black hostility may be the result of the
tendency to downplay variations in the size and strength of black-white
differences in attitudes toward the police. It might also be the result of a
tendency to ignore the proportion of African Americans holding favorable
attitudes toward police.

This chapter investigates the use of police assistance by members of the
black community as a help resource during stressful situations. This inquiry

was based on crisis theory, which states that an individual undergoing a stressful event discovers that former coping mechanisms are no longer effective. This reduced ability to cope results in feelings of vulnerability that, in turn, trigger help-seeking behavior (Mechanic, 1978; Roughman & Hagerty, 1975). The primary assumption of this chapter is that African Americans who experience psychological distress as a result of threats to themselves or members of their family are likely to request assistance from the police after exhausting other available resources. The present analysis is unique because it is the only national study available that involves a cross section of African American adults who requested police assistance for a variety of situations. It is also significant that a number of requests for police assistance do not involve matters of law (Bittner, 1974; Goldstein, 1979; Guyot, 1991; Hartjen, 1978; Reiss, 1977; Scott, 1975; Wilson, 1968).

Regulus et al.'s (1986) review of the nonenforcement activities of the police within black communities suggested that satisfaction with police did not differ for blacks and whites. Furthermore, their study provided evidence of "substantial support for the police among the majority of blacks" (p. 2). The inclusion of factors such as age, experience with police, and crime proved to be critical in determining which members of the black community held less than favorable attitudes toward the police. Ritchey-Mann (1993), however, reached a somewhat different conclusion after reviewing a different set of writings (Bayley & Mendelsohn, 1969; Georges-Abeyie, 1984) from Regulus et al. (1986). Specifically, Ritchey-Mann concluded that the attitude of many African Americans toward the police has been that of distrust and hostility. According to Ritchey-Mann, these attitudes are based on perceived discriminatory behaviors of the police toward blacks and have contributed to animosity and disrespect for police officers among African Americans (p. 138).

A number of factors may be used to explain these contradictory interpretations. Police officers are often the only community resources available 24 hours a day, 7 days a week. They are required to respond to requests for assistance in crisis situations. Police officers respond to what they consider to be routine requests for assistance with standardized responses to resolve the perceived crisis. These routine behaviors sometimes require force or activities that disrupt the kinship-friendship network of those who requested assistance. Assistance that results in a resolution that is less than satisfactory may create feelings of hostility toward police officers (Bittner, 1974; Reiss, 1977). Regulus et al. (1986) noted this phenomenon in their study:

> Public perceptions are sensitive to these different dimensions of police activities, and attitudes may be held separately and independently for each. Further, the extent to which attitudes regarding any particular dimension of police performance are favorable or unfavorable is influenced by . . . quality of their performance . . . structurally based experience and status predispositions of the public. (p. 4)

In other words, routine police activities may be regarded as harassment or unauthorized intervention even though police assistance has been requested by African Americans in crisis. These factors must be taken into consideration when reviewing the literature pertaining to attitudes toward the police.

The assumption of an unfavorable or hostile attitude toward the police is important for this chapter because it suggests that African Americans would be reluctant to request police assistance. A negative attitude toward the police also supports the idea that African Americans in distress will ask for help from police only after exhausting the resources of their informal network. The purpose of this chapter is to present findings on requesting police assistance from a nationally representative sample of African Americans. These findings create a profile of those most likely to request police assistance during periods of distress. The role of the informal referral system in the decision to request nonenforcement assistance from the police is also examined.

Measures and Methods

The help-seeking section of the National Survey of Black Americans (NSBA) questionnaire was used to obtain information on police assistance. The independent variables include measures of problem type, experience with the police, assistance from the informal network, and sociodemographic variables. Respondents were asked whether they experienced an event that had caused them a significant amount of stress and, if so, the nature of the problem. Respondents with problems were also asked if they had sought assistance from their informal network (family, friends, neighbors, or coworkers) and whether they had contacted the police or any other formal systems for help. Those who contacted the police were asked who initiated the contact and what services were provided. These variables were selected to focus on one stressful life event and to obtain baseline data on the respondents' use of the police in dealing with their problems.

It is important to note that the analysis takes into consideration the fact that requests for police assistance do not occur in a vacuum. Respondents often requested assistance from family, friends, or social service-mental health professionals in addition to assistance from the police. Thus, qualitative techniques were also used along with quantitative analyses to further explore how the respondents used the police. This involved reading the verbatim responses to selected open-ended questions from the NSBA questionnaires. The questionnaires of all 43 respondent police users were explored. Of these, 29 described interpersonal problems and were looked at in more depth. Because this is a labor-intensive and time-consuming process, it was decided to limit the presentation of these results to respondents with interpersonal problems. This method was used to specify the nature of the personal problems that respondents stated and the actual experiences that they had with the police. It also provided further insight into whether informal network help and formal system help seeking were linked.[1]

Results

Sociodemographics and Police Involvement

Of respondents who reported experiencing a stressful event, 30% ($n = 632$) sought assistance from formal systems (hospital emergency rooms, mental health agencies, social service agencies, police, etc.). Seven percent (43 people) of those who sought professional help requested police assistance. Table 12.1 reveals that respondents who requested police help were similar to those who sought other sources of formal help. Family income was evenly distributed across both groups of help seekers. The main conclusion drawn from Table 12.1 is that police users do not differ much demographically from users of other formal helping systems.

There was, however, a statistically significant relationship between the type of personal problem experienced by respondents and the type of formal help consulted. Table 12.2 shows that although 39% of those who used other formal systems sought help for interpersonal problems, 76% of those who contacted the police did so for that reason. Only 3% of the police users contacted police because

Table 12.1 Sociodemographic Characteristics of Police Users and Users of Other Formal Systems

	Formal Systems			
	Police		Other Formal Systems	
Demographics	%	N	%	N
Gender				
Women	74.4	32	81.3	478
Men	25.6	11	18.7	110
Age				
18-34	44.2	19	41.5	244
35-54	41.9	18	34.7	204
55+	13.9	6	23.8	140
Education				
0-11 years	51.2	22	41.8	244
12 years	32.6	14	28.6	167
13-15 years	11.5	5	18.5	108
16 years or more	4.7	2	11.1	65
Total household income				
< $5, 000	25.6	11	24.2	142
$5,000-$9,999	23.3	10	27.7	163
$10,000-$19,999	30.2	13	27.9	164
$20,000+	20.9	9	20.2	119
Employment status				
Working	55.8	24	50.7	298
Not working	44.2	19	49.3	290
Marital status				
Married	25.6	11	35.7	209
Not married	74.4	32	64.3	276
Urban/rural				
Urban	81.4	25	82.5	485
Rural	18.6	8	17.5	103

of physical health problems, which was a sharp contrast to how problem type was distributed for respondents who sought help from other formal sources; physical health problems were 23% of that distribution. Similarly, there were no emotional problems among users of the police, but emotional difficulties accounted for 10.5% of the people using other formal systems. Rates of use for death and economic problems were roughly similar for both groups. In summary, African Americans seeking the help of police were much more likely than other users of professional help to do so because of interpersonal problems. This issue will be explored in greater depth later in the chapter.

Table 12.2 Problem Type and Use of Formal Help Sources

Problem Type	Formal Systems			
	Police		Other Formal Systems	
	%	N	%	N
Physical	2.6	1	23.2	128
Interpersonal/family	76.3	29	39.1	216
Emotional	—	—	10.5	58
Death	5.3	2	7.8	43
Economic	15.8	6	19.4	107

NOTE: $\chi^2 (4) = 16.63, p < .05$.

Table 12.3 focuses on sources of referral among police users. More than half (68.4%) of those requesting police assistance initiated the contact themselves. A little more than one quarter (26.3%) were referred by their informal network, and very few (5%) were referred by a member of the formal system. The reactions of the police to requests for assistance showed that most help seekers (76%) received some type of help—either advice (20%) or having the police take action (56%).

Table 12.4 explores the relationship between the referral source and the type of assistance offered by the police and type of assistance provided by police. The tendency for the police to take specific action on behalf of respondents was not substantially influenced by referral source. The majority of the self-referrals (52%) and informal referrals (70%) received specific action by the police in response to their requests for assistance.[2] Although these data provide insight into the various interactions between African American respondents and the police, the reader should be cautious in overgeneralizing these data because of the small sample size.

Use of Informal Networks

In addition to contacting the police, the vast majority of these respondents (93%) sought assistance from members of their informal networks (Table 12.5). In fact, 83% contacted two or more members of their informal networks. These data are consistent with the assumption that police contact is initiated only after the respondents and their informal helpers are unable to resolve the problem satisfactorily. In addition to seeking the assistance of family, friends, and coworkers, Table 12.5 also reveals that police users made multiple use of

Table 12.3 Referral Source and Assistance by Police

	%	N
Source of referral		
Self	68.4	26
Informal	26.3	10
Formal	5.3	2
Total	100.0	38
Assistance provided by police		
Advice	19.5	8
Action	56.1	23
No help	24.4	10
Total	100.0	41

Table 12.4 Source of Referral by Assistance Provided (*N* = 37)

	Assistance Provided						
	Advice		Action		No Help		Total
Source of Referral	%	N	%	N	%	N	N
Self	28	7	52	13	20	5	25
Informal	10	1	70	7	20	2	10
Formal	0	0	50	1	50	1	2

formal contacts (70% contacted two or more formal helpers)—for example, ministers, lawyers, social service agencies, and mental health counselors.

The Role of Informal Helpers

Table 12.5 clearly documented the importance of the informal network among people who eventually called on the police for help. As a result, the role of informal helpers in dealing with interpersonal problems was further explored.[3] When the specific source of informal help was investigated, it became clear that respondents limited their requests for informal help almost exclusively to other family members. This is especially the case for the first two interpersonal contacts.[4] Twenty-seven of 29 people (93%) with interpersonal problems contacted at least one informal helper, and 86% (25 people) of those helpers were family members. Among the 24 people who went on to make a second informal contact, 83% (20 people) went to family members.

Table 12.5 Contact With Formal and Informal Networks Among Respondents Who Used Police

| | Networks | | | |
| | Formal System | | Informal System | |
Number Contacted	%	N	%	N
None	0.0	0	7.1	3
One	30.2	13	9.5	4
Two	27.9	12	16.7	7
Three	16.3	7	16.7	7
Four	25.6	11	21.4	9
Five	—[a]		28.6	12
Total	100.0	43	100.0	42

a. Only four mentions were allowed for formal help.

Twenty people made a third informal contact, and it is here that people begin turning to friends, neighbors, and coworkers (nonkin) for help. The proportion of family contacted for help drops to 60% when 3 people were consulted and drops again to 33% among the 15 people who contacted a fourth member of their informal network. There were only 8 people with an interpersonal problem who contacted a fifth informal helper and 6 of them talked to a friend or coworker.

Another trend among these respondents was the degree of reciprocity involved in informal help seeking. For each informal helper contacted, respondents were asked, "Has this person ever come to you to talk about a similar problem?" Interestingly, many of them (48%) said that they had indeed been contacted previously for help with a similar problem by the person they were now contacting. When asked about additional informal helpers, 50% of the 24 people who contacted a second helper, 75% of the 20 people who went to three helpers, 71% of the 14 who used four helpers, and 50% of the 4 who used five helpers had been previously contacted for help with a similar problem.

Further Exploration of Problem Type and Police Use

These findings are provocative because they do not fit with the popular notion that African Americans have a negative attitude toward the police that prevents them from seeking police help in a time of need. These results raise additional questions concerning the exact nature of the respondents' personal problems, particularly the interpersonal difficulties, and their help experiences with informal and formal networks that motivate them to turn to the police for assistance. One cannot help but wonder what types of interpersonal disagreements these were and why they could not be resolved through other means of conflict resolution. To answer these questions, the actual responses of the respondents were analyzed. Although all of the 43 police users' responses were analyzed, only those with interpersonal difficulties will be discussed here primarily because these problems play such a prominent role in the use of police.

Of the 29 people who experienced interpersonal problems, 22 were women. Of these 22 women, 13 (59%) indicated some type of disagreement with a boyfriend or husband with references to divorce or separation being most frequent. For example, one woman stated,

> A man I broke up with was trying to kill me. He broke windows out of the house, threatened me, said he'd shoot my son. I had him arrested and he bailed out of jail. My son was going to kill him. It was more than I could handle. I moved out for a while with a friend.

Of the 13 women who indicated problems with a boyfriend or husband, 7 (54%) were from 18 to 34 years of age, 4 (31%) were from 35 to 54 years of age, and 2 (15%) were over 55 years old. In terms of family income, 5 (42%) were in the lower-income group (below $10,000), 7 (58%) were in the upper-income group (above $10,000), and one woman did not report her income. All 13 women resided in urban areas.

This profile of police users for interpersonal problems mirrors that of the police users regardless of problem type: Most of them were younger women living in urban areas. Women with higher incomes, however, were slightly more likely to use police for marital or romantic relationship problems than women with lower incomes, although this trend is not statistically significant because of the very small sample size. Use of police help was not, however, restricted exclusively to women; two men also stated problems with their wives.

There were also other kinds of interpersonal problems seen in this group of police users. Four people (two women and two men) stated having "family problems": One woman had a dispute with a neighbor, a man dissolved a business partnership, one man's car was damaged while he was in his sister's car, and a woman's brother was arrested and sent to prison. There were six people who said that their problems involved their children, particularly their children's negative behavior toward them and others. There was one woman who had problems with both her children and her husband.

An interesting trend occurred in analyzing how informal network help may have led to decisions to use the police as a resource. The most common kinds of help received from the informal network were advice, problem solving, and general emotional support. Many respondents stated that their families and friends "listened," "prayed," or "gave advice" while they were dealing with their problem(s). Some members of the respondents' informal network, however, also seemed to influence their decision to seek police help either directly by encouraging them to do so or indirectly by helping to make their police contacts more beneficial. In one case, the neighbor of a middle-aged woman helped by speaking to the police on the respondent's behalf, "She witnessed [this incident] . . . and filed [an] affidavit with police." In another case, a middle-aged woman who referred herself to the police stated that "when I came to Detroit, people told me that the police would help if your husband caused you trouble."[5] These two examples lend support to a possible link between obtaining and being satisfied with informal help and the decision to approach police and other formal systems for assistance.

The kind of help that the police provided was more discernible through reading the actual responses. As was reported in Table 12.3, 20% of all police users, regardless of problem type, received advice, whereas 56% received direct action from the police. Among the users with interpersonal problems, the type of action they described was not in the form of arrests. In several cases, the police instead either protected the individuals seeking help or removed troublesome individuals from the situation and "calmed them down."

Summary and Conclusion

Although there is literature to suggest that negative attitudes deter blacks from using the police, the results of this study support the finding that blacks do use police services to deal with personal problems, with the amount of use differing according to problem type. This evidence was gained through both quantitative and qualitative approaches in analysis. The majority of the respondents requesting police assistance experienced interpersonal problems.

These respondents were not social isolates—they sought police assistance only after or while seeking assistance from their informal networks or social service agencies. Most contacts with the police resulted in receiving some assistance in the form of advice, referral, or some other action.

Many police users, especially those seeking help for interpersonal problems, were younger women living in urban areas. Women appear to use police more for protection (both for themselves and members of their families) than to seek punishment of people. There were a few instances in which women requested arrest warrants from the police; this type of request, however, was in the minority. Interpersonal problems were more likely to require nonenforcement police assistance, such as mediation or counseling, than the other types of problems.

The results of this study provide a descriptive profile of how blacks request police assistance. Information on types of problems, the method of initiating police contact, and the referral advice offered by informal network members were incorporated into the analyses. The findings are important because of their contribution to a deeper understanding of how and why African Americans seek police assistance; they also provide implications for understanding other aspects of the relationship between blacks and the police.

The results of this chapter are of practical importance because they can be used by professionals in other disciplines. Similarities in the problem types and demographics of police users and users of other formal systems should be noted especially by mental health professionals. In some cases, the police seemed to provide services in a manner that should be the province of mental health or other human service professionals—the police may have been more accessible to a more "needy" group. Unfortunately, for many low-income African Americans, the police are the only available 24-hour crisis intervention entity that provides service on request and that has little fear of entering the community (Woolf & Rudman, 1977).

Finally, even though there are many types of personal problems, the emphasis in any investigation of this issue should be on interpersonal problems. The three respondents who were recoded into the interpersonal category are good examples of this. Even though the problems stemmed from death-related, physical, and business-related economic difficulties, they fundamentally involved tense situations with family or coworkers, and this may have increased the necessity of contacting the police for help. Furthermore, the fact that one woman had both marital problems and difficulties with her children provides even more support for further explorations into the nature and effects of interpersonal problems. This study only begins to examine the complex relationship that exists between blacks requesting police assistance and the officers called on to provide that assistance.

Future research on this topic should be wary of the limitations of the present analysis. The very small size of the sample (43) must be taken into account. Although there were some interesting findings, there were few statistically significant results. Obviously, much more research is needed to explore why respondents chose to contact the police the way they did, when they did, and whether they were directly motivated to do so by a friend or family member. Questions worth examining in future analyses should include whether the police were contacted first or last among formal and informal network resources. It is our intention to continue researching this subject, and we hope the issues addressed in this chapter will stimulate others to examine this phenomenon. The issues and relationships that influence African Americans to seek police assistance are important ones, especially for those interested in the interaction between minorities, mental health, and the criminal justice system.

Notes

1. The qualitative analysis uncovered three respondents whose problems, although not originally coded as "interpersonal," made explicit reference to difficulties with significant others. These cases consisted of a woman who had an illness that caused marital problems, a woman who referred to her mother dying and her husband being "on the verge of separating," and a man who talked of the "dishonesty" of a partner and the "breakup" of that union. These respondents were originally coded as having physical, death, and business problems, respectively. For the purposes of this study, they were recoded as having interpersonal problems.

2. There were only two formal referrals: One respondent felt that the police were of no help and the other indicated that the officers had taken action on his or her behalf.

3. Specific data analysis runs for this section are available from the editors.

4. Respondents were allowed to mention up to five informal helpers. Although they were not explicitly instructed to mention these helpers in the order they were contacted, it is likely that respondents did indeed recall these helpers in chronological order.

5. Although this person did not state that these "people" were in her informal network, it is likely that friends, neighbors, and coworkers would have advised her to seek police help than her doctor or lawyer. It is also possible, however, that her minister could have given her this advice.

13

Changes in African American Resources and Mental Health
1979 to 1992

James S. Jackson
Harold W. Neighbors

The chapters in this volume have focused on adult African American mental health, including physical and psychological well-being, coping resources, coping, and help-seeking. The data used were from 1979-1980. We have emphasized in this volume that African Americans are disproportionately exposed to environmental and social conditions considered to be important risk factors for mental dysfunction, but they exhibit prevalence rates of serious mental disorders that are similar to whites (Kessler et al., 1994; Williams, 1995). These findings emphasize, we believe, the need for concerted attention to the material conditions, cultural strengths, and psychological health-enhancing resources that provide protection from these negative risk factors. Much of the prior race-related mental health research has focused only on pathology and the deficits of blacks. We have always believed that a myopic attention to black problems and inadequacies provides a distorted view of the struggles and strengths of individuals and groups in an oppressed community (Small, 1994; Williams, 1995).

The research reported in this volume has tied together distinct and disparate literatures to assess the contributions of psychosocial factors to the mental health of African American adults. This integrative approach is essential to understanding the processes by which psychosocial factors affect health status. Most prior research has studied different types of health-enhancing resources in isolation. This has created gaps and paradoxes in our knowledge base. It is known, for example, that social relationships, religiosity, self-esteem, and perceptions of mastery and control may all affect the psychological well-being of blacks (Jones, 1992), but it is not understood how these factors relate to each other and how they combine to affect the relationship between stress and mental health.

We suggested in the beginning of this book that previous research had not identified what types, amounts, and aspects of psychosocial resources are most consequential for mental health among African Americans (Jones, 1992). For example, the mechanisms and processes by which religion affects psychological well-being are unknown (Williams & House, 1991). Likewise, there has been some dispute as to whether psychosocial resources act to (a) insulate people from exposure to circumstances that threaten health, (b) "buffer" them from the adverse consequences of such circumstances to which they have been exposed, or (c) promote health and well-being by meeting basic needs for social integration and making sense out of one's world (Antonucci & Jackson, 1990). The mechanisms and processes through which psychosocial factors produce these types of effects have not been identified (Antonucci & Jackson, 1987; Jones, 1992). In the case of the buffering hypothesis, for example, we do not know if social support modifies the perceptions of stress, facilitates coping and adaptation, or enhances bodily resistance.

The race comparison paradigm has been the central and dominant focus of most of the research on black mental health (Jackson, Neighbors, & Gurin, 1986). In this framework, the mental health status of the white population is used as a standard of comparison for the mental health of the African American population. The overreliance of epidemiologic studies on a race-comparative paradigm masks the heterogeneity of the black population. African Americans are not a monolithic group, and an approach that identifies the variations within the population can facilitate the identification of risk factors associated with illness and promotive factors associated with well-being. This level of detail could provide etiologic clues and improved targeting of effective intervention and prevention efforts.

Addressing these concerns, the reviews and analyses in this book contribute a great deal to our understanding of factors related to mental health and disorders in African American populations during a significant historical period. Importantly, these results suggest a prominent role of material well-being (Chapter 3, for example) while explicating the role that formal and informal association may play in life satisfactions and dissatisfactions. The numerous analyses in the book also point to gender differences in the experiences and expression of disorder and the ways that marriage and nonmarriage may serve different buffering functions. The important contributions of coping capacity and informal assistance for African Americans is clearly documented, as is a more contextualized view of how public agencies, such as the police and formal speciality mental health professionals, may play complex roles in the lives of blacks.

Many of the relationships found in this book, we expect, are enduring and have continuing relevance. However, the life course model that has been a large part of our thinking (Jackson, 1993) dictates that historical time and events should play a major role in the nature of individual and group responses of African Americans. The purpose of this final chapter is to bring together the basic themes of the volume into a coherent focus—one that examines the continuities and discontinuities over the period 1979-1980 to 1992.

Much of our recent work is based on the 13-year (1979 to 1992), four-wave National Survey of Black Americans (NSBA) panel study (Jackson et al., 1996). Using data from this study, we are investigating changes over time in the nature of mental health problems and reported receipt of mental health services among different age segments of the African American population. Some of our earlier work (e.g., Neighbors & Jackson, 1984) pointed to an important role of the patterns of informal and formal help among African Americans in the receipt of help for serious personal problems. We concluded that the informal network may serve as an important facilitating mechanism for the entry of African Americans into the professional network of mental health services. In a recent article (Jackson & Wolford, 1992), we noted that over a 7-year interval from 1979-1980 to 1987 there was a precipitous drop, especially among older age groups, in the report of informal help for serious problems. We suggested that the loss of roles among older age groups, geographical dispersion, reduction in the size of potential informal helping networks, and a decline in financial resources may have contributed to the decrease in informal assistance for serious personal problems.

Mental Health Over the Life Course

A major focus of our research (e.g., Jackson, Antonucci, & Gibson, 1995) has been on mental and physical health and functioning, stress, internal and external coping capacities, and adaptations of blacks at various ages, points in the individual life span, and role positions (e.g., youth, parents, workers, retirees, etc.). This interest has been heightened by the progressive aging of the original NSBA sample as we follow the cohort. Analyses in this volume of the original NSBA 1979-1980 data suggest differences in exposure to stressors, responses to these stressors, and consequent adaptations that may be linked to age group, life cycle stage, and position in the social structure.

We also found differences due to age and life cycle stage in the ways in which internal and external resources, individual coping strategies, sense of personal efficacy, self-esteem, informal support, and "religiosity" buffer or insulate against stressful conditions (Antonucci & Jackson, 1987; Gibson & Jackson, 1987; Kasl & Berkman,1981; Langer, 1981; Rodin, 1986; Satariano & Syme, 1981). Informal support, in fact, may operate differently on the relationship between stress and effective functioning for blacks at different ages (Jackson & Wolford, 1992).

Age and aging-related processes may also change the strength of the ties between physical and mental health. For example, Gibson (1986) reported that stress seems to play less of a role in the physical health of younger and very old blacks than in the health of blacks aged 65 to 74. Perhaps not so coincidentally, the death rate from stress-related diseases is also high during these years for blacks. Age and life cycle stage may also make a difference in the epidemiology of mental health and mental disorders (Jackson, Antonucci, & Gibson, 1990; Kahana & Kahana, 1982; LaRue, Dessonville, & Jarvik, 1985).

We have suggested that age group, aging, and cohort membership have independent and interactive influences on the mental health status of blacks and affect stress and adaptation responses (Gibson, 1986). Stress and adaptation responses, in fact, could also vary at different ages or times in the life course, among different cohorts, and in different sociohistorical periods. Thus, the mental health problems of American blacks of all ages have to be understood within changing historical, political, social, and economic contexts because mental health is influenced by one's interaction with the social environment (Jackson, 1988; Jackson et al., 1996; Riley, 1994). The mental illness of ethnic and racial minorities must be examined using theoretical models that take a life course perspective (Gibson & Jackson, 1987; Jackson & Wolford, 1992; Jackson et al., 1990).

Over this period, socioenvironmental problems such as poverty, joblessness, single-parent households, and other decrements in the material quality of life of African Americans have increased (Adams, 1996; Jackson & Adams, 1992; Jaynes & Williams, 1989; National Heart, Lung, and Blood Institute [NHBLI], 1995; Small, 1994). It is important to remember that slavery, Jim Crow, and de facto segregation, which ended less than 30 years ago, have created a sort of pseudoimmigrant status, especially in material resources, for generations of black Americans. The United States passed its last major civil rights bill in 1965, 30 years ago, and only one generation of black Americans has reached workforce age with this bill as a historical fact rather than as part of their life experience. In addition, because Americans of African descent have little in the way of acquired wealth (Small, 1994; Williams & Collins, 1995), each succeeding generation that comes to age, does so with an absence of inherited resources. Blacks, unlike many "true" immigrant groups, thus are historically acculturated in the United States on many social, cultural, and language dimensions but have to struggle in each succeeding generation from a base of zero material resources. In many ways, it places African Americans behind some of the more recent external groups that have immigrated to the United States. The lack of material resources, increased competition for job opportunities and housing, and the psychological consequences of observing new immigrant groups making significant progress can be debilitating to the motivation and expectation of new generations of African Americans.

By 2020, the American population will include 44 million African Americans and 47 million Hispanic Americans. Both groups on average will be younger than the white population. During the 1990s, 90% of the net additions to the workforce will be nonminority women, members of racial and ethnic minorities, and new immigrants. By the turn of the century, it is estimated that as many as one third of a 140-million-member workforce will be nonwhite. By the mid-1990s, it is estimated that there will be 3 workers for each retiree and 1 of 3 will be a member of a minority group. By the year 2000, 1 of 3 college-aged persons will be a person of color, and it is estimated that between 40% and 50% of K-12 school-aged children will be African American or Hispanic. Yet, today, the African American population is worse off than whites on almost every social, health, and economic indicator—infant mortality, crude death rates, health care, wealth and income, housing stock, and poverty (Danziger & Gottschalk, 1995).

Although none would deny that improvements have occurred during this century, ethnic and racial minorities continue to have higher high school dropout rates, lower college participation rates, higher college attrition rates, and lower bachelor degree attainment rates. The failure to gain educational resources can have profound influences on the ability of individuals from African American and other racial and ethnic groups to capitalize on changes in the economy or to respond to other unexpected opportunities.

In sum, we examine in this final chapter the relationships of social, economic, and demographic factors to the changes in status of significant personal problems, stress and coping, and mental health among black Americans during a significant historical period. We use data from the NSBA (Jackson et al., 1996; Jackson & Wolford, 1992) to examine changes over four waves, from the original data collection in 1979-1980 to the final one in 1992. Over this period, African Americans suffered tremendous structural reversals in socioeconomic and social statuses (Adams, 1996; Jackson & Adams, 1992; Jaynes & Williams, 1989). The data reveal increased deterioration of the family, falling job opportunities and jobs among African American males, increased teen pregnancy and drug-related problems, and deteriorating inner-city neighborhoods (Adams, 1996; Danziger & Gottschalk, 1995; Jackson & Adams, 1992; Jaynes & Williams, 1989). For this reason, and given the predicted negative relationships between social and economic contexts and mental health functioning, we hypothesized that there would be lowered health status, increased reports of problem severity, increased stress, a decrease in available supports, and lowered levels of psychological well-being.

Sample and Analyses

Respondents from the original NSBA were interviewed at four points in time, beginning in 1979-1980. As indicated in Chapter 1, the 1979-1980 face-to-face NSBA survey was based on a national multistage household probability sample of 2,107 self-identified black American adults living in the continental United States. The overall response rate was approximately 67%. Nearly 80% of the sample resided in urban areas, geographical locations that tend to be the most difficult locations for face-to-face interviewing. The 1979-1980 NSBA data collection was followed by three more waves of smaller, yet comprehensive, telephone data collections in 1987-1988, 1988-1989, and 1992. The relatively large number of black Americans in the initial cross-sectional sample, its wide age range (18 to 101 years of age), and the 13-year time span provide a comprehensive base for the panel analyses conducted in this chapter.

Of the original 2,107 Wave 1 respondents, 951 were reinterviewed in 1987 (Wave 2). Of these, 87 refused to participate, 102 were reported to have died, and 134 were too sick to complete the interview. The high rate of attrition at Wave 2 was largely due to an inability to locate many of the cross-sectional respondents; 783 Wave 1 respondents were lost to tracking. Three primary factors contributed to this inability to locate Wave 1 respondents. First, a period of 8 years transpired between Wave 1 and Wave 2 data collections. Second, the initial study was not designed as a panel study, and therefore very limited recontact information was obtained in 1979-1980. Third, over half of the initial 1979-1980 cross-sectional sample were not homeowners and thus were highly mobile. Wolford and Torres (1994) found that home ownership was the main predictor of nonresponse in subsequent waves.

The third wave of data was collected 1 year later, and 793 (84%) of the 951 second-wave respondents were reinterviewed. The fourth wave of data was collected 3 years later; the sample size was 630 respondents. Seven of these respondents were individuals who were interviewed at Wave 2 but not at Wave 3. Thus, the panel data represent 623 respondents over four waves (Jackson et al., 1996).

To avoid possible problems due to changes in sample composition, we restricted the analyses in this chapter to the 623 respondents who participated in all four waves of data collection. In a prior article, we reported on comparisons of the variables used in the analyses between the full cross-sectional and panel samples at the 1980 Wave 1 time (Jackson et al., 1996). The panel sample differed significantly from the full cross-sectional sample on several variables. The panel respondents have a higher income-to-needs ratio (lower poverty), have more years of education, are somewhat younger, are more likely to be female, are more happy, and have fewer health problems, lower health disability, and marginally less psychological distress.

The panel sample represents survivors over the 13-year period. Thus, it was not unexpected to find females, those with higher socioeconomic resources, and those with fewer chronic health conditions to be overrepresented. On the other hand, the panel and cross-sectional samples did not differ significantly in regional distribution, perceptions and experiences of racism, and life satisfaction. Our major concern in the panel analyses was avoiding possible spurious effects due to changes in sample composition over time. Some of the effects of differences in the panel sample, compared to the full cross-sectional sample, were controlled in the multivariate analyses through inclusion of relevant sociodemographic variables. Because the panel sample represents a somewhat better-off group of African Americans, however, our analyses are conservative and may underestimate the extent of the relationships of interest.

We used five sociodemographic variables in these analyses, representing major subgroupings of African Americans: (a) self-reports of total family income grouped into four categories, (b) education measured at Wave 1 by the number of years of education completed and grouped into three categories, (c) marital status collapsed into married versus those who were not married in 1980, (d) age measured by the number of years since birth and grouped into three categories, and (e) gender as interviewer reported in the Wave 1 data collection.

In the multivariate analyses of variance reported in Tables 13.1 to 13.8, we examine the independent effects of each sociodemographic resource variable measured in 1979-1980 on each health outcome (high blood pressure, high environmental stress, high health satisfaction, health problems), coping, and subjective well-being outcomes (high self-esteem, serious problem severity, high happiness, and life satisfaction), while controlling for the influences of the remaining sociodemographic resource factors. The purpose of our analyses was to examine the trajectories of change among African Americans in different status resource (income, marital status, and education) and sociodemographic positions (age and gender) as they aged over the period 1979-1980 to 1992. Several significance tests on these multivariate analyses are reported in each table. For example, in Table 13.1 the first row (Overall) shows the changes in our sample independent of all the sociodemographic factors over the four waves in the percentage of individuals reporting three or more environmental problems. The F ratio at the end of this row is the test of whether this overall change is significant or not.

For each of the sociodemographic factors, we report two significance tests. The first provides a test of whether there are significant average differences between levels of each sociodemographic factor collapsed across the 13-year period. The second (F ratio interaction) provides a test of whether there are differences in the average trajectories of change over the four waves (1979-1980, 1987, 1988-1989, and 1992) among individuals in the different levels of the sociodemographic factors (e.g., the four income levels) across time, controlled for all the other sociodemographic factors.

Table 13.1 Changes in High Number of Environmental Problems From 1979 to 1992, Across Wave 1 Sample Characteristics

Variables	N	%	Wave 1 1979-80 (%)	Wave 2 1987-88 (%)	Wave 3 1988-89 (%)	Wave 4 1992 (%)	F Ratio
Overall	621	100	23.2	28.7	25.3	28.0	3.09*
Income							1.96
$0-$4,999	78	13	26.9	28.2	26.9	28.2	
$5-$9,999	141	23	23.4	32.6	31.2	29.1	
$10-$19,999	194	31	20.1	29.4	20.6	27.8	
$20,000+	208	33	24.5	25.5	25.0	27.4	
F ratio interaction							0.82
Education							1.51
No high school diploma	191	31	18.3	25.7	25.7	25.7	
High school diploma	214	34	22.9	28.5	22.4	25.7	
Some college	216	35	27.8	31.5	27.8	32.4	
F ratio interaction							0.60
Marital status							0.06
Not married	314	51	24.8	30.9	27.1	29.0	
Married	307	49	21.5	26.4	23.5	27.0	
F ratio interaction							0.14
Age							22.53**
18-34	235	38	27.2	38.3	34.0	39.1	
35-54	254	41	25.2	29.1	24.0	24.0	
55+	132	21	12.1	10.6	10.6	15.9	
F ratio interaction							2.04+
Gender							3.54+
Male	195	31	20.5	19.0	20.0	28.7	
Female	426	69	24.4	33.1	27.7	27.7	
F ratio interaction							4.25**

+$p < .10$; *$p < .05$; **$p < .01$.

Findings and Discussion

Environmental Problems

An index was constructed from reports of problems during the previous month in several domains of life (health, money, job, family, neighbors, crime, children, police, love life, and racist treatment [treated badly because of race]). Table 13.1 shows a significant increase for the total population (23.2% in 1979-1980 to 28.0% in 1992) of those reporting having three or more of these problems. Although not statistically significant, on average over the 13 years, those of higher income reported fewer problems, whereas those of higher education tended to report more problems. No significant effects were found for marital status. However, over the period, there was a tendency for a slightly higher number of those not married in 1979-1980 to report consistently having more problems at each point of data collection. Younger blacks reported more environmentally stressful events and over time showed a larger proportionate increase than older blacks. We propose that younger blacks are more likely to be in work and social situations and thus are exposed to more potentially stressful events than are older blacks (Jackson, 1993). Overall, women reported more stressful events than men. There was a tendency over time for males to report having more stressful events in 1992 than in 1979-1980, with the largest increase occurring between 1988-1989 (20.0%) and 1992 (28.7%). Women, on the other hand, showed a curvilinear relationship. The largest increase in problems reported occurred between 1979-1980 and 1987 (24.4% to 33.1%) and then tapered off.

Health

We examined three indicators of health status changes over the period 1980 to 1992. As indicated earlier, during this period, African Americans continue to show significantly poorer health than the general population (NHBLI, 1995).

High Blood Pressure. High blood pressure is both an outcome and an important factor implicated in a large number of other health disorders. Recent research has pointed to the negative influences of racism and discrimination on blood pressure reactivity (Jackson et al., 1996). As shown in Table 13.2, the population overall showed a significant increase in doctor-reported high blood pressure over the period. An adjustment for all the demographic factors

Table 13.2 Changes in Doctor-Reported High Blood Pressure From 1979 to 1992, Across Wave 1 Sample Characteristics

Variables	N	%	Wave 1 1979-80 (%)	Wave 2 1987-88 (%)	Wave 3 1988-89 (%)	Wave 4 1992 (%)	F Ratio
Overall	618	100	27.0	37.7	30.7	37.1	15.95**
Income							1.42
$0-$4,999	78	13	41.0	46.2	38.5	47.4	
$5-$9,999	138	22	31.9	46.4	34.1	41.3	
$10-$19,999	193	32	25.9	37.8	32.6	37.8	
$20,000+	209	34	19.6	28.7	23.9	29.7	
F ratio interaction							0.65
Education							0.16
No high school diploma	189	31	37.0	50.3	37.6	46.6	
High school diploma	212	34	25.0	35.8	33.0	33.5	
Some college	217	35	20.3	28.6	22.6	32.3	
F ratio interaction							1.66
Marital status							0.88
Not married	311	50	29.9	37.3	28.6	35.7	
Married	307	50	24.1	38.1	32.9	38.4	
F ratio interaction							3.22*
Age							41.90**
18-34	235	38	9.4	17.9	15.7	19.6	
35-54	251	41	31.9	45.0	36.3	44.6	
55+	132	21	49.2	59.1	47.0	53.8	
F ratio interaction							1.39
Gender							5.89*
Male	192	31	19.8	35.4	25.5	27.1	
Female	426	69	30.3	38.7	33.1	41.5	
F ratio interaction							3.10*

$*p < .05; **p < .01.$

revealed a 10% increase in the proportion of black Americans indicating a doctor-reported problem with elevated blood pressure. Although at every data point, lower income and lower education were linked to slightly higher percentages of reports, the increase was fairly uniform over different income and education groups, and there were no significant differential effects over time. There were no average marital status differences. Those who were married in 1979-1980, however, showed a larger increase (24.1% in 1979-1980 to 38.4% in 1992) over time than those who were not married (29.9% in 1979-1980 to 35.7% in 1992). As might be expected, overall, the two older age groups were more likely to report high blood pressure than the youngest age group. Although there were increased reports among all age groups, the relative ordering remained the same at each of the four waves. The lack of a significant interaction effect indicated that this effect was uniform across all three of the large age groupings. Because the entire sample aged over the period, the average age of those in the younger age category is higher at the end of the period (1992) than it was in 1979-1980. This undoubtedly accounted for the increased percentage (from 9.4% to 19.6%) of those reporting having high blood pressure within the younger age group. Gender differences were large, with females being significantly more likely than men at each year of measurement to report having high blood pressure during this period. The significant interaction effect ($F = 3.10$, $p < .05$) indicated that the increase over time for females is greater than the change for males.

Health Satisfaction. As shown in Table 13.3, for the entire sample, the decrement in individuals reporting high health satisfaction was large (52% in 1979-1980 and 39.1% in 1992). In general, regardless of age, income, education, marital status, and gender, African Americans are less likely over this period to report having high health satisfaction. There were no average differences by income, education, marital status, or gender. Those in the younger age group, however, showed a more precipitous decline than the other two age groups in the numbers of blacks reporting high health satisfaction.

Health Problems. In the entire sample, the average number of doctor-reported health problems increased over the 13 years (see Table 13.4). This increase was linked to lower income and lower education; having fewer of these resources is related to more health problems. Over time, there was a tendency in the upper-income brackets, however, to show a greater proportionate increase than those in lower-income brackets. On the other hand, the low-education group showed a steeper proportionate increase than the two higher-education groups. Although those who were not married reported

Table 13.3 Changes in Reports of High Health Satisfaction From 1979 to 1992, Across Wave 1 Sample Characteristics

Variables	N	%	Wave 1 1979-80 (%)	Wave 2 1987-88 (%)	Wave 3 1988-89 (%)	Wave 4 1992 (%)	F Ratio
Overall	612	100	52.0	45.3	42.6	39.1	12.61**
Income							0.45
$0-$4,999	74	12	41.9	40.5	39.2	41.9	
$5-$9,999	140	23	49.3	42.1	38.6	40.7	
$10-$19,999	193	32	53.4	46.6	40.9	34.7	
$20,000+	205	33	56.1	47.8	48.3	41.0	
F ratio interaction							1.16
Education							1.38
No high school diploma	186	30	52.2	45.2	45.2	45.2	
High school diploma	212	35	50.9	45.8	38.7	36.3	
Some college	214	35	52.8	44.9	44.4	36.4	
F ratio interaction							1.08
Marital status							1.89
Not married	309	50	52.4	45.3	41.4	39.5	
Married	303	50	51.5	45.2	43.9	38.6	
F ratio interaction							0.27
Age							0.08
18-34	233	38	57.1	44.2	39.9	38.2	
35-54	250	41	53.2	46.4	44.0	38.8	
55+	129	21	40.3	45.0	45.0	41.1	
F ratio interaction							2.98**
Gender							10.80**
Male	193	32	57.0	53.9	53.4	45.1	
Female	419	68	49.6	41.3	37.7	36.3	
F ratio interaction							1.29

+$p < .10$; *$p < .05$; **$p < .01$.

201

Table 13.4 Changes in the Number of Health Problems From 1979 to 1992, Across Wave 1 Sample Characteristics

Variables	N	%	Wave 1 1979-80 (%)	Wave 2 1987-88 (%)	Wave 3 1988-89 (%)	Wave 4 1992 (%)	F Ratio
Overall	621	100	0.87	1.10	0.83	1.09	20.69**
Income							2.54[+]
$0-$4,999	78	13	1.64	1.91	1.32	1.87	
$5-$9,999	140	23	1.04	1.19	0.96	1.12	
$10-$19,999	194	31	0.70	0.97	0.75	1.00	
$20,000+	209	34	0.62	0.84	0.63	0.87	
F ratio interaction							1.77[+]
Education							1.82
No high school diploma	192	31	1.25	1.63	1.17	1.51	
High school diploma	212	34	0.76	0.97	0.85	1.02	
Some college	217	35	0.63	0.75	0.51	0.78	
F ratio interaction							2.63*
Marital status							0.08
Not married	312	50	0.96	1.13	0.83	1.13	
Married	309	50	0.77	1.06	0.83	1.05	
F ratio interaction							1.55
Age							61.31**
18-34	235	38	0.41	0.46	0.35	0.50	
35-54	252	41	0.90	1.24	0.97	1.29	
55+	134	22	1.60	1.93	1.42	1.75	
F ratio interaction							4.48**
Gender							6.30*
Male	194	31	0.64	0.95	0.66	0.83	
Female	427	69	0.97	1.16	0.91	1.21	
F ratio interaction							1.55

$+p < .10$; $*p < .05$; $**p < .01$.

slightly more health problems, these differences were not significant, and there were no differences in the trends over time between married and not married. Overall, at every period, the two older groups reported more health problems than the younger group. The significant interaction for age and time indicated that over time the two older age groups showed a steeper increase in the average number of reported health problems than the younger age group. Finally, females tended to report on average, at every point in time, significantly more health problems than men, and this difference was uniform over time.

Self-Esteem. As shown in Table 13.5, self-esteem showed an overall significant negative change over time. This change is not linear. The largest drop was between 1979-1980 to 1987 (40.9% to 25.6%). At Waves 3 (34.8%) and 4 (35.3%) there was an overall increase as compared to 1987 but still not a return to the original 40.9% level of 1979-1980. There were no overall average significant differences among income groups. However, after 1979-1980, there was at all points in time higher self-esteem reported among those in the higher income groups. Those in the lowest income group showed the most precipitous decline (45.8% to 22.2%). Similarly, higher education was associated with higher average levels of self-esteem; this was true at every point in time. Like income, those in lower-education categories showed a more abrupt decline in high levels of self-esteem over the 13-year period. Although there were no average differences, those who were married in 1979-1980 showed a greater decrease in self-esteem than those not married. There were no average differences by age. However, older African Americans showed a greater decline in self-esteem in comparison to those in the two younger groups. There were no significant effects of gender, although on average men showed a slightly greater percentage in each year of measurement. In sum, having greater socioeconomic status was associated with increased overall self-esteem and either no decline or less decline than those with lower status. The only resource that differed from this pattern was marital status in that those married in 1980 showed greater declines than those not married. Similarly, those in the oldest age group showed the most precipitous decline in self-esteem.

Serious Personal Problem Severity. As shown in Table 13.6, proportionate reports of serious personal problem severity increased over the period (26.2% in 1979-1980 and 34.1% in 1992). There was a tendency for this increase over time to be localized among low-income and less educated blacks. Marital status was not significantly related, although there was a trend for those who

Table 13.5 Changes in Reports of High Self-Esteem From 1979 to 1992, Across Wave 1 Sample Characteristics

Variables	N	%	Wave 1 1979-80 (%)	Wave 2 1987-88 (%)	Wave 3 1988-89 (%)	Wave 4 1992 (%)	F Ratio
Overall	609	100	40.9	25.6	34.8	35.3	15.26**
Income							0.30
$0-$4,999	72	12	45.8	15.3	22.2	22.2	
$5-$9,999	139	23	38.8	23.0	27.3	29.5	
$10-$19,999	191	31	33.0	23.6	41.4	38.7	
$20,000+	207	34	47.8	32.9	38.2	40.6	
F ratio interaction							3.08**
Education							10.21**
No high school diploma	184	30	38.0	18.5	28.3	22.8	
High school diploma	211	35	39.8	19.9	29.9	33.2	
Some college	214	35	44.4	37.4	45.3	48.1	
F ratio interaction							2.43*
Marital status							0.04
Not married	305	50	38.4	23.6	34.4	34.8	
Married	304	50	43.4	27.6	35.2	35.9	
F ratio interaction							0.43
Age							0.67
18-34	233	38	36.5	26.2	35.2	41.2	
35-54	252	41	43.7	29.0	37.7	36.5	
55+	124	20	43.5	17.7	28.2	21.8	
F ratio interaction							3.13**
Gender							1.19
Male	194	32	43.3	28.9	36.6	40.7	
Female	415	68	39.8	24.1	34.0	32.8	
F ratio interaction							0.45

+$p < .10$; *$p < .05$; **$p < .01$.

Table 13.6 Changes in Reports of High Problem Severity From 1979 to 1992, Across Wave 1 Sample Characteristics

Variables	N	%	Wave 1 1979-80 (%)	Wave 2 1987-88 (%)	Wave 3 1988-89 (%)	Wave 4 1992 (%)	F Ratio
Overall	610	100	26.2	41.3	34.3	34.1	18.30**
Income							2.17+
$0-$4,999	76	12	35.5	48.7	47.4	46.1	
$5-$9,999	138	23	29.7	57.2	39.1	39.9	
$10-$19,999	191	31	23.0	35.6	32.5	30.9	
$20,000+	205	34	23.4	33.2	27.8	28.8	
F ratio interaction							1.72+
Education							1.31
No high school diploma	186	30	29.0	46.2	39.8	37.6	
High school diploma	211	35	27.0	41.7	30.3	32.7	
Some college	213	35	23.0	36.6	33.3	32.4	
F ratio interaction							0.73
Marital status							0.59
Not married	305	50	28.9	44.9	39.0	39.0	
Married	305	50	23.6	37.7	29.5	29.2	
F ratio interaction							0.56
Age							3.39*
18-34	231	38	26.4	47.6	38.1	38.5	
35-54	251	41	26.3	38.2	30.7	31.9	
55+	128	21	25.8	35.9	34.4	30.5	
F ratio interaction							1.20
Gender							17.50**
Male	195	32	14.4	29.7	22.1	26.2	
Female	415	68	31.8	46.7	40.0	37.8	
F ratio interaction							0.89

+p < .10; *p < .05; **p < .01.

were not married to report more serious problems over the period. Those in the youngest age group also reported significantly more high-problem severity, and this difference was fairly uniform over the 13 years. Gender was significantly related and showed more than a twofold difference for more problems to be reported by females than males. Although not significant, this difference between men and women had narrowed by 1992.

Happiness. As shown in Table 13.7, there was a decrease in happiness for the entire sample. Generally, at all points in time those individuals having greater income tended to report higher happiness. There were no effects for education. Marital status showed a curious interaction. Those individuals initially married in 1979-1980 showed large decreases in happiness; nonmarried individuals showed no changes. Overall, those in the oldest age group showed significantly higher levels of happiness at each point in time than those in the two younger groups. There were no differences across time by age in reports of happiness. On average over the 13 years, men tended to report higher levels of happiness than women, and this difference was consistent at each point in time. In addition, there were no differences between men and women in the changes over time.

In sum, happiness showed a significant decrease among African Americans from 1979-1980 to 1992. This decrease was sharpest among those who were married in 1979-1980. We can only speculate that changes in marital status or the structural changes noted earlier had much more impact among those who were married than those who were not married in accounting for these different trends.

Life Satisfaction. Life satisfaction showed a totally different pattern than the other subjective well-being measure, happiness, and the personal resources of health and self-esteem (see Table 13.8). Over the same period of decreased social and economic resources, increased environmental stress, physical and mental health problems, and unhappiness, life satisfaction actually increased for the entire sample. On average, those in the lowest income and education groups actually reported the highest levels of life satisfaction. The increase over time was most noticeable among those not married. Although nonsignificant trends for females, the older age group, and the higher educated group showing greater increases in comparison to their respective counterparts, were also found. These results suggest that life satisfaction might be more than a subjective well-being outcome. In fact, based on these and other analyses not reported here (Jackson & Adams, 1992), life satisfaction might form part of an adjustment mechanism used to protect African

Table 13.7 Changes in High Reports of Happiness From 1979 to 1992, Across Wave 1 Sample Characteristics

Variables	N	%	Wave 1 1979-80 (%)	Wave 2 1987-88 (%)	Wave 3 1988-89 (%)	Wave 4 1992 (%)	F Ratio
Overall	603	100	30.0	23.7	23.2	24.7	4.87**
Income							1.68
$0-$4,999	74	12	32.4	28.4	23.0	25.7	
$5-$9,999	136	23	27.2	21.3	16.9	22.8	
$10-$19,999	188	31	29.8	23.9	25.5	25.0	
$20,000+	205	34	31.2	23.4	25.4	25.4	
F ratio interaction							0.36
Education							1.76
No high school diploma	182	30	40.1	29.7	28.0	33.0	
High school diploma	210	35	26.7	21.4	22.4	21.4	
Some college	211	35	24.6	20.9	19.9	20.9	
F ratio interaction							0.64
Marital status							1.24
Not married	299	50	22.7	21.1	20.7	22.7	
Married	304	50	37.2	26.3	25.7	26.6	
F ratio interaction							3.00*
Age							14.33**
18-34	230	38	25.2	14.3	16.5	20.0	
35-54	249	41	27.3	23.7	22.5	23.3	
55+	124	21	44.4	41.1	37.1	36.3	
F ratio interaction							0.88
Gender							7.07**
Male	193	32	33.7	31.1	29.5	30.1	
Female	410	68	28.3	20.2	20.2	22.2	
F ratio interaction							0.58

+$p < .10$; *$p < .05$; **$p < .01$.

207

Table 13.8 Changes in Reports of High Life Satisfaction From 1979 to 1992, Across Wave 1 Sample Characteristics

Variables	N	%	Wave 1 1979-80 (%)	Wave 2 1987-88 (%)	Wave 3 1988-89 (%)	Wave 4 1992 (%)	F Ratio
Overall	607	100	29.3	36.7	37.9	38.7	8.31**
Income							1.76
$0-$4,999	74	12	35.1	35.1	37.8	45.9	
$5-$9,999	135	22	27.4	33.3	34.1	40.0	
$10-$19,999	191	32	27.7	37.7	40.8	36.1	
$20,000+	207	34	30.0	38.6	37.7	37.7	
F ratio interaction							0.89
Education							1.79
No high school diploma	181	30	40.9	43.1	47.0	47.5	
High school diploma	212	35	25.0	37.3	34.9	33.5	
Some college	214	35	23.8	30.8	33.2	36.4	
F ratio interaction							1.01
Marital status							0.59
Not married	301	49	23.3	33.6	34.6	39.2	
Married	306	51	35.3	39.9	41.2	38.2	
F ratio interaction							3.21*
Age							14.98**
18-34	234	39	23.1	27.4	29.1	30.3	
35-54	247	41	26.7	37.7	38.1	38.9	
55+	126	21	46.0	52.4	54.0	54.0	
F ratio interaction							0.40
Gender							0.04
Male	189	31	28.6	42.3	39.7	37.6	
Female	418	69	29.7	34.2	37.1	39.2	
F ratio interaction							1.95

+$p < .10$; *$p < .05$; **$p < .01$.

Americans from more serious mental disorders due to the structural changes that so clearly produce decrements in other well-being, mental and physical health, and coping resource outcomes (Adams, 1996; Bowman, in press; Jackson & Adams, 1992).

Conclusions

The results of the analyses examining change over the 13-year period 1979 to 1992 were largely consistent with the cross-sectional results reported in prior chapters in this volume. Overall, the findings reveal increased reports of problems and major deterioration in both physical and psychological health status for the population in general. Those African Americans with significant resources, however, tend to be somewhat better off. On the other hand, consistent with the complicated gender and marital status results reported by Brown (Chapter 6, this volume), those who were married in 1979-1980 actually showed poorer outcome trajectories. It could be, as Brown points out, that being nonmarried results in the development of a set of potent coping skills or that those who were married in 1979-1980 had significant changes in the nature and quality of their relationships and therefore were at more risk for the development of poor health. Our analyses do not permit us to disentangle these explanations. For the most part, having higher income and more education—and to some extent, being male—are related to positive physical and psychological health. We expected that material resources would be health protective. Because the sample is based on those who survived the entire period, however, the results may overstate the positive association with being male.

The fact that high education was linked to greater reports of environmental problems may be similar to the exposure hypothesis offered to account for why younger, compared to older, age groups show increased problems. Some have argued that increased education may lead to increased exposure to stress from whites in work, residential, and social situations for African Americans (Essed, 1991; Feagin, 1991; Jackson et al., 1996).

A substantial portion of the African American population resides in environments where people are likely to be exposed to a relatively large number of stressors (Jackson et al., 1996). Low socioeconomic status affects the options that an individual has in terms of the type and location of housing and in the quality of life. Intertwined with low socioeconomic status are stressful lifestyles that may include poor nutrition, poor education, exposure to crime, traffic hazards, substandard and overcrowded housing, low-paying jobs, unemployment and underemployment, and a lack of health insurance and access to basic health services. It is frequently suggested that these factors contribute to the development of a wide range of problems in the black community, but empirical evidence in support of these notions is sparse (Jackson, 1993; Williams & Collins, 1995).

Wilson (1987) proposes that blacks have been increasingly concentrated in depressed inner-city neighborhoods, whereas the white urban poor are more evenly dispersed throughout the city, with many residing in relatively safe and comfortable neighborhoods. There are important suggestions in the literature that the stress of residing in urban residential areas may significantly affect health status. Studies by Harburg and his colleagues (e.g., Harburg, Erfurt, Hauenstein, et al., 1973) found that residence in stressful urban areas (characterized by factors such as low median income and few years of formal education, residential instability, marital instability, and crime) was adversely related to health. The findings of increased perceptions of environmentally stressful problems and increased reports of doctor-reported problems with blood pressure are consistent with the negative environmental changes over this period (Danziger & Gottschalk, 1995).

It has been suggested that the perception and experience of racism adversely affect the health status of African Americans. However, there have been few attempts to empirically assess racism or racial discrimination and to explore the consequences, if any, for the psychological well-being of African American children, adolescents, and adults (Jackson et al., 1996; Williams & Chung, in press). There is a clear consensus in the early literature on black mental health that racial discrimination and racism adversely affect the psychological health of blacks (e.g., McCarthy & Yancey, 1971).

Related to our findings of increased doctor-reported high blood pressure in our panel data, some findings suggest that the experience of unfair treatment is positively related to blood pressure (Harburg, Erfurt, Hauenstein, et al., 1973; James, LaCroix, Kleinbaum, & Strogatz, 1984; Krieger, 1990). Recent analyses of data from the NSBA also reveal that the experience of racial discrimination in the previous month, as well as the experience of racial discrimination in employment settings, is adversely related to multiple indicators of physical and mental health (Williams & Chung, 1996). That is, persons who reported experiencing discrimination had higher levels of chronic health problems, disability, and psychological distress and lower levels of happiness and life satisfaction. In a related study of perceived discrimination in the workplace and job satisfaction in the NSBA, Kirby and Jackson (1995) found that perceptions of job discrimination lowered reports of job satisfaction among blacks and that racial composition of the immediate work group had a salutary effect on this observed adverse relationship. Anderson and his colleagues (Anderson, McNeilly, Armstead, Clark, & Pieper, 1993; McNeilly et al., 1996) have found direct effects of racist provocation on cardiovascular and emotional responses among African Americans. Although social support appeared to reduce the influence of racist provocation on emotional responses, support had no influence on cardiovascular reactivity.

At the present time, the mechanisms and processes by which racial discrimination may affect health are not known. The full range of responses to racial discrimination have not been documented. Racism is ingrained in the social structures and culture of American society, and racial discrimination is relatively ubiquitous in everyday life (Essed, 1991; Feagin, 1991; Jones, 1992). Racial discrimination is not randomly distributed in the African American population (Jackson et al., 1996; Williams & Chung, 1996). Adams and Dressler (1988) found that persons under financial strain, as well as those who perceived their neighborhoods to be unsafe and deficient in basic services, were more likely to be upset by racial discrimination.

The longitudinal and cross-sectional findings in this chapter and volume paint a complex picture of mental health among African Americans. Clearly, the environment and material resources matter in the expression and experience of distress and lowered physical and psychological health. The lack of similar relationships with more serious mental disorders (Kessler et al., 1994; Williams, 1995) suggests the presence of material, social, and psychological factors that may play ameliorative and buffering roles in reducing mental dysfunction. Specific mechanisms may include personal coping resources, such as mastery and efficacy; informal social supports; and cognitive readjustments in expectations and environmental appraisal mechanisms (e.g., life satisfaction). Before the somewhat paradoxical results can be understood, we need increased understanding of racial and cultural influences on diagnosis, the specific cultural patterning of symptom expression, and better studies of African Americans (Williams, 1995).

As the chapters in this volume make clear, we have come a long way in the past 20 years in understanding the nature of symptoms, the distribution of serious personal problems, the use of personal and group resources, and the specific survival mechanisms that African Americans employ (Jones, 1992). We expect that research over the next 20 years will contribute to making important strides in understanding disease-specific psychiatric epidemiology, clinical assessment, informal assistance, formal treatment, and follow-up among African Americans.

References

Acosta, F. (1980). Self-described reasons for premature termination of psychotherapy by Mexican American, Black American, and Anglo-American patients. *Psychological Reports, 47*(2), 435-443.

Adams, J. P., Jr., & Dressler, W. W. (1988). Perceptions of injustice in a black community: Dimensions and variation. *Human Relations, 41*(10), 753-767.

Adams, R. G. (1989). Conceptual and methodological issues in studying friendships of older adults. In R. G. Adams & R. Blieszner (Eds.), *Older adult friendship* (pp. 17-41). Newbury Park, CA: Sage.

Adams, V. H. (1996). *African American quality of life: A paradox in social accounting systems.* Manuscript submitted for publication.

Adebimpe, V. (1981). Overview: White norms and psychiatric diagnosis of black patients. *American Journal of Psychiatry, 138*(3), 279-285.

Adebimpe, V. (1994). Race, racism and epidemiological surveys. *Hospital and Community Psychiatry, 45*(1), 27-31.

Ahlbrandt, R. S., Jr. (1984). *Neighborhoods, people, and community.* New York: Plenum.

Ahlbrandt, R. S., & Cunningham, J. V. (1979). *A new public policy for neighborhood preservation.* New York: Praeger.

Albrecht, S. L. (1979). Correlates of marital happiness among the remarried. *Journal of Marriage and the Family, 41*(4), 857-867.

Alexander, F. G. (1939). Emotional factors in essential hypertension: Presentation of a tentative hypothesis. *Psychosomatic Medicine, 1,* 175-179.

Alexander, F. G. (1948). Emotional factors in hypertension. In F. Alexander & T. M. French (Eds.), *Studies in psychosomatic medicine. An approach to the cause and treatment of vegetative disturbances* (pp. 289-297). New York: Ronald Press. (Original work published 1939)

Allan, G. A. (1989). *Friendship: Developing a sociological perspective.* Hempstead, NY: Harvester Wheatsheaf.

Allan, G. A., & Adams, R. G. (1989). Aging and the structure of friendship. In R. G. Adams & R. Blieszner (Eds.), *Older adult friendship* (pp. 45-64). Newbury Park, CA: Sage.

213

Alwin, D. F., & Hauser, R. N. (1975). The decomposition of effects in path analysis. *American Sociological Review, 40*(1), 37-47.

American Psychiatric Association. (1987). *Diagnostic and statistical manual of mental disorders* (3rd. ed., rev.) Washington, DC: Author.

Andersen, R., & Newman, J. (1973). Societal and individual determinants of medical care utilization in the United States. *Milbank Memorial Fund Quarterly, 51*(1), 95-124.

Anderson, L. P. (1991). Acculturative stress: A theory of relevance to black Americans. *Psychology Review, 11*(6), 685-702.

Anderson, N. B., McNeilly, M. D., Armstead, C., Clark, R., & Pieper, C. (1993). Assessment of cardiovascular reactivity: A methodological overview. *Ethnicity and Disease, 3,* 29-37.

Andrews, F. M. (1981). Subjective social indicators, objective social indicators, and social accounting systems. In F. T. Juster & K. C. Land (Eds.), *Social accounting systems: Essays on the state of the art* (pp. 317-419). New York: Academic Press.

Andrews, F. M., & Withey, S. B. (1976). *Social indicators of well-being: America's perception of life quality.* New York: Plenum.

Antonucci, T. C., & Depner, C. (1982). Social support and informal helping relationships. In T. A. Wills (Ed.), *Basic process in helping relationships* (pp. 233-253). New York: Academic Press.

Antonucci, T. C., & Jackson, J. S. (1987). Social support, interpersonal efficacy and health. In L. L. Carstensen & B. A. Edelstein (Eds.), *Handbook of clinical gerontology* (pp. 299-311). Elmsford, NY: Pergamon.

Antonucci, T. C., & Jackson, J. S. (1990). The role of reciprocity in social support. In I. G. Sarason, B. R. Sarason, & G. R. Pierce (Eds.), *Social support: An interactive view* (pp. 173-198). New York: John Wiley.

Armstrong, H. E., Ishiki, D., Heiman, J., Mundt, J., & Womack, W. (1984). Service utilization by black and white clientele in an urban community mental health center: Revised assessment of an old problem. *Community Mental Health Journal, 20*(4), 269-281.

Aschenbrenner, J. (1975). *Lifelines: Black families in Chicago.* New York: Holt, Rinehart & Winston.

Asher, H. B. (1976). *Causal modeling.* Beverly Hills, CA: Sage.

Autunes, G., Gordon, C., Gaitz, C., & Scott, J. (1974). Ethnicity, socioeconomic status and the etiology of psychological distress. *Sociology and Social Research, 58*(4), 361-368.

Ax, A. F. (1953). The physiological differentiation between fear and anger in humans. *Psychosomatic Medicine, 15*(3), 433-442.

Bachrach, K. M., & Zautra, A. J. (1985). Coping with a community stressor: The threat of a hazardous waste facility. *Journal of Health and Social Behavior, 26*(2), 127-141.

Baer, P. E., Collins, F. H., Bourianoff, G. G., & Ketchel, M. (1979). Assessing personality factors in essential hypertension with a brief self-report instrument. *Psychosomatic Medicine, 41*(4), 321-331.

Bailey, E. J. (1987). Sociocultural factors and health care seeking behavior among black Americans. *Journal of the National Medical Association, 79*(4), 389-392.

Bailey, M. B., Haberman, P., & Alkane, H. (1965). The epidemiology of alcoholism in an urban residential area. *Quarterly Journal of Studies on Alcohol, 26*(1), 19-40.

Ball, R. E., & Robbins, L. (1986). Marital status and life satisfaction among black Americans. *Journal of Marriage and the Family, 48*(2), 389-394.

Balswick, J. O., & Peek, C. W. (1971). The inexpressive male: A tragedy of American society. *Family Coordinator, 20*(4), 363-368.

Bankoff, E. A. (1983). Social support and adaptation to widowhood. *Journal of Marriage and the Family, 45*(4), 827-839.

Barbarin, O. A. (1983). Coping with ecological transitions by black families: A psychological model. *Journal of Community Psychology, 11*(4), 308-322.

Baum, A., Singer, J. E., & Baum, C. S. (1981). Stress and the environment. *Journal of Social Issues, 37*(1), 4-35.

Bayley, D. H., & Mendelsohn, H. (1969). *Minorities and the police: Confrontation in America.* New York: Free Press.

Bell, C. (1987). Preventive strategies for dealing with violence among blacks. *Community Mental Health Journal, 23,* 217-228.

Bell, C., & Mehta, H. (1980). The misdiagnosis of black patients with depressive illness. *Journal of the National Medical Association, 72*(2), 141-145.

Bell, C., & Mehta, H. (1981). Misdiagnosis of black patients with manic depressive illness: Second in a series. *Journal of the National Medical Association, 73*(2), 101-107.

Bell, R. A. (1981). *Worlds of friendship.* Newbury Park, CA: Sage.

Bell, R. A., Leroy, J. B., & Stephenson, J. J. (1982). Evaluating the mediating effects of social support upon life events and depressive symptoms. *Journal of Community Psychology, 10*(4), 325-340.

Bernard, J. (1972). *The future of marriage.* New York: Bantam.

Bettes, B. A., Dusenbury, L., Kerner, J., James-Ortiz, S., & Botvin, G. J. (1990). Ethnicity and psychosocial factors in alcohol and tobacco use in adolescence. *Child Development, 61*(2), 557-565.

Biafora, F. A., Jr., Warheit, G. J., Zimmerman, R. S., Gil, A. G., Apospori, E., & Taylor, D. (1993). Racial mistrust and deviant behaviors among ethnically diverse black adolescent boys. *Journal of Applied Social Psychology, 23*(11), 891-910.

Billings, A. G., & Moos, R. H. (1981). The role of coping responses and social resources in attenuating the stress of life events. *Journal of Behavioral Medicine, 4*(2), 139-157.

Billingsley, A. (1992). *Climbing Jacob's ladder: The enduring legacy of African American families.* New York: Simon & Schuster.

Birkel, R. C., & Reppucci, N. D. (1983). Social networks, information seeking, and the utilization of services. *American Journal of Community Psychology, 11*(2), 185-205.

Bittner, E. (1974). Florence Nightingale in pursuit of Willie Sutton: A theory of the police. In H. Jabob (Ed.), *The potential for reform in criminal justice* (pp. 125-126). Beverly Hills, CA: Sage.

Blalock, H. M., Jr. (Ed.). (1971). *Causal models in the social sciences.* Chicago: Aldine.

Blauner, R., & Wellman, D. (1973). Toward the decolonization of social research. In J. A. Ladner (Ed.), *The death of white sociology* (pp. 310-330). New York: Vintage.

Block, C. B. (1981). Black Americans and the cross-counseling and the psychotherapy experience. In A. J. Marsella & P. B. Pedersen (Eds.), *Cross-cultural counseling and psychotherapy.* New York: Pergamon.

Blot, W. J. (1992). Alcohol and cancer. *Cancer Research, 52*(Suppl. 7), 2119S-2123S.

Bowman, P. J. (in press). Toward a cognitive theory of role strain: Implications of research on black male providers. In R. L. Jones (Ed.), *Advances in black psychology.* Berkeley: University of California Press.

Boyd-Franklin, N. (1989). *Black families in therapy: A multisystems approach.* New York: Guilford.

Boyle, E. (1979). Biological patterns in hypertension by race, sex, body weight, and skin color. *Journal of the American Medical Association, 213*(10), 1637-1643.

Bradburn, N. M. (1969). *The structure of psychological well-being.* Chicago: Aldine.

Bradburn, N. M., & Caplovitz, D. (1965). *Reports on happiness.* Chicago: Aldine.

Braithwaite, R., & Taylor, S. (Eds.). (1992). *Health issues in the black community.* San Francisco: Jossey-Bass.

Brenner, G. F., Norvell, N. K., & Limacher, M. (1989). Supportive and problematic social interaction: A social network analysis. *American Journal of Community Psychology, 17*(6), 831-836.

Breznitz, S. (Ed.). (1983). *The denial of stress.* New York: International Universities Press.

Broman, C. L. (1987). Race differences in professional help seeking. *American Journal of Community Psychology, 15*(4), 473-489.

Broman, C. L. (1989). Race and responsiveness to life stress. *National Journal of Sociology, 3,* 49-64.

Broman, C. L., Hoffman, W. S., & Hamilton, V. L. (1994). Impact of mental health services use on subsequent mental health of autoworkers. *Journal of Health and Social Behavior, 35*(1), 80-95.

Broman, C. L., Neighbors, H. W., & Jackson, J. S. (1988). Racial group identification among black adults. *Social Forces, 67*(1), 146-158.

Broman, C. L., Neighbors, H. W., & Taylor, R. J. (1989). Race differences in seeking help from social workers. *Journal of Sociology and Social Welfare, 16*(3), 109-123.

Brown, D. R., Ahmed, F., Gary, L. E., & Milburn, N. G. (1995). Major depression in a community sample of African Americans. *American Journal of Psychiatry, 152*(3), 373-378.

Brown, D. R., Eaton, W., & Sussman, L. (1990). Racial differences in prevalence of phobic disorders. *Journal of Nervous and Mental Disease, 178*(7), 434-441.

Brown, D. R., & Gary, L. E. (1985). Social support network differentials among married and nonmarried black females. *Psychology of Women Quarterly, 9*(2), 229-241.

Brown, D. R., & Gary, L. E. (1988). Unemployment and psychological distress among black American women. *Sociological Focus, 21,* 209-221.

Brown, D. R., Milburn, N. G., Ahmed, F., Gary, L. E., & Booth, J. (1990). Depression and marital status among black females. *Urban Research Review, 21*(2), 11-16.

Brown, L. A., & Moore, E. G. (1970). The intra-urban migration process: A perspective. *Geografiska Annaler, 52*(B), 1-13.

Brummell, A. C. (1981). A method of measuring residential stress. *Geographical Analysis, 13,* 248-261.

Brunswick, A. F. (1977). Health and drug behavior: A study of urban black adolescents. *Addictive Diseases, 3*(2), 197-214.

Brunswick, A. F., & Collette, P. (1972). Psychological correlates of elevated blood pressure: A study of urban black adolescents. *Journal of Human Stress, 3*(4), 19-31.

Bruun, K., Edward, G., Lumio, M., Makela, K., Pan, L., Popham, R. E., Room, R., Schmidt, W., Skog, O. J., Sulkunen, P., & Osterberg, E. (1975). *Alcohol control policies in public health perspectives.* Helsinki: Forssa, Finnish Foundation for Alcohol Studies.

Bryant, F. B., & Veroff, J. (1982). The structure of psychological well-being: A sociohistorical analysis. *Journal of Personality and Social Psychology, 43*(4), 653-673.

Bui, K. T., & Takeuchi, D. T. (1992). Ethnic minority adolescents and use of community mental health care services. *American Journal of Community Psychology, 20*(4), 403-417.

Burke, R. J., & Weir, T. (1977). Marital helping relationships: The moderator between stress and well-being. *Journal of Psychology, 95*(1), 121-130.

Burnett, P., Carr, J., Sinapi, J., & Taylor, R. (1976). Police and social workers in community outreach program. *Social Casework, 57*(1), 41-49.

Caldwell, C. H., Chatters, L. M., Billingsley, A., & Taylor, R. J. (1995). Church-based support programs for elderly black adults: Congregational and clergy characteristics. In M. A. Kimble, S. H. McFadden, J. W. Ellor, & J. J. Seeber (Eds.), *Aging, spirituality, and religion: A handbook* (pp. 306-324). Minneapolis, MN: Augsburg Fortress.

Caldwell, C. H., Greene, A. D., & Billingsley, A. (1994). Family support programs in black churches: A new look at old functions. In S. L. Kagan & B. Weissbourd (Eds.), *Putting families first: America's family support movement and the challenge of change* (pp. 137-160). San Francisco: Jossey-Bass.

Calnan, M. (1983). Social networks and patterns of help-seeking behavior. *Social Science and Medicine, 17*(1), 25-28.

Campbell, A. (1980). *Sense of well-being in America: Recent patterns and trends.* New York: Russell Sage Foundation.

Campbell, A., Converse, P. E., & Rodgers, W. L. (1976). *The quality of American life: Perceptions, evaluations, and satisfactions.* New York: Russell Sage Foundation.

Campbell, A., & Schuman, H. (1969). Racial attitudes in 15 American cities. In *The Kerner Commission Survey. Supplemental studies for the National Advisory Commission on Civil Disorders* (p. 44). Washington, DC: Government Printing Office.

Campinha-Bacote, J. (1991). Community mental health services for the underserved: A culturally specific model. *Archives of Psychiatric Nursing, 5*(4), 229-235.

Cannon, M., & Locke, B. (1977). Being black is detrimental to one's mental health: Myth or reality? *Phylon, 38*(4), 408-428.

Cantor, M. H. (1979). Neighbors and friends. *Research on Aging, 1,* 434-463.

Capers, C. F. (1991). Nurses' and lay African Americans' views about behavior. *Western Journal of Nursing Research, 13*(1), 123-135.

Carp, F. M., & Carp, A. (1982a). Perceived environmental quality of neighborhoods: Development of assessment scales and their relation to age and gender. *Journal of Environmental Psychology, 2*(4), 295-312.

Carp, F. M., & Carp, A. (1982b). A role for technical environmental assessment in perceptions of environmental quality and well-being. *Journal of Environmental Psychology, 2*(3), 171-191.

Carp, F. M., & Carp, A. (1982c). Test of a model of domain satisfactions and well-being. *Research on Aging, 4*(4), 503-533.

Carr, J. J. (1979). An administrative retrospective on police crisis teams. *Social Casework, 9,* 416-422.

Carver, C. S., Scheier, M. F., & Weintraub, J. K. (1989). Assessing coping strategies: A theoretically based approach. *Journal of Personality and Social Psychology, 56*(2), 267-283.

Cassel, J. C., Heyden, S., & Bartel, A. G. (1971). Incidence of coronary heart disease by ethnic group, social class, and sex. *Archives of Internal Medicine, 128*(6), 901.

Catalano, R., & Dooley, D. (1983). Health effects of economic instability: A test of economic stress hypothesis. *Journal of Health and Social Behavior, 24*(1), 46-60.

Cavanagh, J., & Clairmonte, F. (1985). *Alcoholic beverages: Dimensions of corporate power.* New York: St. Martin's.

Chappell, N. L. (1983). Informal support networks among the elderly. *Research on Aging, 5*(1), 77-99.

Chatters, L. M., & Taylor, R. J. (1993). Intergenerational support: The provision of assistance to parents by adult children. In J. S. Jackson, L. M. Chatters, & R. J. Taylor (Eds.), *Aging in black America* (pp. 69-83). Newbury Park, CA: Sage.

Chatters, L. M., Taylor, R. J., & Jackson, J. S. (1985). Size and composition of the informal helper networks of elderly blacks. *Journal of Gerontology, 40*(5), 605-614.

Chatters, L. M., Taylor, R. J., & Jackson, J. S. (1986). Aged blacks' choices for an informal helper network. *Journal of Gerontology, 41*(1), 94-100.

Chatters, L. M., Taylor, R. J., & Neighbors, H. W. (1989). Size of informal helper network mobilized during a serious personal problem among black Americans. *Journal of Marriage and the Family, 51,* 667-676.

Checkoway, B., & Van Til, J. (1978). What do we know about citizen participation? A selective review of research. In S. Langton (Ed.), *Citizen participation in America.* Lexington, MA: Lexington Books.

Cheung, F. K., & Snowden, K. R. (1990). Community mental health and ethnic minority populations. *Community Mental Health Journal, 26*(3), 277-291.

Cheung, Y. W. (1990-1991). Ethnicity and alcohol/drug use revisited: A framework for future research. *International Journal of the Addictions, 25*(5A-6A), 581-605.

Clark, K. B. (1965). *Dark ghetto.* New York: Harper Torch.

Clark, W. A. V., & Cadwallader, M. (1973). Locational stress and residential mobility. *Environment and Behavior, 5*(1), 29-41.

Cleary, P. D., & Mechanic, D. (1983). Sex differences in psychological distress among married people. *Journal of Health and Social Behavior, 24*(2), 111-121.

Clopton, L. P. (1978). The impact of ecological influences on the mental health of urban black communities. In L. E. Gary (Ed.), *Mental health: A challenge to the black community* (pp. 196-211). Philadelphia: Dorrance.

Cochran, S. D., & Mays, V. M. (1994). Depressive distress among homosexually active African Americans. *American Journal of Psychiatry, 151*(4), 524-529.

Cochrane, R. (1973). Hostility and neuroticism among unselected essential hypertensives. *Journal of Psychosomatic Research, 17*(3), 215-218.

Comas-Diaz, L. (1992). The future of psychotherapy with ethnic minorities. *Psychotherapy: Theory, Research, and Practice, 29*(1), 88-94.

Comer, J. (1970). Research and the black backlash. *American Journal of Orthopsychiatry, 40*(1), 8-11.

Comstock, G. W. (1957). An epidemiologic study of blood pressure levels in a bi-racial community in the southern United States. *American Journal of Hygiene, 65,* 271.

Cooper, J. L. (1980). *The police and the ghetto.* Port Washington, NY: Kennikat.

Cooper, R. (1984). A note on the biologic concept of race and its application in epidemiologic research. *American Heart Journal, 108*(3 pt. 2), 715-722.

Coulton, C., & Frost, A. K. (1982). Use of social and health services by the elderly. *Journal of Health and Social Behavior, 23*(4), 330-339.

Cox, K. R., & McCarthy, J. J. (1980). Neighborhood activism in the American city: Behavioral relationships and evaluation. *Urban Geography, 1*(1), 22-38.

Cox, T. (1978). *Stress.* Baltimore, MA: University Park Press.

Crane, R. S. (1982). *The role of anger, hostility and aggression essential hypertension.* Unpublished doctoral dissertation, University of South Florida, Tampa.

Crohan, S. E., & Antonucci, T. C. (1989). Friends as a source of social support in old age. In R. G. Adams & R. Blieszner (Eds.), *Older adult friendship* (pp. 129-146). Newbury Park, CA: Sage.

Crohan, S. E., Antonucci, T. C., Adelmann, P. K., & Coleman, L. M. (1989). Job characteristics and well-being at midlife: Ethnic and gender comparisons. *Psychology of Women Quarterly, 13*(2), 223-235.

Cronkite, R. C., & Moos, R. H. (1984). The role of predisposing and moderating factors in the stress-illness relationship. *Journal of Health and Social Behavior, 25*(4), 372-393.

Cruickshank, J. K., & Beevers, D. G. (1982). Epidemiology of hypertension: Blood pressure in blacks and whites. *Clinical Science, 62*(1), 1-6.

Cullen, K., Steinhouse, N. S., & Wearne, K. L. (1982). Alcohol and mortality in the Busselton study. *International Journal of Epidemiology, 11*(10), 67-70.

Danziger, S., & Gottschalk, P. (1995). *America unequal.* New York: Russell Sage.

Dawkins, M., Dawkins, M. P., & Terry, J. A. (1979). Personality and lifestyle characteristics of users and nonusers of mental health services in an urban black community. *Western Journal of Black Studies, 8,* 43-52.

Deane, G. D. (1990). Mobility and adjustments: Path to the resolution of residential stress. *Demography, 27,* 65-79.

Diener, E. (1984). Subjective well-being. *Psychological Bulletin, 95*(3), 542-575.

Dillman, D. A., & Hobbs, D. J. (Eds.). (1982). *Rural society in the U.S.: Issues for the 1980s.* Boulder, CO: Westview.

Dilworth-Anderson, P., Burton, L. M., & Johnson, L. M. (1993). Reframing theories for understanding race, ethnicity and families. In P. G. Boss, W. J. Doherty, R. LaRossa, W. R. Schumm, & S. K. Steinmetz (Eds.), *Sourcebook of family theories and methods: A conceptual approach* (pp. 627-646). New York: Plenum.

Doherty, W. J. (1992). Linkages between family theories and primary health care. In R. J. Sawa (Ed.), *Family health care* (pp. 30-39). Newbury Park, CA: Sage.

Dohrenwend, B. P., & Dohrenwend, B. S. (1969). *Social status and psychological disorder: A causal inquiry.* New York: John Wiley.

Dohrenwend, B. S. (1973). Social status and stressful life events. *Journal of Personality and Social Psychology, 28*(2), 225-235.

Dohrenwend, B. S., & Dohrenwend, B. P. (1974a). *Life stress and illness: Formulation of the issue.* New York: John Wiley.

Dohrenwend, B. S., & Dohrenwend, B. P. (Eds.). (1974b). *Stressful life events: Their nature and effects.* New York: John Wiley.

Dohrenwend, B. S., & Dohrenwend, B. P. (1978). Some issues in research on stressful life events. *Journal of Nervous Mental Disorders, 166*(1), 7-15.

Dohrenwend, B. S., & Dohrenwend, B. P. (Eds.). (1981). *Stressful life events and their contexts.* New York: Prodist.

Dohrenwend, B. S., Krassnoff, L., Askenasy, A. R., & Dohrenwend, B. P. (1978). Exemplification of a method for scaling life events: The PERI Events Scale. *Journal of Health and Social Behavior, 19*(2), 205-229.

Dressler, W. W. (1985a). Extended family relationships, social support and mental health in a southern black community. *Journal of Health and Social Behavior, 26*(1), 39-48.

Dressler, W. W. (1985b). The social and cultural context of coping: Action, gender, and symptoms in a southern black community. *Social Science and Medicine, 21*(5), 499-506.

Dressler, W. W. (1986). Unemployment and depressive symptoms in a southern black community. *Journal of Nervous and Mental Disease, 174*(11), 639-645.

Dressler, W. W. (1987). Stress process in a southern black community: Implications for prevention research. *Human Organization, 46*(3), 211-220.

Dressler, W. W. (1991). *Stress and adaptation in the context of culture: Depression in a southern black community.* Albany: State University of New York Press.

Dressler, W. W., Viteri, F., Chavez, A., Grell, G., & Dos Santos, J. (1991). Comparative research in social epidemiology: Measurement issues. *Ethnicity and Disease, 1*(4), 379-393.

Duncan, O. D. (1966). Path analysis: Sociological examples. *American Journal of Sociology, 72*(1), 1-16.

Eaton, W. W. (1975). Marital status and schizophrenia. *Acta Psychiatria Scandinavia, 52*(5), 320-329.

Eaton, W. W., Holzer, C. E., Von Korff, M., Anthony, J. C., Helzer, J. E., George, L., Burnam, M. A., Boyd, J. H., Kessler, L. G., & Locke, B. Z. (1984). The design of the epidemiologic catchment area surveys. *Archives of General Psychiatry, 41*(10), 942-948.

Eaton, W. W., & Kessler, L. G. (1981). Rates of symptoms of depression in a national sample. *American Journal of Epidemiology, 114*(14), 528-538.

Eng, E., Hatch, J., & Callan, A. (1985). Institutionalizing social support through the church and into the community. *Health Education Quarterly, 12*(1), 81-92.

Ensel, W. M. (1982). The role of age in the relationship of gender and marital status to depression. *Journal of Nervous and Mental Disease, 170*(9), 536-543.

Esler, M., Julius, S., Zweifler, A., Randall, O., Harburg, E., Gardiner, H., & deQuattro, V. (1977). Mild high-renin essential hypertension. *New England Journal of Medicine, 296*(8), 405-411.

Essed, P. (1991). *Understanding everyday racism: An interdisciplinary theory.* Newbury Park, CA: Sage.

Evans, G. W. (Ed.). (1982). *Environmental stress.* Cambridge, UK: Cambridge University Press.

Eve, S. B. (1984). Age strata differences on utilization of health care services among adults in the United States. *Sociological Focus, 17*(2), 105-120.

Eve, S. B. (1988). A longitudinal study of use of health cares services among older women. *Journal of Gerontology: Medical Sciences, 43*(2), M31-M39.

Eysenck, H. J. (1983). Stress, disease, and personality: The "inoculation effect." In C. L. Cooper (Ed.), *Stress research* (pp. 121-146). New York: John Wiley.

Fairchild, H. H., & Tucker, M. B. (1982). Black residential mobility: Trends and characteristics. *Journal of Social Issues, 38*(3), 51-74.

Faris, R. E. L., & Dunham, H. W. (1939). *Mental disorders in urban areas: An ecological study of schizophrenia and other psychoses.* Chicago: University of Chicago Press.

Feagin, J. R. (1991). The continuing significance of race: Antiblack discrimination in public places. *American Sociological Review, 56*(1), 101-116.

Feldstein, L., Harburg, E., & Hauenstein, L. (1980). Parity and blood pressure among four race-stress groups of females in Detroit. *American Journal of Epidemiology, 111*(3), 356-366.

Finney, J. M. (1972). Indirect effects in path analysis. *Sociological Methods and Research, 1,* 175-186.

Fischer, C. S. (1982). *To dwell among friends: Personal networks in town and city.* Chicago: University of Chicago Press.

Fischer, C. S. (1984). *The urban experience* (2nd ed.). San Diego, CA: Harcourt Brace.

Fischer, J. (1969). Negroes and whites and rates of mental illness: Reconsideration of a myth. *Psychiatry, 32*(4), 428-446.

Flaherty, J. A., Gaviria, M., Pathak, D., Mitchell, T., Wintrob, D., Richman, J., & Birz, S. (1988). Developing instruments for cross-cultural psychiatric research. *Journal of Nervous and Mental Disease, 176*(5), 257-263.

Flaherty, J. A., Naidu, J., Lawton, R., & Pathak, D. (1981). Racial differences in perception of ward atmosphere. *American Journal of Psychiatry, 138*(6), 815-817.

Flaskerud, J. H. (1980). Perceptions of problematic behavior by Appalachians. *Nursing Research, 29*(1), 4-5.

Flaskerud, J. H., & Hu, L. (1992). Racial/ethnic identity and amount and type of psychiatric treatment. *American Journal of Psychiatry, 149*(3), 379-384.

Fleishman, J. A. (1984). Personality characteristics and coping patterns. *Journal of Health and Social Behavior, 25*(2), 229-244.

Franklin, A. J., & Jackson, J. S. (1990). Factors contributing to positive mental health among black Americans. In D. Ruiz (Ed.), *Handbook of mental health and mental disorder among black Americans* (291-307). New York: Greenwood.

Freedman, D. X. (1984). Psychiatric epidemiology counts. *Archives of General Psychiatry, 41*(10), 931-933.

Freud, A. (1946). *The ego and the mechanisms of defense.* New York: International Universities Press.

Friedman, S. (1994). *Anxiety disorders in African Americans.* New York: Springer.

Frye, M. (1992). Oppression. In P. S. Rothenberg (Ed.), *Racism and sexism: An integrated study* (pp. 54-57). New York: St. Martin's.

Funkenstein, D. H., King, S. H., & Drolette, M. E. (1957). *Mastery of stress.* Cambridge, MA: Harvard University Press.

Galster, G. C., & Hesser, G. W. (1981). Residential satisfaction: Compositional and contextual correlates. *Environment and Behavior, 13*(6), 735-758.

Gary, L. E. (1978a). *Mental health: A challenge to the black community.* Philadelphia: Dorrance.

Gary, L. E. (1978b). Mental health: The problem and the product. In L. E. Gary (Ed.), *Mental health: A challenge to the black community* (pp. 26-47). Philadelphia: Dorrance.

Gary, L. E. (1985). Correlates of depressive symptoms among a select population of black men. *American Journal of Public Health, 25*(10), 1220-1222.

Gentry, W. D. (1972). Biracial aggression: I. Effect of verbal attack and sex of victim. *Journal of Social Psychology, 88*(5), 75-82.

Gentry, W. D. (1985). Relationship of anger-coping styles and blood pressure among black Americans. In M. A. Chesney & R. H. Rosenman (Eds.), *Anger and hostility in cardiovascular and behavioral disorders* (pp. 139-147). New York: Hemisphere/McGraw-Hill.

Gentry, W. D., Chesney, A. P., Gary, H. G., Hall, R. P., & Harburg, E. (1982). Habitual anger-coping styles: I. Effect on mean blood pressure and risk for essential hypertension. *Psychosomatic Medicine, 44*(2), 195-202.

Gentry, W. D., Chesney, A. P., Hall, R. P., & Harburg, E. (1981). Effect of habitual anger-coping pattern on blood pressure in black/white, high/low stress area respondents. *Psychosomatic Medicine, 44*(2), 195-202.

Gentry, W. D., Harburg, E., & Hauenstein, L. (1973). Effects of anger expression/inhibition of guilt on elevated blood diastolic pressure in high/low stress and black/white females. *Proceedings of the American Psychological Association, 8,* 115-116.

Gentry, W. D., Julius, S., & Johnson, E. H. (Eds.). (1992). *Personality, elevated blood pressure, and essential hypertension.* Washington, DC: Hemisphere.

George, L. K., Okun, M. A., & Landerman, R. (1985). Age as a moderator of the determinants of life satisfaction. *Research on Aging, 7*(2), 209-233.

Georges-Abeyie, D. E. (1984). *The criminal justice system and blacks.* Boardman.

Gibson, R. C. (1982). Black at middle and late life: Resources and coping. *Annals of the American Academy of Political and Social Science, 464,* 79-90.

Gibson, R. C. (1986). *The physical disability of older blacks.* Final Report to the National Institute of Aging (Grant no. AGO3553). Ann Arbor: University of Michigan.

Gibson, R. C., & Jackson, J. S. (1987). The black oldest old: Informal support, physical health and functioning. *Milbank Memorial Quarterly, 65*(Suppl. 2), 421-454.

Gibson, R. C., & Jackson, J. S. (1992). Informal support, health and functioning among the black elderly. In R. Suzman, D. Willis, & K. Manton (Eds.), *The oldest old* (pp. 321-340). New York: Oxford University Press.

Gillum, R. F. (1979). Pathophysiology of hypertension in blacks and whites: A review of the basics of racial blood pressure differences. *Hypertension, 5,* 468-475.

Glenn, N. D. (1975). The contribution of marriage to the psychological well-being of males and females. *Journal of Marriage and the Family, 37*(3), 594-600.

Glenn, N. D., & Weaver, C. N. (1978). A multivariate, multisurvey study of marital happiness. *Journal of Marriage and the Family, 40*(2), 269-282.

Glenn, N. D., & Weaver, C. N. (1981). The contribution of marital happiness to global happiness. *Journal of Marriage and the Family, 43*(2), 161-168.

Goldstein, H. (1979). Improving policing: A problem-oriented approach. *Crime & Delinquency, 25*, 236-258.

Gordon, T., & Kannel, W. B. (1984). Drinking and mortality: The Framingham study. *American Journal of Epidemiology, 120*(1), 97-107.

Gourash, N. (1978). Help-seeking: A review of literature. *American Journal of Community Psychology, 6*(5), 413-425.

Gove, W. R. (1972). The relationship between sex roles, marital status, and mental health. *Social Forces, 52*(1), 34-44.

Gove, W. R., Hughes, M., & Style, C. B. (1983). Does marriage have positive effects on the psychological well-being of the individual? *Journal of Health and Social Behavior, 24*(2), 122-131.

Graham, S. (1992). Most of the subjects were white and middle class: Trends in published research on African Americans in selected APA journals, 1979-1989. *American Psychologist, 47*(5), 629-639.

Greene, B. A. (1990). Special issues in feminist therapy. 1: What has gone before: The legacy of racism and sexism in the lives of black mothers and daughters. *Women & Therapy, 9*(1-2), 207-230.

Greene, R. L., Jackson, J. S., & Neighbors, H. W. (1993). Mental health and health-seeking behavior. In J. S. Jackson, L. M. Chatters, & R. J. Taylor (Eds.), *Aging in black America* (pp. 185-200). Newbury Park, CA: Sage.

Greenley, J. R., Mechanic, D., & Cleary, P. D. (1988). Seeking help for psychologic problems. *Medical Care, 25*(12), 1113-1128.

Grier, W. H., & Cobbs, P. M. (1969). *Black rage.* New York: Bantam.

Griffith, E. H., & Baker, F. M. (1993). Psychiatric care of African Americans. In A. C. Gaw (Ed.), *Culture, ethnicity and mental illness* (pp. 147-173). Washington, DC: American Psychiatric Press.

Griffith, J. (1985). A community survey of psychological impairment among Anglo and Mexican Americans and its relationship to service utilization. *Community Mental Health Journal, 21*(1), 28-41.

el-Guebaly, N., & el-Guebaly, A. (1981). Alcohol abuse in ancient Egypt: The recorded evidence. *International Journal of the Addictions, 16*(7), 1207-1221.

Gurin, G., Veroff, J., & Feld, S. (1960). *Americans view their mental health.* New York: Basic Books.

Gurin, P., Miller, A. H., & Gurin, G. (1980). Stratum identification and consciousness. *Social Psychology Quarterly, 43*(1), 30-47.

Guttentag, M., & Secord, P. (1983). *Too many women? The sex ratio question.* Beverly Hills, CA: Sage.

Guyot, D. (1991). *Policing as though people mattered.* Philadelphia: Temple University Press.

Hacker, A. (1992). *Two nations: Black and white: Separate, hostile, unequal.* New York: Ballantine.

Hackett, T. P., & Cassem, N. H. (1970). Psychological reactions to life-threatening illness: Acute myocardial infarction. In H. S. Abram (Ed.), *Psychological aspects of stress* (pp. 29-43). Springfield, IL: Charles C Thomas.

Hahn, B. A. (1993). Marital status and women's health: The effect of economic marital acquisitions. *Journal of Marriage and the Family, 55*, 495-504.

Hahn, R. (1992). The state of federal health statistics on racial and ethnic groups. *Journal of the American Medical Association, 267*(2), 268-271.

Hamilton, V. L., Broman, C. L., Hoffman, W. S., & Renner, D. S. (1990). Hard times and vulnerable people: Initial effects of plant closings on autoworkers' mental health. *Journal of Health and Social Behavior, 31*(2), 123-140.

Harburg, E., Blakelock, E. H., & Roeper, P. J. (1979). Resentful and reflective coping with arbitrary authority and blood pressure: Detroit. *Psychosomatic Medicine, 3,* 189-202.

Harburg, E., Erfurt, J. C., Chape, C., Schull, W., & Schork, M. A. (1973). Socio-ecological stressor areas and black-white blood pressure: Detroit. *Journal of Chronic Diseases, 26*(9), 596-611.

Harburg, E., Erfurt, J. C., Hauenstein, L. S., Chape, C., Schull, W. J., & Schork, M. A. (1973). Socio-ecological stress, suppressed hostility, skin color, and black-white male blood pressure: Detroit. *Psychosomatic Medicine, 35*(4), 276-296.

Harburg, E., & Hauenstein, L. (1980). Parity and blood pressure among four race-stress groups of females in Detroit. *American Journal of Epidemiology, 111,* 356-366.

Harburg, E., Julius, S., McGinn, N. F., McLeod, J., & Hoobler, S. W. (1964). Personality traits and behavioral patterns associated with systolic blood pressure levels in college males. *Journal of Chronic Diseases, 17,* 405-414.

Harford, T. C. (1992). Family history of alcoholism in the United States: Prevalence and demographic characteristics. *British Journal of Addiction, 87*(6), 931-935.

Harper, F. D. (1976). Overview: Alcohol and blacks. In F. D. Harper (Ed.), *Alcohol abuse and black America* (pp. 1-12). Alexandria, VA: Douglas.

Hartjen, C. A. (1978). *Crime and criminalization* (2nd ed.). New York: Holt, Reinhart & Winston.

Hatch, L. R. (1991). Informal support patterns of older African-American and white women: Examining the effects of family, paid work, and religious participation. *Research on Aging, 13*(2), 144-170.

Hatchett, S. J., & Jackson, J. S. (1993). African American extended kin systems: An assessment. In H. P. McAdoo (Ed.), *Family ethnicity: Strength in diversity* (pp. 90-108). Newbury Park, CA: Sage.

Health Resources Administration. (1980). *Health of the disadvantaged* (DHHS Pub. No. HRA 80-633, Public Health Service). Washington, DC: Government Printing Office.

Heath, D. B. (1990-1991). Uses and misuses of the concept of ethnicity in alcohol studies: An essay in deconstruction. *International Journal of the Addictions, 25*(5A-6A), 607-628.

Herd, D. (1985). We cannot stagger to freedom: A history of blacks and alcohol in American politics. In L. Brill & C. Winick (Eds.), *Yearbook of substance use and abuse* (Vol. 3, pp. 141-186). New York: Human Services Press.

Herd, D. (1990). Subgroup differences in drinking patterns among black and white men: Results from a national survey. *Journal of Studies on Alcohol, 51*(3), 221-232.

Herd, D. (1994). Predicting drinking problems among black and white men: Results from a national survey. *Journal of Studies on Alcohol, 55*(1), 61-71.

Herzog, A. R., & Rodgers, W. L. (1981). The structure of subjective well-being in different age groups. *Journal of Gerontology, 36*(4), 472-479.

Heyman, A., Karp, H. R., & Heyden, S. (1971). Cerebrovascular disease in the bi-racial population of Evans County, Georgia. *Archives of Internal Medicine, 128*(6), 949-955.

Higginson, J. (1966). Etiological factors in gastrointestinal cancer in man. *Journal of the National Cancer Institute, 37*(4), 527-545.

Hilliard, T. (1981). Political and social action in the prevention of psychopathology of blacks: A mental health strategy for oppressed people. In J. Joffee & G. Albee (Eds.), *Prevention through political action and social change* (Primary Prevention of Psychopathology, Vol. 5, pp. 135-152). Hanover, NH: University of New England Press.

Hobfoll, S. E., & Walfisch, S. (1984). Coping with a threat to life: A longitudinal study of self-concept, social support, and psychological distress. *American Journal of Community Psychology, 12*(1), 87-100.

Hollingshead, A. B., & Redlich, F. C. (1958). *Social class and mental illness.* New York: John Wiley.

Horwitz, A. (1977). The pathways into psychiatric treatment: Some differences between men and women. *Journal of Health and Social Behavior, 18*(2), 169-178.

Hough, R. L., Landsverk, J. A., Karno, M., Burnam, A. A., Timbers, D. M., & Escobar, J. I.(1987). Utilization of health and mental health services by Los Angeles Mexican-Americans and non-Hispanic Whites. *Archives of General Psychiatry, 44*(8), 702-709.

Howard, C. S. (1983). *Locus of control and informal familial support as determinants of help-seeking behavior among black women.* Unpublished manuscript.

Hypertension Detection and Follow-Up Cooperative Group. (1977). Race, education, and prevalence of hypertension. *American Journal of Epidemiology, 106*(5), 351-361.

Hypertension Detection and Follow-Up Cooperative Group. (1979). Mortality by race, sex, and age. *Journal of the American Medical Association, 242*(23), 2572-2577.

Israel, B., & Rounds, K. (1987). Social networks and social support. *Advances in Health Education and Health Promotion, 2,* 311-351.

Jackson, J. J. (1981). Urban black Americans. In A. Harwood (Ed.), *Ethnicity and medical care* (pp. 37-129). Cambridge, MA: Harvard University Press.

Jackson, J. S. (1988). Mental health problems among black Americans: Research needs. *Division of Child and Family Services Newsletter, 11*(2), 18-19.

Jackson, J. S. (1989). Race, ethnicity, and psychological theory and research [Editorial]. *Journal of Gerontology: Psychological Sciences, 44*(1), 1-2.

Jackson, J. S. (Ed.). (1991). *Life in black America.* Newbury Park, CA: Sage.

Jackson, J. S. (1993). Racial influences on adult development and aging. In R. Kastenbaum (Ed.), *The encyclopedia of adult development* (pp. 18-26). Phoenix, AZ: Oryx.

Jackson, J. S., & Adams, V. H. (1992). Changes in reports of subjective well-being among African Americans: 1979 to 1989. In *Quality of life and psychological well-being among ethnic and racial groups in the United States.* Symposium conducted at the American Psychological Association Annual Meetings, Washington, DC.

Jackson, J. S., Antonucci, T. C., & Gibson, R. C. (1995). Ethnic and cultural factors in research on aging and mental health: A life-course perspective. In D. K. Padgett (Ed.), *Handbook on ethnicity, aging and mental health* (pp. 22-46). Westport, CT: Greenwood.

Jackson, J. S., Antonucci, T. C., & Gibson, R. C. (1990). Cultural, racial and ethnic minority influences on aging. In J. E. Birren & K. W. Schaie (Eds.), *Handbook of the psychology of aging* (3rd ed., pp. 103-123). New York: Academic Press.

Jackson, J. S., Brown, T., Williams, D. W., Torres, M., Sellers, S., & Brown. K. (1996). Perceptions and experiences of racism and the physical and mental health status of African Americans: A thirteen-year national panel study. *Ethnicity and Disease, 6*(1, 2), 132-147.

Jackson, J. S., Chatters, L. M., & Neighbors, H. W. (1986). The subjective life quality of black Americans. In F. M. Andrews (Ed.), *Research on the quality of life* (pp. 193-203). Ann Arbor: University of Michigan Press.

Jackson, J. S., Chatters, L. M., & Taylor, R. J. (1993). *Aging in black America.* Newbury Park, CA: Sage.

Jackson, J. S., & Hatchett, S. J. (1986). Intergenerational research: Methodological considerations. In N. Datan, A. L. Green, & H. W. Reese (Eds.), *Intergenerational relations* (pp. 51-75). Hillsdale, NJ: Lawrence Erlbaum.

Jackson, J. S., & Neighbors, H. W. (1989). Sociodemographic predictors of psychological distress in black adults. In A. O. Harrison (Ed.), *Proceedings from the eleventh conference on empirical research in black psychology* (pp. 120-128). Rockville, MD: National Institute of Mental Health.

Jackson, J. S., Neighbors, H. W., & Gurin, G. (1986). Findings from a national survey of black mental health: Implications for practice and training. In M. R. Miranda & H. L. Kitano (Eds.), *Mental health research and practice in minority communities: Development of culturally sensitive training programs* (DHHS Publication No. ADM 86-1466, pp. 91-115). Rockville, MD: National Institute of Mental Health.

Jackson, J. S., Tucker, M. B., & Bowman, P. (1982). Conceptual and methodological problems in survey research on black Americans. In W. T. Liu (Ed.), *Methodological problems in minority research* (pp. 11-39). Chicago: Pacific/Asian American Mental Health Research Center.

Jackson, J. S., Tucker, M. B., & Gurin, G. (1987). *National survey of black Americans, 1979-80.* Ann Arbor, MI: Inter-University Consortium for Political and Social Research, Institute for Social Research.

Jackson, J. S., & Wolford, M. L. (1992). Changes from 1979 to 1987 in mental health status and help-seeking among African Americans. *Journal of Geriatric Psychiatry, 25*(1), 15-67.

James, S. A. (1985). Psychosocial and environmental factors in black hypertension. In E. Saunders & N. Shulman (Eds.), *Hypertension in blacks: Epidemiology, pathophysiology, and treatment* (pp. 132-143). Chicago: Yearbook Medical Publishers.

James, S. A. (1993, November). The narrative of John Henry Martin. *Southern Cultures, Inaugural Issues,* pp. 83-106.

James, S. A. (1994). John Henryism and the health of African-Americans. *Culture, Medicine, and Psychiatry, 18*(2), 163-182.

James, S. A., Hartnett, S. A., & Kalsbeek, W. D. (1983). John Henryism and blood pressure differences among black men. *Journal of Behavioral Medicine, 6*(3), 259-278.

James, S. A., Keenan, N. L., Strogatz, D. S., Bowning, S. R., & Garrett, J. M. (1992). Socioeconomic status, John Henryism, and blood pressure in black adults: The Pitt County study. *American Journal of Epidemiology, 135*(1), 59-67.

James, S. A., & Kleinbaum, D. G. (1976). Socioecologic stress and hypertension-related mortality rates in North Carolina. *American Journal of Public Health, 66*(4), 354-358.

James, S. J., LaCroix, A. Z., Kleinbaum, D. G., & Strogatz, D. S. (1984). John Henryism and blood pressure differences among black men II: The role of occupational stressors. *Journal of Behavioral Medicine, 7*(3), 259-275.

Janson, P., & Mueller, K. R. (1983). Age, ethnicity, and well-being. *Research on Aging, 5*(3), 353-367.

Jaynes, G. D., & Williams, R. M. (1989). *A common destiny: Blacks and American society.* Washington, DC: National Academy Press.

Johnson, E. H. (1984). *Anger and anxiety as determinants of elevated blood pressure in adolescents: The Tampa study.* Unpublished doctoral dissertation, University of South Florida, Tampa.

Johnson, E. H. (1987). Behavioral factors associated with hypertension in black Americans. *Handbook of Hypertension, 9*(13), 181-197.

Johnson, E. H. (1989a). Cardiovascular reactivity, emotional factors, and home blood pressure in black males with and without a parental history of hypertension. *Psychosomatic Medicine, 51*(4), 390-403.

Johnson, E. H. (1989b). The role of the experience and expression of anger and anxiety in elevated blood pressure among black and white adolescents. *Journal of the National Medical Association, 81*(5), 573-584.

Johnson, E. H. (1990). Interrelationships between psychological factors, body mass and overweight, and blood pressure in black and white adolescents. *Journal of Adolescent Health Care, 11*(4), 310-318.

Johnson, E. H., Spielberger, C. D., Worden, T. J., & Jacobs, G. A. (1987). Emotional and familial determinants of elevated blood pressure in black and white adolescent males. *Journal of Psychosomatic Research, 31*(3), 287-300.

Jonas, K. (1979). Factors in development of community among elderly persons in age-segregated housing: Relationships between involvement in friendship roles within the community and external social roles. *Anthropological Quarterly, 52*(1), 29-38.

Jones, B. E., & Gray, B. A. (1984). Similarities and differences in black men and women in psychotherapy. *Journal of the National Medical Association, 76*(1), 21-27.

Jones, J. M. (1992). Understanding the mental health consequences of race: Contributions of basic social psychological research. In D. N. Ruble, P. H. Constanzo, & M. E. Oliveri (Eds.), *The social psychology of mental health: Basic mechanisms and applications* (pp. 199-240). New York: Guilford.

Kahana, E., & Kahana, B. (1982). Clinical issues of middle age and later life. *Annals of the American Academy of Political and Social Science, 464*, 140-161.

Kasl, S. V., & Berkman, L. F. (1981). Some psychosocial influences on the health status of the elderly: The perspective of social epidemiology. In J. L. McGaugh & S. B. Kiesler (Eds.), *Aging, biology and behavior* (pp. 345-385). New York: Academic Press.

Kasl, S. V., & Harburg, E. (1972). Perceptions of the neighborhood and the desire to move out. *Journal of the American Institute of Planners, 38*, 318-324.

Kessler, R. C. (1979a). A strategy for studying differential vulnerability to the psychological consequences of stress. *Journal of Health and Social Behavior, 20*, 100-108.

Kessler, R. C. (1979b). Stress, social status, and psychological distress. *Journal of Health and Social Behavior, 20*(3), 259-272.

Kessler, R. C., & Cleary, P. D. (1980). Social class and psychological distress. *American Sociological Review, 45*, 463-478.

Kessler, R. C., McGonagle, K., Zhao, S., Nelson, C., Hughes, M., Eshleman, S., Wittchen, H., & Kendler, K. (1994). Lifetime and 12-month prevalence of DSM-III-R psychiatric disorders in the United States: Results from the National Comorbidity Survey. *Archives of General Psychiatry, 51*(1), 8-19.

Kessler, R. C., & Neighbors, H. (1986). A new perspective on the relationships among race, social class, and psychological distress. *Journal of Health and Social Behavior, 27*(2), 107-115.

Kessler, R. C., Price, R. H., & Wortman, C. B. (1985). Social factors in psychopathology: Stress, social support, and coping processes. *Annual Review of Psychology, 36*, 531-572.

King, L. (1982). Alcoholism: Studies regarding black Americans. In *Special population issues, Monograph 4* (DHHS Publication No. ADM 82-1193, pp. 385-407). Washington, DC: Government Printing Office.

Kirby, D., & Jackson, J. S. (1995). *Racial discrimination in the workplace: Workgroup racial composition and supervisor race.* Unpublished manuscript.

Kiyak, H. A., & Hooyman, N. R. (1994). Minority and socioeconomic status: Impact on quality of life in aging. In R. P. Abeles, H. C. Gift, & M. G. Ory (Eds.), *Aging and quality of life.* New York: Springer.

Kramer, M., Brown, H., Skinner, A., Anthony, J., & German, P. (1986). *Changing living arrangements in the population and the potential effect on the prevalence of mental disorder: Findings of the Eastern Baltimore Mental Health Study.* Unpublished manuscript.

Kramer, M., Rosen, B., & Willis, E. (1973). Definitions and distributions of mental disorders in a racist society. In C. Willie, M. Kramer, & B. Brown (Eds.), *Racism and mental health* (pp. 353-459). Pittsburgh: University of Pittsburgh Press.

Krause, N. (1993). Race differences in life satisfaction among aged men and women. *Journal of Gerontology, 48*(5), S235-S244.

Krieger, N. (1990). Racial and gender discrimination: Risk factors for high blood pressure? *Social Science and Medicine, 30*(12), 1273-1281.

Langer, E. H. (1981). Old age: An artifact? In J. L. McGaugh & S. B. Kiesler (Eds.), *Aging, biology and behavior* (pp. 255-282). New York: Academic Press.

Langner, T. (1962). A twenty-two item screening score of psychiatric symptoms indicating impairment. *Journal of Health and Human Behavior, 3,* 269-276.

LaRue, A., Dessonville, C., & Jarvik, L. (1985). Aging and mental disorders. In J. Birren & K. Schaie (Eds.), *Handbook of the psychology of aging* (pp. 664-702). New York: Van Nostrand Reinhold.

Lawson, W. B. (1986). Racial and ethnic factors in psychiatric research. *Hospital and Community Psychiatry, 37*(1), 50-54.

Lawson, W. B., Hepler, N., Holladay, J., & Cuffel, B. (1994). Race as a factor in inpatient and outpatient admissions and diagnosis. *Hospital Community Psychiatry, 45*(1), 72-74.

Lawton, M. P. (1978). The housing problems of community resident elderly. In R. P. Boynton (Ed.), *Occasional papers in housing and community affairs* (pp. 39-74). Washington, DC: Government Printing Office.

Lawton, M. P. (1980a). *Environment and aging.* Pacific Grove, CA: Brooks/Cole.

Lawton, M. P. (1980b). Housing the elderly: Residential quality and residential satisfaction. *Research on Aging, 2,* 309-328.

Lazarus, R. S. (1981). The costs and benefits of denial. In B. S. Dohrenwend & B. P. Dohrenwend (Eds.), *Stressful life events and their contexts* (pp. 131-156). New York: Prodist.

Lazarus, R. S., & Folkman, S. (1984). *Stress, appraisal, and coping.* New York: Springer.

Leaf, P. J., Bruce, M. L., Tischler, G. L., Freeman, D. H., Weissman, M. M., & Myers, J. K. (1988). Factors affecting the utilization of specialty and general medical mental health services. *Medical Care, 26*(1), 9-26.

Lee, S. G., Carstairs, G. M., & Pickersgill, M. J. (1971). Essential hypertension and the recall of motives. *Journal of Psychosomatic Research, 15*(1), 95-105.

Lee, T., & Marans, R. W. (1980). Objective and subjective indicators: Effects of scale discordance on interrelationships. *Social Indicators Research, 8*(1), 47-64.

Levine, S., & Scotch, N. A. (1970). *Social stress.* Chicago: Aldine.

Levinson, D. H. (1978). Studies based on the human relations area files. *Behavior Science Research, 13*(4), 295-301.

Lewis, D. O., & Shanok, S. S. (1980). The use of correctional setting for follow-up care of psychiatrically disturbed adolescents. *American Journal of Psychiatry, 137*(8), 953-955.

Liang, J., Dvorkin, L., Kahana, E., & Mazian, F. (1980). Social integration and morale: A re-examination. *Journal of Gerontology, 35*(5), 746-757.

Liebow, E. (1967). *Tally's corner.* Boston: Little, Brown.

Lillie-Blanton, M., Mackenzie, E., & Anthony, J. C. (1991). Black-white differences in alcohol use by women: Baltimore survey findings. *Public Health Reports, 106*(2), 124-133.

Lin, K. M., Inui, T. S., Kleinman, A. M., & Womack, W. M. (1982). Sociocultural determinants of the help-seeking behavior of patients with mental illness. *Journal of Nervous and Mental Disease, 170*(2), 78-85.

Litwak, E. (1970). Differential structures and tasks of primary groups: The principle of matching task and group structures. In E. Litwak (Ed.), *Helping the elderly: The complementary roles of informal networks and formal systems* (pp. 31-53). New York: Guilford.

Litwak, E., & Szelenyi, I. (1969). Primary group structures and their functions: Kin, neighbors, and friends. *American Sociological Review, 34*(4), 465-481.

Locke, D. (1992). *Increasing multicultural understanding: A comprehensive model.* Newbury Park, CA: Sage.

Loggie, J. M. H. (1971). Systemic hypertension in children and adolescents. *Pediatric Clinics of North America, 18*(4), 1273-1310.

Londe, S., Bourgoignie, J. J., Robson, A. M., & Goldring, D. (1971). Hypertension in apparently normal children. *Journal of Pediatrics, 78*(4), 569.

Londe, S., & Goldring, D. (1976). High blood pressure in children: Problems and guidelines for evaluation and treatment. *American Journal of Cardiology, 37*(4), 650-657.

Lopata, H. Z. (1973). Self-identity in marriage and widowhood. *Sociological Quarterly, 14*(3), 407-418.

Louis Harris and Associates. (1978). *A survey of citizens' views and concerns about urban life* (Final Report). Washington, DC: U.S. Department of Housing and Urban Development.

Lowenthal, M., & Robinson, B. (1976). Social networks and isolation. In R. Bengston & E. Shanas (Eds.), *Handbook of aging and the social sciences* (pp. 432-456). New York: Van Nostrand Reinhold.

Makela, K., Room, R., Single, E., Sulkunen, P., & Walsh, B. (1981). *Alcohol, society and the state. Vol. 1. A comparative study of alcohol control.* Toronto, Canada: Addiction Research Foundation.

Malgady, R., Rogler, L., & Tryon, W. (1992). Issues of validity in the Diagnostic Interview Schedule. *Journal of Psychiatric Research, 26*(1), 59-67.

Malin, H., Coakley, J., Yaelber, C., Munch, N., & Holland, W. (1982). An epidemiologic perspective on alcohol use and abuse in the U.S. In *Alcohol consumption and related problems, alcohol and health monograph 1* (DHHS Publication No. ADM 82-1190, pp. 99-153). Washington, DC: Government Printing Office.

Marans, R. W. (1976). Perceived quality of residential environments: Some methodological issues. In K. H. Craik & E. H. Zube (Eds.), *Perceiving environmental quality: Research and applications* (pp. 123-147). New York: Plenum.

Marans, R. W. (1979). *The determinants of neighborhood quality: An analysis of the 1976 annual housing survey* (Annual Housing Survey Studies No. 3). Washington, DC: U.S. Department of Housing and Urban Development.

Marans, R. W., & Rodgers, W. (1975). Toward an understanding of community satisfaction. In A. H. Hawley & V. P. Rock (Eds.), *Metropolitan America in contemporary perspective* (pp. 299-352). New York: John Wiley.

Markush, R. E., & Favero, R. V. (1974). Epidemiologic assessment of stressful life events, depressed mood, and psycho-physiological symptoms—A preliminary report. In B. S. Dohrenwend & B. P. Dohrenwend (Eds.), *Stressful life events: Their nature and effects* (pp. 171-190). New York: John Wiley.

Marsella, A. J., Kinzie, D., & Gordon, P. (1973). Ethnic variations in the expression of depression. *Journal of Cross-Cultural Psychology, 4*(4), 435-458.

Matthews, S. H. (1986). *Friendships through the life course: Oral biographies in old age.* Beverly Hills, CA: Sage.

Mattson, J. A. (1975). Hostility and aggression in black essential hypertensive diabetics and general medical patients. *Dissertation Abstracts International, 36*(5B), 2477.

Mayer, N., & Lee, O. (1980). *The effectiveness of federal home repair and improvement programs in meeting elderly homeowner needs* (Final Project Report No. 1283-1). Washington, DC: The Urban Institute.

Mays, V. M. (1985). The black American and psychotherapy: The dilemma. *Psychotherapy: Theory, Research, Practice and Training, 22*(2S), 69-78.

Mays, V. M. (1995). Black women, work stress and perceived discrimination: The focused support group model as an intervention for stress reduction. *Cultural Diversity and Mental Health, 1*(1), 53-65.

Mays, V. M., & Albee, G. W. (1992). Ethnic minorities and psychotherapy: A question of policy and a matter of relevance. In D. K. Freedheim (Ed.), *History of psychotherapy: A century of change* (pp. 552-570). Washington, DC: American Psychological Association.

Mays, V. M., & Cochran, S. D. (1995). HIV/AIDS in the African American community: Changing concerns, changing behaviors. In M. Stein & A. Baum (Eds.), *Chronic diseases* (pp. 259-272). Hillside, NJ: Lawrence Erlbaum.

Mays, V. M., & Cochran, S. D. (1996). *Is there a legacy of Tuskegee? AIDS misbeliefs among inner city African Americans and Hispanics.* Manuscript submitted for publication.

Mays, V. M., Coleman, L. M., & Jackson, J. S. (1996). *Perceived discrimination, employment status, and job stress in a national sample of black women.* Unpublished manuscript.

Mays, V. M., & Comas-Diaz, L. (1988). Feminist therapy with ethnic minority population: A closer look at blacks and Hispanics. In M. A. Douglas & L. Walker (Eds.), *Feminist psychotherapies: Integration of therapeutic and feminist systems* (pp. 228-251). Norwood, NJ: Ablex.

McAdoo, H. P. (1980). Black mothers and the extended family support network. In L. F. Rodgers-Rose (Ed.), *The black woman* (pp. 125-144). Beverly Hills, CA: Sage.

McCarthy, J. D., & Yancey, W. L. (1971). Uncle Tom and Mr. Charlie: Metaphysical pathos in the study of racism and personal disorganization. *American Journal of Sociology, 76,* 648-672.

McDaniels, A. (1989, June 26). The court spins right. *Newsweek, 113,* 18-19.

McDonough, J. R., Garrison, G. E., & Hames, C. G. (1964). Blood pressure and hypertensive disease among Negroes and whites. *Annals of Internal Medicine, 61,* 208.

McKeigue, P. M., & Karmi, G. (1993). Alcohol consumption and alcohol-related problems in Afro-Caribbeans and south Asians in the United Kingdom. *Alcohol and Alcoholism, 28*(1), 1-10.

McLoyd, V. (1990). The impact of economic hardship on black families and children: Psychological distress, parenting and socioemotional development. *Child Development, 61*(2), 311-346.

McNeilly, M., Anderson N. B., Armstead, C., Clark, R., Corbett, M., Robinson, E., Pieper, C., & Lepisto, E. (in press). The perceived racism scale: A multidimensional assessment of the experience of white racism among African Americans. *Ethnicity and Disease.*

Mechanic, D. (1978). *Medical sociology* (2nd ed.). New York: Free Press.

Mechanic, D., Cleary, P. D., & Greenley, J. R. (1982). Distress syndrome, illness behavior, access to care, and medical utilization in a defined population. *Medical Care, 20*(4), 361-372.

Medley, M. L. (1980). Life satisfaction across four stages of adult life. *International Journal of Aging and Human Development, 11*(3), 193-209.

Menaghan, E. G. (1982). Measuring coping effectiveness: A panel analysis of marital problems and coping efforts. *Journal of Health and Social Behavior, 23*(3), 220-234.

Menaghan, E. G. (1983). Individual coping efforts: Moderators of the relationship between life stress and mental health outcomes. In H. B. Kaplan (Ed.), *Psychosocial stress* (pp. 157-191). New York: Academic Press.

Menaghan, E. G., & Merves, E. S. (1984). Coping with occupational problems: The limits of individual efforts. *Journal of Health and Social Behavior, 25*(4), 406-423.

Meriyama, I., Krueger, D. E., & Stamler, J. (1971). *Cardiovascular diseases in the United States.* Cambridge, MA: Harvard University Press.

Messer, M. (1968). Race differences in selected attitudinal dimensions of the elderly. *The Gerontologist, 8*(4), 245-249.

Michalos, A. C. (1980). Satisfaction and happiness. *Social Indicators Research, 8,* 385-422.

Michigan State University. National Center on Police and Community Relations, School of Police Administration and Public Safety. (1967). *A national survey of police and community relations; field survey A.* Washington, DC: Government Printing Office.

Midanik, L. T., & Clark, W. B. (1994). The demographic distribution of U.S. drinking patterns in 1990: Description and trends from 1984. *American Journal of Public Health, 84*(8), 1218-1222.

Miller, C. L., Stein, R. F., & Grim, G. (1979). Personality factors of the hypertensive patient. *International Journal of Nursing Studies, 16*(3), 235-241.

Miller, F. T., Bentz, W. K. Aponte, J. F., & Brogan, D. R. (1974). Perception of life crisis events: A comparative study of rural and urban samples. In B. S. Dohrenwend & B. P. Dohrenwend (Eds.), *Stressful life events—Their nature and effects* (pp. 259-274). New York: John Wiley.

Miller, F. T., Tsemberis, S., Malia, G., & Grega, D. (1980). Neighborhood satisfaction among urban dwellers. *Journal of Social Issues, 36*(3), 101-117.

Miller, T. W. (Ed.). (1989). *Stressful life events.* New York: International Universities Press.

Mindel, C. H., & Wright, R. J. (1982). The use of social services by black and white elderly: The role of social support systems. *Journal of Gerontological Social Work, 4*(3-4), 107-125.

Mindel, C. H., Wright, R., Jr., & Starrett, R. A. (1986). Informal and formal health and social support systems of black and white elderly: A comparative cost approach. *The Gerontologist, 26*(3), 279-285.

Mirowsky, J., & Ross, C. E. (1980). Minority status, ethnic culture, and distress: A comparison of blacks, whites, Mexicans, and Mexican-Americans. *American Journal of Sociology, 86*(3), 479-495.

Mitchell, R., & Trickett, E. (1980). Social networks as mediators of social support: An analysis of the effects and determinants of social networks. *Community Mental Health Journal, 16*(1), 27-44.

Morgan, D. J. (1978). *Patterns of population distribution: A residential preference model and its dynamic* (Research Paper No. 176). Chicago: Department of Geography, the University of Chicago.

Morgan, J. N., Dickinson, K., Dickinson, J., Benus, J., & Duncan, G. (1974). *Five thousand American families—Patterns of economic progress: An analysis of the first five years of the panel study of income dynamics.* Ann Arbor: University of Michigan Press.

Moser, J. (1980). *Prevention of alcohol-related problems.* Toronto, Canada: Addiction Research Foundation.

Mukherjee, S., Shukla, S., Woodle, J., Rosen, A. M., & Olarte, S. (1983). Misdiagnosis of schizophrenia in bipolar patients: A multiethnic comparison. *American Journal of Psychiatry, 140*(12), 1571-1574.

Murphy, G. E., & Wetzel, R. D. (1990). The lifetime risk of suicide in alcoholism. *Archives of General Psychiatry, 47*(4), 383-392.

Murray, C. B., Khatib, S., & Jackson, M. (1989). Social indices and the black elderly: A comparative life cycle approach to the study of double jeopardy. In R. L. Jones (Ed.), *Black adult development and aging* (pp. 167-187). Berkeley, CA: Cobb & Henry.

Murray, S. R., & Harrison, D. D. (1981). Black women and the future. *Psychology of Women Quarterly, 6*(1), 113-122.

Mutchler, J. E., & Burr, J. A. (1991). Racial differences in health and health care service utilization in later life: The effect of socioeconomic status. *Journal of Health and Social Behavior, 32*(4), 342-356.

Myers, H. F. (1982). Stress, ethnicity and social class: A model for research with black populations. In E. Jones & S. Korchin (Eds.), *Minority mental health* (pp. 118-148). New York: Praeger.

Myers, H. F. (1986). Coronary heart disease in black populations: Current research, treatment and prevention needs. In *Health & human services secretary's task force report on black and minority health: Vol. IV: Cardiovascular and cerebrovascular diseases* (pp. 302-344). Washington DC: Government Printing Office.

Myers, H. F., Bastien, R., & Miles, R. (1992). Life stress, health and blood pressure in black college students. In A. K. Burlew, W. Banks, H. McAdoo, & D. Azibo (Eds.), *African American psychology: Theory, research and practice* (pp. 370-391). Newbury Park, CA: Sage.

Myers, J. K., Lindenthal, J. J., & Pepper, M. P. (1971). Life events and psychiatric impairment. *Journal of Nervous Mental Disorders, 152*(3), 149-157.

Naranjo, C. A., & Bremer, K. E. (1993). Behavioral correlates of alcohol intoxication. *Addiction, 88*(1), 25-35.

National Center for Health Statistics, Division of Vital Statistics. (1967). *Vital statistics of the United States: 1967.* Washington, DC: Government Printing Office.

National Heart, Lung, and Blood Institute. (1995). *Chartbook of U.S. national data on socioeconomic status and cardiovascular health and disease.* Washington, DC: Author.

National Institute of Alcohol and Alcohol Abuse. (1979). *Alcohol treatment and black Americans* (DHEW Publication No. 79-853). Washington, DC: Government Printing Office.

National Institute on Drug Abuse. (1991a). *Drug use among American high school seniors, college students and young adults, 1975-1990. Vol. 1: High school seniors.* Rockville, MD: U.S. Department of Health and Human Services.

National Institute on Drug Abuse. (1991b). *National household survey on drug abuse: Population estimates 1991.* Rockville, MD: U.S. Department of Health and Human Services.

Neal, A. N., & Turner, S. M. (1991). Anxiety disorders research with African Americans: Current status. *Psychological Bulletin, 109*(3), 400-410.

Neff, J. A. (1985). Race and vulnerability to stress: An examination of differential vulnerability. *Journal of Personality and Social Psychology, 49*(2), 481-491.

Neighbors, H. W. (1984a). The distribution of psychiatric morbidity in black Americans: A review and suggestions for research. *Community Mental Health Journal, 20*(3), 5-18.

Neighbors, H. W. (1984b). Professional help use among black Americans: Implications for unmet need. *American Journal of Community Psychology, 12*(5), 551-566.

Neighbors, H. W. (1985). Seeking professional help for personal problems: Black Americans' use of health and mental health services. *Community Mental Health Journal, 21*(3), 156-166.

Neighbors, H. W. (1986). Ambulatory medical care among adult black Americans: The hospital emergency room. *Journal of the National Medical Association, 78*(4), 275-282.

Neighbors, H. W. (1987). Improving the mental health of black Americans: Lessons from the community mental health movement. *Milbank Quarterly, 65*(2), 348-380.

Neighbors, H. W. (1988). The help-seeking behavior of black Americans: A summary of findings from the National Survey of Black Americans. *Journal of the National Medical Association, 80*(9), 1009-1012.

Neighbors, H. W. (1990). The prevention of psychopathology in African Americans: An epidemiologic perspective. *Community Mental Health Journal, 26*(2), 167-179.

Neighbors, H. W. (1991). Mental health. In J. S. Jackson (Ed.), *Life in black America* (pp. 221-237). Newbury Park, CA: Sage.

Neighbors, H. W., Bashshur, R., Price, R., Selig, S., Donabedian, A., & Shannon, G. (1992). Ethnic minority mental health service delivery: A review of the literature. *Research in Community and Mental Health, 7*(1), 55-71.

Neighbors, H. W., Caldwell, C. H., Thompson, E., & Jackson, J. S. (1994). Help-seeking behavior and unmet need. In S. Friedman (Ed.), *Anxiety disorders in African Americans* (pp. 26-39). New York: Springer.

Neighbors, H. W., & Howard, C. S. (1987). Sex differences in professional help seeking among adult black Americans. *American Journal of Community Psychology, 15*(4), 403-417.

Neighbors, H. W., & Jackson, J. S. (1984). The use of informal and formal help: Four patterns of illness behavior in the black community. *American Journal of Community Psychology, 12*(6), 629-644.

Neighbors, H. W., & Jackson, J. S. (1986). Uninsured risk groups in a national survey of Black Americans. *Journal of the National Medical Association, 78*(10), 979-983.

Neighbors, H. W., Jackson, J. S., Bowman, P., & Gurin, G. (1983). Stress, coping and black mental health: Preliminary findings from a national study. *Prevention in Human Services, 2*(3), 5-29.

Neighbors, H. W., Jackson, J. S., Broman, C. L., & Thompson, E. (1996). Racism and the mental health of African Americans: The role of self and system blame. *Ethnicity and Disease, 6*(1, 2), 167-175.

Neighbors, H. W., Jackson, J. S., Campbell, L., & Williams, D. (1989). The influence of racial factors on psychiatric diagnosis: A review and suggestions for research. *Community Mental Health Journal, 25*(4), 301-311.

Neighbors, H. W., & Taylor, R. J. (1985). The use of social service agencies by black Americans. *Social Service Review, 59,* 258-268.

Neugarten, B. L., Havighurst, R. J., & Tobin, S. S. (1961). The measurement of life satisfaction. *Journal of Gerontology, 16,* 134-143.

Nichaman, M. Z., Boyle, E., Lesne, P. T., & Sauer, H. I. (1962). Cardiovascular disease mortality by race: The Charleston Heart Study, Phase I. *Geriatrics, 17,* 724-731.

Nickerson, K. J., Helms, J. E., & Terrell, F. (1994). Cultural mistrust, opinions about mental illness, and black students' attitudes toward seeking psychological help from white counselors. *Journal of Counseling Psychology, 41*(3), 378-385.

Obot, I. S. (1991). *Drinking behaviour and attitudes in Nigeria.* Jos, Nigeria: Centre for Development Studies, University of Jos.

O'Hare, W. P., Pollard, K. M., Mann, T. L., & Kent, M. M. (1991). African Americans in the 1990's. *Population Bulletin, 46,* 1-40.

Orbell, J. M., & Uno, T. (1972). A theory of neighborhood problem solving: Political action vs. residential mobility. *American Political Science Review, 61,* 471-489.

Outlaw, F. H. (1993). Stress and coping: The influence of racism on the cognitive appraisal processing of African Americans. *Issues in Mental Health Nursing, 14*(4), 399-409.

Pearlin, L. I., Lieberman, M. A., Menaghan, E. G., & Mullen, J. T. (1981). The stress process. *Journal of Health and Social Behavior, 22*(4), 337-356.

Pearlin, L. I., & Schooler, C. (1978). The structure of coping. *Journal of Health and Social Behavior, 19*(1), 2-21.

Phillips, G. Y. (1991). *Black Americans' perceptions of residential life quality.* Unpublished manuscript.

Pilowsky, I., Spalding, D., Shaw, J., & Komer, P. I. (1973). Hypertension and personality. *Psychosomatic Medicine, 35*(1), 50-56.

Poikolainen, K. (1991). Epidemiologic assessment of population risks and benefits of alcohol use. *Alcohol and Alcoholism, 1*(Suppl.), 27-34.

Pollans, C. H. (1983). *The psychometric properties and factors structure of the anger expression scale.* Unpublished master's thesis, University of South Florida, Tampa.

Popkin, C. L., & Council, F. M. (1993). A comparison of alcohol-related driving behavior of white and non-white North Carolina drivers. *Accident Analysis and Prevention, 25*(4), 355-364.

Powell, D. R., & Eisenstadt, J. (1983). Predictors of help-seeking in an urban setting: The search for child care. *American Journal of Community Psychology, 11*(4), 401-422.

Procidano, M. E., & Heller, K. (1983). Measures of perceived social support from friends and from family: Three validation studies. *American Journal of Community Psychology, 11*(1), 1-24.

Rachal, J. V., Hubbard, R. L., Williams, J. R., & Tuchfeld, B. S. (1976). Drinking levels and problem drinking among junior and senior high school students. *Journal of Studies on Alcohol, 37*(11), 1751-1761.

Radelet, L. A. (1973). *The police and the community.* Encino, CA: Glencoe.

Rahe, R. H. (1974). The pathway between subjects' recent life changes and their near-future illness reports: Representative results and methodological issues. In B. S. Dohrenwend & B. P. Dohrenwend (Eds.), *Stressful life events: Their nature and effects* (pp. 73-86). New York: John Wiley.

Rahe, R. H. (1978). Life change measurement clarification [Editorial]. *Psychosomatic Medicine, 40*(2), 95-98.

Rahe, R. H. (1979). Life change events and mental illness: An overview. *Journal of Human Stress, 5*(3), 2-10.

Rahe, R. H., Meyer, M., Smith, M., Kjaer, G., & Holmes, T. H. (1964). Social stress and illness onset. *Journal of Psychosomatic Research, 8*(1), 35-44.

Rainwater, L. (1970). *Behind ghetto walls: Black families in a federal slum.* Chicago: Aldine.

Ralph, J. R. (1983, December). Mental illness—A growing concern for minorities. In *Mental health commentaries.* (Available from the Center for Studies of Minority Group Mental Health, NIMH, Rockville, MD 20857)

Rao, V. P., & Rao, V. N. (1983). *Determinants of life satisfaction among black elderly.* New York: Haworth.

Regulus, T., Taylor, R., & Jackson, J. (1986). *Black Americans' attitudes toward the police.* Unpublished manuscript.

Reiss, A. J. (1977). *The police and the public.* New Haven, CT: Yale University Press.

Reskin, B., & Coverman, S. (1985). Sex and race in the determinants of psychophysical distress: A reappraisal of the sex-role hypothesis. *Social Forces, 63*(4), 1038-1059.

Rice, D. P., Kelman, S., Miller, L. S., & Dunmeyer, S. (1990). *The economic costs of alcohol and drug abuse and mental illness: 1985* (DHHS Publication No. ADM 90-1694). Washington, DC: Government Printing Office.

Riley, M. W. (1994). Changing lives and changing social structures: Common concerns of social science and public health. *American Journal of Public Health, 84*(8), 1214-1217.

Ritchey-Mann, C. R. (1993). *Unequal justice: A question of color.* Bloomington: Indiana University Press.

Roberts, J., & Rowland, M. (1981). *Vital and health statistics (Series I 1. No. 22 1), hypertension in adults 25-74 years of age: United States, 1971-75* (DHEW Publication No. PHS 811671). Washington, DC: Government Printing Office.

Roberts, R., Stevenson, J., & Breslow, L. (1981). Symptoms of depression among blacks and whites in an urban community. *Journal of Nervous and Mental Disease, 169*(12), 774-779.

Robins, L., & Regier, D. (1991). *Psychiatric disorders in America: The epidemiologic catchment area study.* New York: Free Press.

Robinson, C. R. (1983). Black women: A tradition of self-reliance strength. In J. H. Robbins & R. J. Siegel (Eds.), *Women changing therapy: New assessment, values, and strategies in feminist therapy.* New York: Haworth.

Robinson, J. D. (1962). A study of neuroticism and causal arterial blood pressure. *British Journal of Social and Clinical Psychology, 2*(1), 56-64.

Robyak, J. E., Byers, P. H., & Prange, M. E. (1989). Patterns of alcohol abuse among black and white alcoholics. *International Journal of the Addictions, 24*(7), 715-724.

Rodin, J. (1986). Aging and health: Effects of the sense of control. *Science, 233,* 1271-1276.

Rosen, B., Goldsmith, H. F., & Redlick, R. W. (1979). Demographics and social indicators. Uses in mental health planning in small areas. In *World health statistics, quarterly report, 31* (No. l). Geneva: World Health Organization.

Rosenberg, M. (1965). *Society and adolescent self-image.* Princeton, NJ: Princeton University Press.

Rosenblatt, S. M., Gross, M. M., Malenowski, B., Broman, M., & Lewis, E. (1971). Marital status and multiple psychiatric admissions for alcoholism: A cross validation. *Quarterly Journal of Studies on Alcohol, 32*(4), 1092-1096.

Rosenstein, M. J., & Milazzo-Sayre, L. J. (1981). *Characteristics of admissions to selected mental health facilities* (DHHS Publication No. 81-1005). Washington, DC: Government Printing Office.

Rosow, I. (1967). *Social integration of the aged.* New York: Free Press.

Roughman, P., & Hagerty, J. (1975). *Child health and the community.* New York: John Wiley.

Rubin, L. B. (1985). *Just friends.* New York: Harper & Row.

Rudov, R., & Santangelo, A. (1978). Health status of minorities and low-income groups (DHEW publication HRA 79-627). Washington, DC: U.S. Department of Health, Education, and Welfare Office of Health Research Opportunity.

Ruiz, D. (Ed.). (1990). *Handbook of mental health and mental disorder among black Americans.* New York: Greenwood.

Russell, S. F. (1981). *The factor structure of the Buss-Durkee hostility inventory.* Unpublished master's thesis, University of South Florida, Tampa.

Sainsburg, P. (1960). Psychosomatic disorders and neurosis in outpatients attending a general hospital. *Journal of Psychosomatic Research, 4,* 261-273.

Sarason, I. G., Johnson, J. H., & Siegel, J. M. (1978). Assessing the impact of life changes: Development of the life experiences survey. *Journal of Consulting and Clinical Psychology, 46*(5), 932-946.

Satariano, W. A., & Syme, S. L. (1981). Life changes and disease in elderly populations: Coping with change. In J. I. McGaugh & S. B. Kiesler (Eds.), *Aging, biology, and behavior* (pp. 311-328). New York: Academic Press.

Scheffler, R. M., & Miller, A. B. (1991). Differences in mental health service utilization among ethnic subpopulations. *International Journal of Law and Psychiatry, 14*(4), 363-376.

Scheidt, R. J., & Windley, P. G. (1983). The mental health of small-town rural elderly residents: An expanded ecological model. *Journal of Gerontology, 38*(4), 472-479.

Schneider, R., Egan, B., Johnson, E. H., Drobney, H., & Julius, S. (1986). Anger and anxiety in borderline hypertension. *Psychosomatic Medicine, 48*(3-4), 242-248.

Schonecke, O. W., Schuffel, W., Schafer, N., & Winter, K. (1972). Assessment of hostility in patients with functional cardiac complaints. *Psychotherapy and Psychosomatics, 20*(5), 272-281.

Scott, J. (1975). Police authority and the low income black family: An area of needed research. In L. Gary & L. Brown (Eds.), *Crime and its impact on the black community* (pp. 155-164). Washington, DC: Howard University Institute for Urban Affairs.

Seixas, F. A. (1980). The medical complications of alcoholism. In S. E. Getlow & H. S. Peyser (Eds.), *Alcoholism: A practical treatment guide* (pp. 124-141). New York: Grune & Stratton.

Seller, S. C. (1985). Alcohol abuse in the Old Testament. *Alcohol and Alcoholism, 20*(1), 69-76.

Selye, H. (1956). *The stress of life.* New York: McGraw-Hill.

Shanas, E. (1979). The family as support system in old age. *The Gerontologist, 19*(2), 169-174.

Shaper, A. G. (1990). Alcohol and mortality: A review of prospective studies. *British Journal of Addictions, 85*(7), 837-847.

Small, S. (1994). *Racialized barriers: The black experience in the United States and England in the 1980s.* London: Routledge.

Smith, E. J. (1981). Mental health and delivery systems for black women. *Journal of Black Studies, 12*(2), 126-141.

Smith, E. J. (1985). Ethnic minorities: Life stress, social support, and mental health issues. *The Counseling Psychologist, 13*(4), 537-579.

Smith, J. C., & Johns, R. L. (1995). *Statistical record of black America.* Detroit: Gale Research.

Snowden, L. (1982). *Reaching the underserved.* Beverly Hills, CA: Sage.

Snowden, L., & Cheung, F. (1990). Use of inpatient mental health services by members of ethnic minority groups. *American Psychologist, 45*(3), 291-298.

Snowden, L., & Holschuh, J. (1992). Ethnic differences in emergency psychiatric care and hospitalization in a program for the severely mentally ill. *Community Mental Health Journal, 28*(4), 281-291.

Solomon, P. (1988). Racial factors in mental health service utilization. *Psychosocial Rehabilitation Journal, 11*(3), 3-12.

Sonquist, J. A., Baker, E. L., & Morgan, J. N. (1973). *Searching for structure: An approach to analysis of substantial bodies of micro-data and documentation for a computer program.* Ann Arbor, MI: Survey Research Center.

Speare, A., Jr. (1974). Residential satisfaction as an intervening variable in residential mobility. *Demography, 11,* 173-188.

Spielberger, C. D., Crane, R. S., Kearns, W. D., Pellegrin, K. L., Rickman, R. L., & Johnson, E. H. (1991). Anger and anxiety in essential hypertension. In C. D. Spielberger & I. G. Sarason (Eds.), *Stress and emotion* (Vol. 14, pp. 266-283). New York: Hemisphere/Taylor & Francis.

Spielberger, C. D., Jacobs, G., Russell, S., & Crane, R. (1983). Assessment of anger: The state-trait anger scale. In J. N. Butcher & C. D. Spielberger (Eds.), *Advances in personality assessment* (Vol. 2, pp. 159-187). Hillsdale, NJ: Lawrence Erlbaum.

Spielberger, C. D., Johnson, E. H., Russell, S. F., Crane, R., Jacobs, G. A., & Worden, T. J. (1985). The experience and expression of anger: Construction and validation of an anger expression scale. In M. A. Chesney & R. H. Rosenbaum (Eds.), *Anger and hostility in cardiovascular and behavioral disorders* (pp. 5-30). New York: Hemisphere/McGraw-Hill.

Spreitzer, E., & Snyder, E. C. (1974). Correlates of life satisfaction among the aged. *Journal of Gerontology, 29*(4), 454-458.

Srole, L., Langner, T., Michael, S., Opler, M., & Rennie, T. (1962). *Mental health in the metropolis: The midtown Manhattan study.* New York: McGraw-Hill.

Stack, C. (1974). *All our kin.* New York: Harper & Row.

Stamler, J., Stamler, R., & Pullman, T. (1967). *The epidemiology of essential hypertension.* New York: Grune & Stratton.

Stanford, E. P. (1978). *The elder black.* San Diego, CA: Campanile Press, San Diego State University.

Staples, R. (1981a). Race and marital status. In H. P. McAdoo (Ed.), *Black families* (pp. 173-175). Beverly Hills, CA: Sage.

Staples, R. (1981b). *The world of black singles.* Westport, CT: Greenwood.

Staples, R., & Johnson L. (1993). *Black families at the crossroads: Challenges and prospects.* San Francisco: Jossey-Bass.

Steinglass, P. (1992). Family systems theory and medical illness. In R. J. Sawa (Ed.), *Family health care* (pp. 18-29). Newbury Park, CA: Sage.

Stipak, B., & Hensler, C. (1983). Effect of neighborhood racial and socioeconomic composition on urban residents' evaluations of their neighborhoods. *Social Indicators Research, 12*(3), 311-320.

Stoller, E. P., & Earl, L. L. (1983). Help with activities of everyday life: Sources of support for noninstitutionalized elderly. *The Gerontologist, 23*(1), 64-70.

Strakowski, S. M., Lonczak, H. S., Sax, K. W., West, S. A., Crist, A., Mehta, R., & Thienhaus, O. J. (1995). The effects of race on diagnosis and disposition from a psychiatric emergency service. *Journal of Clinical Psychiatry, 56*(3), 101-107.

Strakowski, S. M., Shelton, R. C., & Kolbrener, M. L. (1993). The effects of race and comorbidity on clinical diagnosis in patients with psychosis. *Journal of Clinical Psychiatry, 54*(3), 96-102.

Struyk, R. J., & Soldo, B. J. (1980). *Improving the elderly's housing: A key to preserving the nation's housing stock and neighborhoods.* Cambridge, MA: Ballinger.

Sue, S. (1977). Community mental health service to minority groups: Some optimism, some pessimism. *American Psychologist, 32*(8), 616-624.

Sue, S., Fujino, D. C., Hu, L., Takeuchi, D. T., & Zane, N. W. S. (1991). Community mental health services for ethnic minority groups: A test of the cultural responsiveness hypothesis. *Journal of Consulting and Clinical Psychology, 59*(4), 533-540.

Sue, S., McKinney, H., Allen, D., & Hall, J. (1974). Delivery of community mental health services to black and white clients. *Journal of Consulting and Clinical Psychology, 42*(6), 794-801.

Sussman, L. K., Robins, L. N., & Earls, F. (1987). Treatment-seeking for depression by black and white Americans. *Social Science and Medicine, 24*(3), 187-196.

Syme, L. S., Oakes, T. W., Friedman, G. D., Feldman, R., Siegelaub, A. B., & Collen, M. (1974). Social class and racial differences in blood pressure. *Public Health Briefs, 64,* 619-620.

Takeuchi, D., Bui, K., & Kim, L. (1993). The referral of minority adolescents to community mental health centers. *Journal of Health and Social Behavior, 34*(2), 153-164.

Taylor, R. B. (1982). Neighborhood physical environment and stress. In G. W. Evans (Ed.), *Environmental stress* (pp. 286-324). Cambridge, UK: Cambridge University Press.

Taylor, R. E., & Fant, M. E. (1975). Hypertension in the black community: An overview. Part I. *Journal of Tennessee Medical Association, 68*(12), 983-986.

Taylor, R. J. (1985). The extended family as a source of support to elderly blacks. *The Gerontologist, 25*(5), 488-495.

Taylor, R. J. (1986a). Church-based informal support among elderly blacks. *The Gerontologist, 26*(6), 637-642.

Taylor, R. J. (1986b). Receipt of support from family among black Americans: Demographic and familial differences. *Journal of Marriage and the Family, 48*(1), 67-77.

Taylor, R. J. (1986c). Religious participation among elderly blacks. *The Gerontologist, 26*(6), 630-636.

Taylor, R. J., & Chatters, L. M. (1986). Patterns of informal support to elderly black adults: Family, friends, and church members. *Social Work, 31*(6), 432-438.

Taylor, R. J., & Chatters, L. M. (1988). Church members as a source of informal social support. *Review of Religious Research, 30*(2), 193-203.

Taylor, R. J., & Chatters, L. M. (1989). Family, friend, and church networks, of black Americans. In R. L. Jones (Ed.), *Black adult development and aging* (pp. 245-271). Berkeley, CA: Cobb & Henry.

Taylor, R. J., & Chatters, L. M. (1991). Extended family networks of older black adults. *Journal of Gerontology: Social Sciences, 46*(4), S210-S217.

Taylor, R. J., Chatters, L. M., & Mays, V. (1988). Parents, children, siblings, in-laws, and non-kin as sources of emergency assistance to black Americans. *Family Relations, 37,* 298-304.

Taylor, R. J., Neighbors, H. W., & Broman, C. L. (1989). Evaluation by black Americans of the social service encounter during a serious personal problem. *Social Work, 34*(3), 205-211.

Theorell, T. (1974). Life events before and after the onset of a premature myocardial infarction. In B. S. Dohrenwend & B. P. Dohrenwend (Eds.), *Stressful life events: Their nature and effects* (pp. 101-117). New York: John Wiley.

Thomas, A., & Sillen, S. (1972). *Racism and psychiatry.* New York: Brunner/Mazel.

Thomas, V. G. (1986). *Sex roles: A synthesis and critique of selective measurements and research.* Washington, DC: Howard University Institute for Urban Affairs and Research.

Thompson, G. E. (1981). Hypertension in the black population. *Cardiovascular Review and Report, 2,* 351-357.

Thompson, M. S., & Peebles-Wilkins, W. (1992). The impact of formal, informal, and societal support networks on the psychological well-being of black adolescent mothers. *Social Work, 37*(4), 322-328.

Tucker, M. B., & Mitchell-Kernan, C. (1995). *The decline in marriage among African Americans: Causes, consequences and policy implications.* New York: Russell Sage.

Tucker, M. B., & Taylor, R. J. (1989). Demographic correlates of relationship status among black Americans. *Journal of Marriage and the Family, 51*(3), 655-665.

Tyroler, H. A., Heyden, S., Bartel, A., Cassel, J., Comoni, J. C., Hames, C. G., & Kleinbaum, D. (1971). Blood pressure and cholesterol as coronary heart disease risk factors. *Archives of Internal Medicine, 128*(6), 907.

Ulbrich, P. M., Warheit, G. J., & Zimmerman, R. S. (1989). Race, socioeconomic status, and psychological distress: An examination of differential vulnerability. *Journal of Health and Social Behavior, 30*(1), 131-146.

Unger, D. G., & Powell, D. R. (1980). Supporting families under stress: The role of social networks. *Family Relations, 29,* 566-574.

U.S. Bureau of the Census. (1994). *Statistical abstracts of the United States: 1994* (114th ed.). Washington, DC: Government Printing Office.

U.S. Department of Commerce. (1994). Households and family characteristics. *Current population reports, population characteristics* (pp. 20-483, Series P, Bureau of the Census). Washington, DC: Government Printing Office.

U.S. Department of Health and Human Services. (1985). *Report of the secretary's task force on black & minority health, Vol. 1: Executive summary.* Washington, DC: Government Printing Office.

U.S. Department of Health and Human Services. (1990). *Seventh special report to the U.S. Congress on alcohol and health* (DHHS Publication No. ADM 90-1656). Washington, DC: Government Printing Office.

U.S. Department of Health, Education, and Welfare. Public Health Service. (1979). *Health status of minorities and low-income groups.* Washington, DC: Government Printing Office.

U.S. Department of Housing and Urban Development. (1979). *How well are we housed? 3. Blacks.* Washington, DC: Government Printing Office.

U.S. Department of Justice, Law Enforcement Assistance Administration. (1979). *Public attitudes about crime.* Washington, DC: Government Printing Office.

U.S. National Advisory Commission on Civil Disorders. (1968). *Report of the National Advisory Commission on Civil Disorders.* Washington, DC: Government Printing Office.

Varady, D. P. (1983). Determinants of residential mobility decisions: The role of government services in relation to other factors. *Journal of the American Planning Association, 49,* 184-200.

Verba, S., & Nie, N. H. (1972). *Participation in America: Political democracy, and social equality.* New York: Harper & Row.

Verbrugge, L. M. (1977). The structure of adult friendship choices. *Social Forces, 56*(2), 576-597.

Vernon, S., & Roberts, R. (1982). Prevalence of treated and untreated psychiatric disorders in three ethnic groups. *Social Science and Medicine, 16*(17), 1575-1582.

Veroff, J., Douvan, E., & Kulka, R. (1981). *The inner American: A self-portrait from 1957-1976.* New York: Basic Books.

Veroff, J., Kulka, R., & Douvan, E. (1981). *Mental health in America: Patterns of help-seeking from 1957 to 1976.* New York: Basic Books.

Wagenfeld, M., Lemkau, P., & Justice, B. (1982). *Public mental health.* Beverly Hills, CA: Sage.

Wallach, I., & Jackson, C. (1973). Perceptions of the police in a black community. In J. Snibbe & H. Snibbe (Eds.), *The urban policeman in transition: A psychological and sociological review.* Springfield, IL: Charles C Thomas.

Wallen, J. (1992). Providing culturally appropriate mental health services for minorities. *Journal of Mental Health Administration, 19*(3), 288-295.

Warheit, G., Holzer, C., & Arey, S. (1975). Race and mental illness: An epidemiologic update. *Journal of Health and Social Behavior, 16*(3), 243-256.

Warheit, G., Holzer, C., & Schwab, J. (1973). An analysis of social class and racial differences in depressive symptomatology: A community study. *Journal of Health and Social Behavior, 14*(4), 291-299.

Warheit, G. J., Holzer, C. E., Bell, R. A., & Arey, S. A. (1976). Sex, marital status and mental health. *Social Forces, 55*(2), 459-470.

Warren, D. I. (1975). *Black neighborhoods: An assessment of community power.* Ann Arbor: University of Michigan Press.

Warren, D. I. (1981). *Helping networks: How people cope with problems in an urban community.* South Bend, IN: University of Notre Dame Press.

Webb, S. D., & Collette, J. (1979). Rural-urban stress: New data and new conclusions. *American Journal of Sociology, 84,* 1446-1452.

Weiner, H. (1977). *Psychobiology of essential hypertension.* New York: Elsevier.

Weinstein, E., & Kahn, R. (1955). *Denial of illness: Symbolic and physiological aspects.* Springfield, IL: Charles C Thomas.

Weissman, M. M. (1987). Advances in psychiatric epidemiology. *American Journal of Public Health, 77*(4), 445-451.

Whitehead, W. E., Blackwell, B., DeSilva, H., & Robinson, A. (1977). Anxiety and anger in hypertension. *Journal of Psychosomatic Research, 21*(5), 383-389.

Wilkinson, C. B. (Ed.). (1986). *Ethnic psychiatry.* New York: Plenum.

Wilkinson, D., & King, G. (1989). Conceptual and methodological issues in the use of race as a variable: Policy implications. In D. Willis (Ed.), *Health policies and black Americans.* New Brunswick, NJ: Transaction Publishing.

Williams, D. H. (1986). The epidemiology of mental illness in Afro-Americans. *Hospital and Community Psychiatry, 37*(1), 42-49.

Williams, D. H. (1995). African American mental health: Persisting questions and paradoxical findings. *African American Research Perspectives, 2*(1), 8-16.

Williams, D. R., & Chung, A. (in press). Racism and health. In R. C. Gibson & J. S. Jackson (Eds.), *Health in black America,* Thousand Oaks, CA: Sage.

Williams, D. R., & Collins, C. (1995). U.S. socioeconomic and racial differences in health: Patterns and explanations. *Annual Review of Sociology, 21,* 349-386.

Williams, D. R., & House J. S. (1991). Stress, social support, control and coping: A social epidemiological view. In B. Badura & I. Kickbusch (Eds.), *Health promotion research: Towards a new social epidemiology* (pp. 147-172). Copenhagen: World Health Organization.

Williams, D. R., Lavizzo-Mourey, R., & Warren, R. (1994). The concept of race and health status in America. *Public Health Reports, 109*(1), 26-41.

Williams, D. R., Takeuchi, D., & Adair, R. (1992a). Marital status and psychiatric disorder among blacks and whites. *Journal of Health and Social Behavior, 33*(2), 140-157.

Williams, D. R., Takeuchi, D. T., & Adair, R. K. (1992b). Socioeconomic status and psychiatric disorder among blacks and whites. *Social Forces, 71*(1), 179-194.

Williams, W. W., Ware, J. E., & Donald, C. A. (1981). A model of mental health, life events, and social supports applicable to general populations. *Journal of Health and Social Behavior, 22*(4), 324-336.

Willie, C., Kramer, M., & Brown, B. (Eds.). (1973). *Racism and mental health.* Pittsburgh: University of Pittsburgh Press.

Wilson, J. Q. (1968). *Varieties of police behavior: The management of law and order in eight communities.* Cambridge, MA: Harvard University Press.

Wilson, W. (1967). Correlates of avowed happiness. *Psychological Bulletin, 67*(4), 294-306.

Wilson, W. J. (1987). *The truly disadvantaged.* Chicago: University of Chicago Press.

Wolford, M. L., & Torres, M. (1994). Nonresponse adjustment in a longitudinal survey of African Americans. *American Statistical Association 1993 Proceedings of the Section on Survey Research Methods, 1,* 520-525.

Wolinsky, F. D. (1982). Racial differences in illness behavior. *Journal of Community Health, 8*(2), 87-101.

Wolpert, J. (1966). Migration as an adjustment to environmental stress. *Journal of Social Issues, 22*(4), 92-102.

Wolpert, J. (1984, July). *Social characteristics as contributors to neighborhood development.* Princeton, NJ: Woodrow Wilson School of Public and International Affairs, Princeton University.

Wood, V., & Robertson, J. F. (1978). Friendship and kinship interaction: Differential effect on the morale of the elderly. *Journal of Marriage and the Family, 40*(2), 367-375.

Woolf, D., & Rudman, M. (1977). A police-social service cooperative program. *Social Work, 22,* 62-64.

Worthington, C. (1992). An examination of factors influencing the diagnosis and treatment of black patients in the mental health system. *Archives of Psychiatric Nursing, 6*(3), 195-204.

Wu, I-Hsin, & Windle, C. (1980). Ethnic specificity in the relative minority use and staffing of community mental health centers. *Community Mental Health Journal, 16*(2), 156-168.

Yamamoto, J., Dixon, F., & Bloombaum (1972). White therapist and Negro patients. *Journal of the National Medical Association, 64*(4), 312-316.

Yamamoto, J., James, Q., & Palley, N. (1968). Cultural problems in psychiatric therapy. *Archives of General Psychiatry, 19*(1), 45-49.

Yancey, W. L., Rigsby, L., & McCarthy, J. D. (1972). Social position and self-evaluation: The relative importance of race. *American Journal of Sociology, 78,* 338-359.

Yee, A., Fairchild, H., Weizmann, F., & Wyatt, G. (1993). Addressing psychology's problems with race. *American Psychologist, 48*(1), 1132-1140.

Zehner, R. B. (1977). *Indicators of the quality of life in new communities.* Cambridge, MA: Ballinger.

Zollar, A. C., & Williams, J. S. (1987). The contribution of marriage to the life satisfaction of black adults. *Journal of Marriage and the Family, 49*(1), 87-92.

Author Index

Subject Index

About the Editors

Harold W. Neighbors is Associate Professor in the Department of Health Behavior and Health Education, School of Public Health, at the University of Michigan. He is also an Adjunct Research Scientist with the Program for Research on Black Americans at the Institute for Social Research, where he is Associate Director of the African American Mental Health Research Center. He received his PhD in social psychology from the University of Michigan in 1982 and did postdoctoral work at the Institute for Social Research, where he was supported by the Rockefeller Foundation and the National Institute of Mental Health (New Investigator Research Award). His current research interests and areas of publication include psychiatric epidemiologic field methods, cultural influences on the diagnosis of mental disorder, and the use of mental health services. He has directed both community and institutional surveys of African American mental health and is currently the recipient of a Research Scientist Development Award from the National Institute of Mental Health to study ethnic differences in the social epidemiology of mental disorder.

James S. Jackson holds a PhD in social psychology from Wayne State University and has been a faculty member at the University of Michigan since 1971. He is the Daniel Katz Distinguished University Professor of Psychology, Director of the Research Center for Group Dynamics Program for Research on Black Americans, Research Scientist at the Institute for Social

Research, Professor of Health Behavior and Health Education in the School of Public Health, and Faculty Associate at the Center for Afro-American and African Studies and at the Institute of Gerontology. He is a Fellow of the American Psychological Society, American Psychological Association, and Gerontology Society of America. In addition, he was a recipient of a 1993-94 Fogarty Senior Postdoctoral International Fellowship for study in France, where he holds the position of *Chercheur Invité, Group d'Études et de Recherches sur la Science, École des Hautes Études en Sciences Sociales.* In 1990, he helped to establish, and continues to direct, the African American Mental Health Research Center, funded by the National Institute of Mental Health. His research interests and areas of publication include race and ethnic relations, health and mental health, adult development and aging, attitudes and attitude change, and African American politics.

About the Contributors

Clifford L. Broman is Associate Professor of Sociology at Michigan State University. In 1984, he received his doctoral degree in sociology from the University of Michigan. He was a National Institute of Mental Health Post-doctoral Scholar from 1984 to 1985. He conducts research and publishes in several areas, including African American families, health-related behavior, and psychological well-being.

Diane R. Brown is Interim Director at the Center for Urban Studies and Associate Professor of Sociology at Wayne State University, Detroit, Michigan. Her research interests focus on sociocultural influences and mental health.

Cleopatra Howard Caldwell is a Research Investigator with the African American Mental Health Research Center, Program for Research on Black Americans, Institute for Social Research, University of Michigan. She has published journal articles in the areas of help-seeking behaviors and informal social support among African Americans, the black church as a social service institution, and race-related socialization and academic achievement among African American youth. Her current research focuses on two areas: (a) inter-generational family influences on early childbearing and (b) self-efficacy, exercise, and the sexual behaviors of African American adolescent females. She received her PhD in social psychology from the University of Michigan in 1986.

Linda M. Chatters is Associate Professor in the Health Behavior-Health Education Department of the School of Public Health and is Faculty Associate with the Institute for Social Research at the University of Michigan. Her research, funded by the National Institutes of Health, focuses on psychological and social-structural determinants and correlates of subjective well-being in African Americans as well as on the uses of survey data in this population. She has published extensively in the areas of subjective well-being, informal social support networks, and the measurement of religious participation. She received her PhD in developmental psychology from the University of Michigan.

Joan E. Crowley received her PhD in social psychology in 1978 from the University of Michigan. She held positions at Ohio State University and the University of Alabama where her areas of research included delinquency, alcohol use, and child abuse. Currently, she is Assistant Professor of Criminal Justice at New Mexico State University, with interests in crime victims and community corrections.

Larry M. Gant is Associate Professor of Social Work at the University of Michigan. He has an extensive familiarity with the academic field of psychology and the professional fields of social work and public health. Since 1985, he has created, implemented, and evaluated programs in the area of HIV primary prevention and harm reduction for sexual minorities, people of color, and injection drug users. His interests and publications include the areas of evaluation of case management systems, caregivers of persons with HIV/ AIDS, the relationship between condom use attitudes and participation in risk reduction activities, the social work response to HIV/AIDS, and the relationship between readiness for behavioral change and intervention outcomes for drug-dependent women. He earned his MSW in interpersonal practice and research, his MA in psychology, and in 1986, his PhD in social work and social psychology from the University of Michigan.

Cheryl Burns Hardison is a doctoral student in the Joint Doctoral Program in Social Work and Sociology at the University of Michigan. She has substantive interests in caregiving to elderly African Americans and in African American friendship networks.

Ernest H. Johnson is Professor in the Department of Family Medicine at Morehouse School of Medicine and Director of the Program for Urban Health Research, Atlanta, Georgia. He is president of Infinite Choices and Possibilities, Inc., a health promotion company that sponsors seminars and workshops. His prinicipal areas of research and clinical activities focus on hypertension, HIV risk behaviors, and the role of emotions in health. He is the founder and Editor-in-Chief of *Ethnic Perspective on Health and Behavior*, a Praeger series. In 1984, he received his PhD in clinical and community psychology, with a special focus on the health of black Americans from the University of South Florida in Tampa.

Rhoda E. Barge Johnson is the former Chair of the Women's Studies Department at the University of Alabama and is Associate Professor of Women's Studies. Her academic activities include a variety of special projects and publications. She has worked with communities and agencies as they have attempted to deal with racial, ethnic, and gender prejudice and discrimination. She participated in a FIPSE (Fund for the Improvement of Post Secondary Education) funded project on the culture of southern black women, and she edited the book *Women's Studies in the South*. Other publications include a study of the postbaccalaureate careers of black graduates and distress on the college campus. She was co-investigator of the National Survey of Women's Studies Programs. She received her doctorate in sociology from the University of Alabama and has completed postdoctoral work in the areas of oppression, stress, and AIDS.

Vickie M. Mays is Professor of Psychology at the University of California, Los Angeles, and was a Fellow in the RAND/UCLA Health Policy Program. She has published several articles investigating behavioral factors in ethnic women's physical and mental health outcomes. Her areas of research on ethnic women have included HIV/AIDS, alcoholism, employment-related stressors, health status/health care access, and the role of perceptions of inequality and race-based discrimination in the health outcomes of African Americans.

Carolyn B. Murray is Associate Professor of the Psychology and Ethnic Studies Departments at the University of California at Riverside (UCR). She was awarded a Ford Fellowship in 1985, the Distinguished Teaching Award at UCR in 1990, and the Riverside County Woman of the Year Award in Education in 1993. In 1993, she also received a National Institutes of Health,

Human Learning and Behavior grant to investigate socialization practices used by African American parents and to determine the normative developmental processes and outcomes for African American children.

Isidore Silas Obot is Senior Lecturer in the Department of General and Applied Psychology, University of Jos, Nigeria. He received his PhD in psychology from Howard University in Washington, D.C. He also holds a Master of Public Health (MPH) degree from the Harvard School of Public Health in Boston. He is a recipient of several awards, including postdoctoral fellowships from the World Health Organization and the National Institute on Drug Abuse/Hubert H. Humphrey Program. His research interests include health and behavior, epidemiology, prevention of substance abuse, and social policy analysis. He is the author of a research monograph titled *Drinking Behaviour and Attitudes in Nigeria* and has edited a book titled *Epidemiology and Control of Substance Abuse in Nigeria.* He is currently Editor-in-Chief of the *Nigerian Journal of Basic and Applied Psychology,* Director of the Centre for Research and Information on Substance Abuse (CRISA) in Nigeria, and President of the Nigerian Psychological Association.

M. Jean Peacock is Assistant Professor of Psychology at California State University, San Bernardino. She received her PhD in social/personality psychology from the University of California at Riverside (UCR). As a graduate student member of the African American Families' Project at UCR, her primary research interest was the development of the Black Family Process Q-Sort. She continues as a member of the African American Families' Project, specializing in race socialization, parenting strategies, and self-esteem in relationship to specific behavior outcomes.

Gayle Y. Phillips received her doctoral degree in social work from the University of Pennsylvania in 1983 and was a National Institute of Mental Health Postdoctoral Research Fellow at the Institute for Social Research, University of Michigan, from 1984 to 1985. Her research interests included quality of life, the elderly, young people, substance abuse prevention, employment and training, housing and community development, and the residential environment. She had an untimely death in 1995.

Robert Joseph Taylor is Associate Professor of Social Work and a Faculty Associate at the Institute for Social Research at the University of Michigan.

His research, funded by the National Institutes of Health, focuses on family and friend social support networks across the life span, with a particular emphasis on the networks of older adults. Another major area of interest is the investigation of the correlates of religious participation and church support among African Americans. He has published articles on these topics in the *Journal of Gerontology: Social Sciences, Journal of Marriage and the Family, Family Relations, Review of Religious Research,* and *Social Work.*

Patricia A. Washington is the Director of the Master of Social Work Program—South Bend Campus at the Indiana University School of Social Work. She received both her MSW and PhD degrees in social work from the University of Pittsburgh School of Social Work. Her areas of research include mental health issues in corrections, incarcerated women, and the impact of institutions on oppressed populations.